2022年度广东省教育科学规划课题（高等教育专项）：秦皇岛港藏耀华英文档案的翻译与研究（项目编号：2022GXJK307）
广州航海学院引进人才科研启动基金

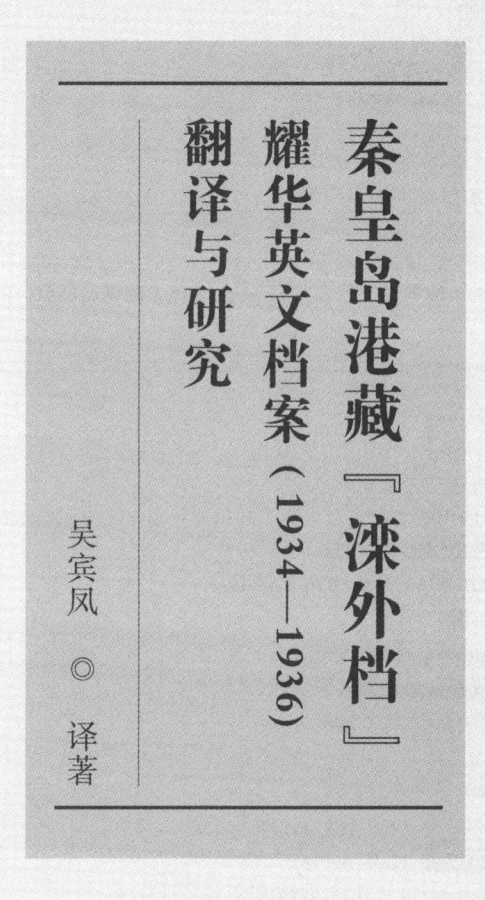

秦皇岛港藏『滦外档』耀华英文档案（1934—1936）翻译与研究

吴宾凤 ◎ 译著

西南交通大学出版社
·成　都·

图书在版编目（CIP）数据

秦皇岛港藏"滦外档"耀华英文档案（1934—1936）翻译与研究 / 吴宾凤译著. --成都：西南交通大学出版社，2023.12
ISBN 978-7-5643-9573-5

Ⅰ. ①秦… Ⅱ. ①吴… Ⅲ. ①玻璃 – 化学工业 – 工业企业 – 档案资料 – 英语 – 翻译 – 研究 – 秦皇岛 – 民国 Ⅳ. ①F426.7

中国国家版本馆 CIP 数据核字（2023）第 229085 号

Qinhuangdao Gangcang "Luanwai Dang" Yaohua Yingwen Dang'an (1934—1936) Fanyi yu Yanjiu
秦皇岛港藏"滦外档"耀华英文档案（1934—1936）翻译与研究

吴宾凤　译著

责 任 编 辑	邵莘越
封 面 设 计	原谋书装
出 版 发 行	西南交通大学出版社
	（四川省成都市金牛区二环路北一段 111 号
	西南交通大学创新大厦 21 楼）
营销部电话	028-87600564　028-87600533
邮 政 编 码	610031
网 　　 址	http://www.xnjdcbs.com
印 　　 刷	成都蜀通印务有限责任公司
成 品 尺 寸	170 mm × 230 mm
印 　　 张	19
字 　　 数	310 千
版 　　 次	2023 年 12 月第 1 版
印 　　 次	2023 年 12 月第 1 次
书 　　 号	ISBN 978-7-5643-9573-5
定 　　 价	88.00 元

图书如有印装质量问题　本社负责退换
版权所有　盗版必究　举报电话：028-87600562

前言

在体量巨大的秦皇岛港藏开滦外文档案中，有 71 卷耀华玻璃公司的英文档案，内容涉及玻璃经销、财务管理、人事管理、生产保障、函件合同等五类。历史档案是世界学术界公认的历史学研究最可靠的资料之一。近现代史研究若要做出重要的理论突破及创新，很大程度上依赖于对史实资料的占有和掌握。我国档案界不断有人探讨提高档案的开放性和利用率问题，不少地方档案馆中极为珍贵的民国档案馆藏很少为学界了解，大多数甚至从未被利用。由于民国半殖民地半封建社会的特殊性，不少民国档案使用英文、法语等多国文字，增加了档案馆工作人员整理的难度，让民国档案的社会利用变得难上加难。民国时期外文历史档案的翻译具有历史、档案、语言、翻译等多学科交叉特征，正成为逐步增长的刚性需求。

对秦皇岛港"滦外档"耀华玻璃公司英文档案的整理、翻译，进而对耀华玻璃公司的发展进行研究，能够丰富中国近代工业科技史内容，能增强国家民族自信心和文化自信，并让这些珍贵的历史档案发挥更大的价值。历史研究无疑需要历史档案作为重要依据，而历史档案也只有被历史研究所利用才能从沉埋中焕发光彩，披沙拣金，二者不可或缺。

本书在撰写过程中得到了广州航海学院外语学院陈丽丽老师、翁靖华老师、吴雪红老师的帮助，她们做了部分翻译工作，这里一并感谢！

作　者

目 录

第一章　秦皇岛港藏"滦外档"的历史形成及耀华公司介绍 …… 001
　　第一节　秦皇岛港开埠 ……………………………………… 001
　　第二节　开滦矿务局的历史发展 …………………………… 003
　　第三节　开滦外文档案 ……………………………………… 010
　　第四节　秦皇岛港藏"滦外档"的历史形成 ……………… 015
　　第五节　耀华机器制造玻璃有限公司介绍 ………………… 018

第二章　秦皇岛港藏"滦外档"之耀华玻璃经销合同 ……… 021
　　第一节　开滦矿务总局耀华机器制造玻璃有限公司与同祥湧
　　　　　　玻璃庄之合同（1934年）………………………… 021
　　第二节　开滦矿务总局耀华机器制造玻璃有限公司与同祥湧
　　　　　　玻璃庄之合同（1936年）………………………… 028
　　第三节　开滦矿务总局耀华机器制造玻璃有限公司与北平地
　　　　　　区经销商之合同（1936年）……………………… 035

第三章　开滦矿务总局耀华公司玻璃经销部门间备忘录（共107份）…… 042

第四章　开滦矿务总局耀华公司玻璃经销函电（共16份）………… 218

第五章　秦皇岛港藏"滦外档"耀华玻璃经销翻译及研究 ……… 248
　　第一节　秦港藏"滦外档"民国时期耀华英文档案中地名、
　　　　　　人名、商号名的翻译规律 ………………………… 248
　　第二节　秦港藏"滦外档"民国时期耀华英文档案合同翻译
　　　　　　中的时代特色 ………………………………………… 250
　　第三节　秦港藏"滦外档"民国时期耀华英文档案中地名的考证
　　　　　　………………………………………………………… 260

第四节　秦港藏"滦外档"民国时期耀华玻璃经销英文档案中"退旧税"的考证 ……………………………………… 265

第五节　秦港藏"滦外档"民国时期耀华英文档案中"Shoko" "昌光"和"Vitrea"的考证 ………………………… 267

第六节　秦港藏"滦外档"民国时期耀华英文档案中"耀华"玻璃销售的考证 …………………………………… 288

参考文献 ……………………………………………………… 296

第一章
秦皇岛港藏"滦外档"的历史形成及耀华公司介绍

第一节 秦皇岛港开埠

19世纪后期,帝国列强频频发动对华战争并不断威胁京师安全,清王朝腐败无能、国家危如累卵,不得不重视起京畿沿海一带的海防建设。当时负责北洋海防事务的李鸿章认为:"直隶之大沽、北塘、山海关一带系京畿门户,是为最要。"

在经过两次鸦片战争、中日甲午战争后,帝国列强掀起了瓜分中国的狂潮,竞相侵权夺地,俄国侵占了旅顺,德国吞并了胶州湾,英国窃据了威海,广州湾等中国沿海重要港口都已被外国侵略者以"约开口岸"之名瓜分殆尽,致使当时中国没有自己的主权港口。通商口岸的开放,使帝国主义侵略势力深入中国内地。

中日甲午战争中北洋水师覆灭,为重建北洋水师,急需寻找建设一座可资利用的良港作为中国的海军基地,以"兴复海军"。秦皇岛港因地处海陆要冲、京畿门户,水深浪缓,不冻不淤,轮船可泊,最初是以作为重建海军的军港为目的建设的。然而中日甲午战争战败后,清政府要赔偿战争赔款2.3亿两白银,大借外债,财政拮据,致使列强控制了中国的经济命脉。因清政府无力筹措资金以修建军港以及商港,清朝政府为"以兴商务""扩充利源",谋求京畿出海通道,最终将筹办秦皇岛商港的权力交付开平矿务局,决定由开平矿务局出资建设,"试办码头,借资利运"。计划在商港建成后以运输煤炭为主,同时转递国家邮政文件及驻扎北洋水师的军舰。开平矿务局接受委托后，先是购置了秦皇岛至北戴河沿海 40 里范围内的 1.5 万余亩土地，又于 1897 年秋冬在烟台与秦皇岛之间试航"永平"号轮船获得成功。

1898 年 3 月 26 日，总理各国事务衙门上奏《秦皇岛自开口岸折》，光绪皇帝朱批"依议钦此"，清政府宣布秦皇岛为自开口岸，如图 1-1 所示。4 月 3 日，总理衙门照会各国驻华使节，宣布秦皇岛自行开埠。6 月 10 日，开平矿务局秦皇岛经理处在秦皇岛附近的东盐务村成立，自此秦皇岛港正式诞生，按照清政府规定实行"实行垄断、专擅兴造、不得呈明、锐意经营，视同己有"的绝对控制式经营模式。秦皇岛成为自开口岸的消息引起了中外媒体的关注，上海《时务报》以"古岛通商"的显著标题做了报道，英国的《泰晤士报》《伦敦中国报》、日本的《经济报》也对此进行了报道。

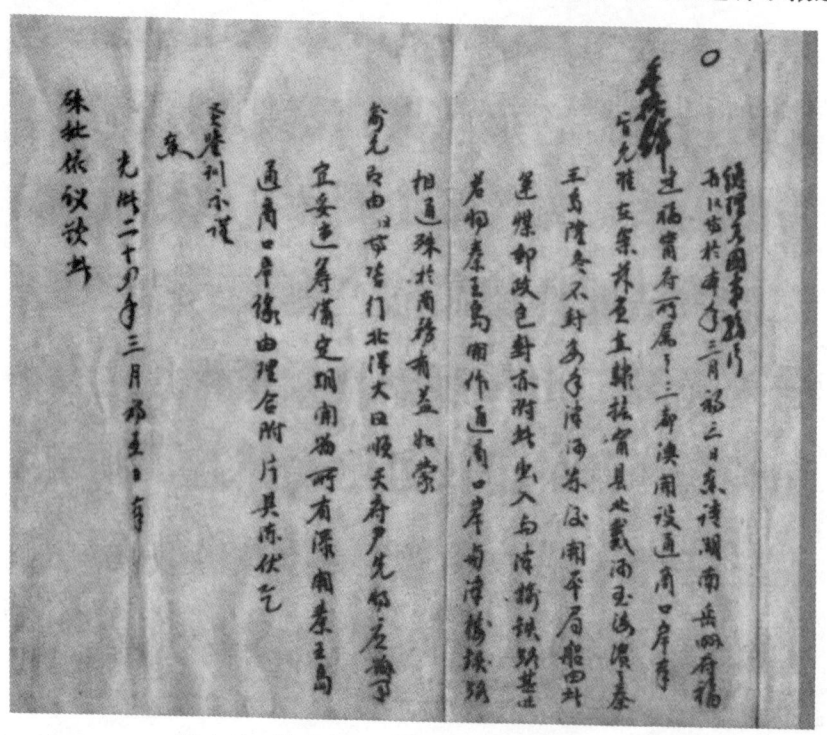

图 1-1　清光绪帝朱批添开秦皇岛通商口岸

1899 年 4 月，秦皇岛建港工程全面启动，到 1900 年上半年，已新修防波堤 300 米，码头 200 米，在码头上铺设了轻铁路，港区内修建了车站一座，接运往来客货。

1899年12月，秦皇岛港修筑了第一条自码头至汤河火车站的4.8公里单线铁路，与1893年中国第一条铁路干线——津榆铁路接轨。这条线路的竣工标志着秦皇岛港口自备铁路的诞生。港区车站同步建成。开平建成一支由6艘船组成的船队，秦皇岛港出现第一批海员工人。

第二节 开滦矿务局的历史发展

一、开平矿务局、滦州煤矿、开滦矿务总局

1. 开平矿务局

早在明永乐年间（1403—1424），河北滦州的开平矿区已用土法开采。开滦始建于1878年，至今已有144年发展历史，以建设"中国第一佳矿"唐山矿为肇始，托举了唐山、秦皇岛两座城市的兴起，被誉为"中国煤炭工业源头""中国近代工业摇篮"。其间，因国家多难，山河破碎，帝国列强横行，在不同阶段，民间、政府、外国列强等各方股东先后上演了一幕幕近代中国煤矿行业主权争夺战，执掌着这座晚清民国时期的"中国第一佳矿"，控制权数易其主，企业生存风雨飘摇。

1876年，直隶总督李鸿章派时任轮船招商局总办的唐廷枢到河北滦州开平镇一带勘探煤矿。1877年10月，唐廷枢拟定开平矿务局招商章程十二条。章程规定：开平矿务局专营煤铁，拟集资80万两。1878年7月24日在直隶唐山开平镇正式成立"开平矿务局"，唐廷枢任总办。1881年全面投产，雇工3 000人。1882年产煤38 000吨，1898年达73万吨。历年扩充设备，改善运输条件，备有运输煤轮，设有专用码头和堆栈。截至1899年，开平煤矿共产煤527万吨，盈利400多万两白银，几乎相当于整个开平矿务局投资（150万两白银）的3倍。质优价廉的开平煤很快将日本煤挤出天津，市场甚至远到华中的汉阳铁厂。到19世纪末，总资产已近600万两白银。

1892年10月7日，唐廷枢在天津病逝，江苏候补道张翼出任矿务局总办，后又升任直隶、热河矿务督办。1900年7月30日，德璀琳以开平矿务局代理总办的身份，仅以8万英镑的价格私下在"卖约"上签字画押，将开平矿务局"卖给"代表墨林公司的胡佛（后来的美国第31任总统、时任张翼技术顾问）。1901年2月19日张翼被逼同时签订了"卖约"和"移交约"。就这样，当时中国最大的、技术最先进的煤矿和秦皇岛"自开口岸"便完全沦入英帝国主义者的手中。1901年2月，胡佛凭借这个"大功"被墨林公司任命为英商开平矿务有限公司总经理。

仅在1906—1910年期间，英国人借助开平矿务局在中国掠夺了大量财富，年均获利有200多万两，股息率年均达12.5%。

2. 滦州煤矿

开平矿务局被英人霸占，大白天下后，迫于各界压力，1904年年底，清廷责成张翼、严复等人去英国高等法院控告墨林公司，收回开平煤矿主权。伦敦高等法院虽承认墨林公司的行为属于欺骗，但又宣称"无法强制执行"，胜诉的判决书只是一纸空文。司法途径失败后，曾做过张翼副手的周学熙对此耿耿于怀，他认为能源是一切工业的基础，"煤为制造之根本，根本不立，他事皆无基础"。他向袁世凯提出"以滦制开"的策略，即在开平煤矿附近，再创办一个比开平煤矿大十倍的滦州煤矿，将开平矿区的矿脉团团围住，然后通过竞争压垮开平煤矿，使其就范，从而实现"以滦收开"。

1907年，滦州煤矿有限公司成立，周学熙出任总经理，以50万两官银为启动金，另募200万两商股，以前车为鉴，滦州煤矿特别规定不许外国人入股，注明"招股权限为华商，概不搭入洋股"。不再聘用英国人，转而聘任德国人，进口德国设备。为了表达支持，已经升任直隶总督兼北洋大臣的袁世凯宣布"滦州煤矿三百三十平方里严禁他人采矿"，同时明定该矿是北洋官矿，为北洋军需服务。滦州煤矿产量猛增，在市场上大受欢迎。

滦州煤矿创办后，一时间在开平煤矿矿区四周矿井星罗棋布，开平煤矿矿区顿呈被围之势。从 1908 年正式投产到 1912 年，滦州煤矿产煤 130 多万吨，在京津市场的销量不断上升。

3. 开滦矿务总局

在 1906—1910 年期间，开平矿务局效益颇丰，年均获利有 200 多万两白银，股息率年均达 12.5%。滦州煤矿与开平矿务局的缠战，斗争到最后，双方利润大减，均难以维持。最终周学熙与英方就两矿合并事宜多次谈判交涉，双方在公司性质、利润分配和管理权三个敏感问题上争执不下。最后，英商同意将开平矿务局交还中方，代价是要"赎款"270 万英镑。周学熙讨价还价，减至 178 万英镑。英方已决定同意。

可是，局势在 1911 年 10 月又发生了 180 度的大转弯，谈判进行期间，武昌爆发了辛亥革命，朝廷岌岌可危，北方港口各国军舰拉响警笛，双方态势对比瞬间发生逆转。先是滦州公司的股东惶恐不安，生怕再次出现当年被洋人枪杆子夺走煤矿的悲剧，希望依靠外国势力在战火和变局中保住自己的利益，滦州公司的股东们匆匆同意再议合并。11 月，开平、滦州达成"合办条件协议十款"，同意合并成中英开滦矿务有限公司，股权对等平分，利润则由开平得六成，滦州得四成，管理权由英方把持。

开滦合并的得失，在商业史上很有争议。开滦案例再次以最直接而残酷的方式证明了——国不强，则商不立。此后 30 多年，开滦煤矿始终被英资公司控制，一直到 1948 年年底才由中国收回。周学熙对开滦合并的结局当然十分伤感，他拒绝出任新公司的督办。在日记中，他慨然曰："吾拂虎须，冒万难，创办滦矿，几濒绝境，始意谓，将以滦收开，今仅成联合营业之局，非吾愿也。"他还在家中写了一副对联："孤忠惟有天知我，万事当思后视今。"

双方遂于 1912 年商定联合营业，签订合同，设立开滦矿务总局。尽管根据合同规定，1922 年后滦州公司有权以双方商定的价格购回开平煤矿。但开滦煤矿此后连年获得高额利润，滦矿股东获利不菲，对"回购"越来越消极。嗣后，北洋政府并未根据合同收回开平公司，1934 年两公司正式合并，结果英商独占开滦矿务局。

1941年，太平洋战争爆发。日本随即对开滦煤矿实行所谓"军管理"。此后的三年零九个月里，开滦煤矿被掠走煤炭2 260多万吨。1945年日本投降后，开滦煤矿由国民党政府接收，交还英商经营。直到1948年唐山解放，开滦煤矿才完全回到中国人手中。

二、开平矿务有限公司被霸占和英国法院控告事件

1900年10月10日，英商墨林将开平矿务局（包括港口）改称为"开平矿务有限公司"，于12月21日在伦敦注册。

1900年，义和团运动掀起了反列强侵略高潮，帝国主义列强借机组成了八国联军入侵中国，懦弱的清朝政府授权李鸿章下令山海关、秦皇岛驻军自行撤退，使得八国联军轻易地从水陆两方面侵占了秦皇岛和山海关，并在此沿海地带肆意圈地为营、割据一方，秦皇岛和山海关地区从此沦为了帝国主义的"国中之国"。在此大背景下，开平煤矿与秦皇岛港也未能摆脱被英帝国殖民者骗占的命运。

英国垄断商行组织毕威克—墨林公司（Bewiek & Moreing.co）早已窥视着中国开平丰富的煤炭资源，为了达到掠夺矿产的目的，有计划有步骤地展开了罪恶的骗占计划。

1897年，英国矿业巨头墨林采矿公司招聘具有长期找矿工作经验的地质学家，后来成为美国第31任总统的胡佛（赫伯特·克拉克·胡佛，Herbert Clark Hoover，美国第31任总统，毕业于斯坦福大学）应聘并获得了这份工作。1899年2月，墨林公司将胡佛派往中国进行探矿事业。3月，胡佛夫妇抵达天津并住在今天的重庆道小学西楼旧址，还给自己取了一个中文名字"胡华"。

首先，墨林采矿公司的胡佛对开平煤矿及秦皇岛地区进行了多次调查。胡佛先是由天津海关德籍税务司德璀琳推荐给张翼的，他以开平煤矿矿师之名收集了大量开平矿务局所属企业的情报。胡佛在给毕威克—墨林公司的《关于中国天津开平煤矿之调查报告》中这样写道："这项产业肯定值得投资一百万磅，这个企业绝不是一种投资事业，而是一个会产生非

常高的盈利的实业企业。"《报告》同时也对秦皇岛港口进行了分析，说它是"形成公司的一个独立的深水不冻港口"。

其次，他们在开平矿务局注入资本，为日后的骗占行为埋下了伏笔。开平矿务局聘请了英国白利工程公司的工程师休兹前来主持建港工程。经过仔细的勘测，休兹将工程分为两期，先行扩建已有的运煤矿及客货码头，投资估计百余万银元；其次全面动工建设军、商兼用港口，投资估计600万银元（约432万两白银）①。开平矿务局由于购买土地建设港口，资金一时困难。于是，毕威克—墨林公司"慷慨"地借给开平矿务局20万英镑（约140万两白银）作为修建秦皇岛港码头的资金，墨林还答应经办一笔为修筑港口码头而发行的20万英镑债券的工程借款，矿务局总办张翼则同意以开平矿务局全部产业作为抵押。这笔工程借款占开平全部资产的36%，加上外国资本家收购了不少开平的股票，开平实际上已经被外国资本家控制。而毕威克—墨林公司为筹措秦皇岛港这笔巨额借款，吸引了比利时资本，比利时资本的背后有包括德、法、意、俄、奥匈、瑞士等国在内的国际财团，组成了帝国主义列强的"资本神圣同盟"。

最后，他们采取威逼利诱的手段，逼迫开平矿务局总办张翼出卖国家权益。义和团运动兴起后，张翼躲进天津外国租界地避难，英国人以"饲养信鸽为义和团传递情报"为由，拘捕了开平矿务局督办张翼。同时，联合对开平矿务局持有债券的外国银行逼迫张翼偿还债务。早就与毕威克—墨林公司勾结的张翼的顾问，曾在天津海关税务司任职的英籍德国人德璀琳接着到拘留处对张翼百般胁迫利诱，让昏聩的张翼签署了"保矿手据"和"备用合同"，在"手据"中，提出要以保矿为名委托德璀琳为开平矿务局总办，全权与英国人进行交涉。而在"合同"中则明确规定，德璀琳有权按其意愿出售、抵押租赁、管理、经营及管辖开平矿务局。英帝国主

---

① 据可靠记载，墨西哥鹰洋在1854—1856年间中英贸易中流入中国，此处银元即指墨西哥鹰洋。墨西哥鹰洋的成色较其他外国银元为佳，而且多年不变，人们都乐于使用。墨西哥鹰洋在中国南部、中部各省流通非常广泛，几乎成为主币。上海的外国银行发行纸币，1919年以前都以墨西哥鹰洋为兑换标准。此处投资预估为英国白利工程公司的工程师休兹所做，所以以银元预计。当时1块鹰洋折合中国白银7钱2分，所以600万银元相当于432万两白银。

义分子达到目的后，第二天便释放了张翼。

德璀琳"受托"后，背着张翼，伙同胡佛共同炮制了一个关于开平矿务局全部产权和港权的"卖约"——《出卖开平矿务局合约》。1900 年 7 月 30 日，胡佛代表毕威克—墨林公司在"卖约"上签字画押，仅仅以 8 万英镑的价格私下签订"卖约"，开平矿务局被"卖给"代表墨林公司的胡佛。旋即，墨林公司转手以 25 万英镑的价格将开平煤矿卖给英国财团"东方辛迪加"。

为了使骗占活动合法化，1901 年，胡佛进一步与张翼密商，要求张翼亲自承认"卖约"，签订"移交约"。张翼开始拒绝承认"卖约"，更拒绝签订"移交约"，但在胡佛等人的威逼和利诱下，于 1901 年 2 月 19 日被逼同时签订了"卖约"和"移交约"。就这样，当时中国最大的、技术最先进的煤矿和秦皇岛"自开口岸"便完全沦入英帝国主义者的手中。1901 年 2 月，胡佛凭借这个"大功"被墨林公司任命为英商开平矿务有限公司总经理。但是胡佛并没有长期在开平矿务有限公司任职。1901 年，比利时商人成为开平矿务有限公司的大股东，胡佛便辞去了总经理一职，于次年带着妻子离开了中国。

按照"卖约"的规定，开平矿务局名下三处煤矿，秦皇岛港以及清朝政府委托开平矿务局经管的 4 万多亩地皮，8 万亩新河地皮以及沿海各城市的 600 亩地皮等均被毕威克—墨林公司非法侵吞和骗占。英帝国主义不费分文，便骗取了开平矿务局的全部产权，这场骗局的始作俑者墨林在事后得意地说："契约的形式以及弄到手的签字盖章可以说是尽善尽美，我敢说，就中国同等重要的产业来说，没有一家外国公司曾获得过这样完美的一份契约。"

1902 年 8 月，英国不许中国军舰停泊秦皇岛，认为中国军队强行闯入英国公司，并拿出"移交约"给前来交涉的直隶总督、北洋大臣袁世凯看，颇为得意地说："开平现在是英国公司，并非中英合办，所以绝不可以悬挂龙旗。"

开平矿被英人骗占后，真相大白。愤怒的袁世凯连续三次参劾张翼。迫于压力，1904 年年底，清廷责成张翼、严复等人去英国高等法院伦敦劳伦斯法庭控告墨林公司，收回开平煤矿主权。开庭 21 次后，伦敦高等法院虽在法律和道义上承认了张翼胜诉，承认墨林公司的行为属于欺骗，但又宣称"无法强制执行"，推脱了事。胜诉的判决书只是一纸空文，清政府根本无法收回开平煤矿。

数年后，清朝政府又曾试图给由周学熙等中国官僚资本组建的滦州矿加筹商股，借以抵制开平矿并伺机收回开平矿权。滦州公司与开平公司的竞争，是中国弱小的工业资本与强大的国际垄断资本的较量，很快便以被开平公司收购而告终。滦州矿被开平公司收购后，开滦矿务总局成立，英国人继续控制着秦皇岛港，作为开滦煤炭的主要出海口。曾经点燃国人自强希望的"自开口岸"沦为帝国主义专用煤炭输出港，据统计，仅开滦煤炭一项，新中国成立前英帝国主义就掠走了 17 000 万吨。秦皇岛港的遭遇，只是当时半殖民地半封建社会的中国无数主权丧失事件中的一个缩影而已。

1901 年 7 月，开平矿务局秦皇岛经理处更名为开平矿务有限公司秦皇岛经理处。12 月，港口小码头 1 号泊位建成投产。

1904 年 12 月，港口小码头 2 号泊位建成投产。

1906 年 12 月，港口修建 6 号泊位，次年竣工投产。

1909 年，大码头铁路由 60 磅改铺 80 磅重轨，设立磅房，计量进出口货物。

1910 年，港区铁路总长 12.5 公里，形成了每年 50 万吨的拖运能力。同年 8 月，2 000 吨山西煤炭第一次经由秦皇岛港装船运往美国旧金山。

1912 年 1 月 27 日，开平矿务有限公司与滦州矿务有限公司"联合"，开滦矿务总局在天津成立。9 月 24 日，孙中山以全国铁路督办身份访问、考察秦皇岛港，预言秦皇岛港如收归国民所有，"就其发展趋势，可使之与国际大港纽约港相媲美"；并建议修筑京秦直达铁路。

1914 年 12 月，港内煤场至码头铁路铺设双线，分上行线和下行线。

1915 年 12 月 7 日，泊位竣工投产，至此秦皇岛港 1～7 号泊位的格局基本形成。

1916 年 9 月，京奉铁路秦皇岛绕线工程通车，汤河火车站废止，新建铁路秦皇岛站，港内自备铁路作业线也由原来的 3 股增至 5 股。

1916年大小码头全景如图 1-2 所示。

图 1-2　1916 年大小码头全景

1929 年 1 月 24 日，港口管理体制改革，设立工务处，取代包工头直接管理装卸工人。

三、英日共管开滦、秦皇岛港

20 世纪 30 年代以后，日本帝国主义入侵中国，英国与日本勾结，推行英日共管开滦的政策，雇佣日本顾问、监督官，大量向日本输出开滦优质煤。港口设施只增添部分船、机，对码头、库场进行维修和改造。

1940 年港口吞吐量达 459.4 万吨，为开滦时期年吞吐量最高纪录。

1941 年 12 月 8 日，日本帝国主义偷袭珍珠港，太平洋战争爆发，日本对英美全面开战。

1942 年 1 月 19 日，日本帝国主义从英国殖民者手中接收开滦与秦皇岛，对港口实行军事管制，实施残酷的法西斯统治。

1942 年 1 月 21 日，开滦矿务局秦皇岛经理处改称军管理秦皇岛港务局。

第三节　开滦外文档案

一、开滦集团简况

开滦（集团）有限责任公司（以下简称开滦集团）始建于 1878 年，为国有特大型煤炭能源企业，被誉为"中国煤炭工业源头"和"北方民族工业摇篮"，创造了多个中国近代工业史上的第一。北京"中华世纪坛"青铜甬道，镌刻着1881年开滦创造的三个第一："开平煤矿建成出煤"，这是中国近代最早最成功的大型煤矿，被誉为"中国第一佳矿"；"开平煤矿至胥各庄铁路投入使用"，这是中国第一条标准轨距铁路；"中国制造'火箭号'蒸汽机车"，这是中国第一台蒸汽机车。2014年，开滦集团位居美国《财富》杂志世界500强企业第394位。

原开滦矿务局大楼如图1-3所示。

图1-3 原开滦矿务局大楼

开滦集团前身是开滦矿务局，1999年年底改制为开滦（集团）有限责任公司。1878年7月24日，开滦的前身——"开平矿务局"成立，后建造了中国企业第一个煤炭码头——秦皇岛港。1906年直隶总督札饬天津官银号筹办滦州煤矿公司，目的在于"以滦制开"，翌年，委周学熙为该公司总经理。1912年开滦矿务局和滦州煤矿公司商定联合营业，签订合同，设立开滦矿务总局。1932年9月12日，开滦矿务总局总经理马克菲在总经理通告第650号中宣布，即日起，秦皇岛经理履行对耀华玻璃厂的行政管理。1934年开平、滦州两大煤矿公司修正联合合同，正式合并，结果英商独占开滦矿务局。

1941年太平洋战争爆发后，开滦矿务局又被日本夺去。1945年日本投降后，开滦矿务局由国民党政府接收，交还英商经营。

1950年8月16日，开滦矿务总局由天津市正式迁入唐山市，与开滦矿区管理机构合并，开除封建把头63人，天津改设开滦办事处。1953年5月28日，开滦天津办事处撤销。1999年年底改制为开滦（集团）有限责任公司。

二、开滦历史老档案的主要内容

开滦历史老档案不仅记录了开滦的历史，实际上也是当时整个社会的一个缩影，反映了开滦所处的社会历史概貌。开滦历史老档案包罗万象，从种类上说包括文件、信函、报告、计划、合同契约、规章规程、证件、董事会议记录、公司组织、矿藏报告等。

从内容上，档案人员把开滦历史档案详细划分为36类，主要有矿权、储量、机械装备、财会缴税等情况，投资贷款捐款及股票融资、人事管理规章制度、经营管理和生产计划、采购及销售、劳资双方关系和罢工纠纷、工资待遇和娱乐及福利、医疗教育和多种副业、房地产、交通运输、通讯、社会和企业间往来、本企业武装力量及防卫事务等。

开滦历史老档案包括唐廷枢1876年在勘察开平煤矿最初的几天内所写给李鸿章的报告，以及相关的资料；滦州煤矿的创办者周学熙作出的指示等重要文件资料，煤炭生产销售及多种经营相关的内容；还包括从各种渠道获得的中国境内各煤田煤量赋存情况，甚至包括东南亚各国，日本的福冈县、北海道，朝鲜以及西伯利亚地区的矿藏情况；也涉及了19世纪末和20世纪上半叶冀东（包括秦皇岛港）、上海、香港的民俗、民风和民情；还反映了中国上层社会中官僚、政客、军阀和民族企业家、外国资本家错综复杂的相互关系，特别是档案中他们之间的来往信件对一些事件描述得事无巨细，无所不包，甚至涉及当时极为重要、极为秘密的军事资料。

三、开滦历史老档案记载采用的文字

1901年英国墨林公司借八国联军入侵中国之机骗占开平煤矿后，开平煤矿一切文件采用英文。1907年成立的周学熙任总经理的滦州煤矿的文件采用中文。1912年联合营业的开滦矿务总局中，英国人占主导地位，全局正式文件均采用英文。所以，开滦遗留下来的历史老档案中，90%采用外文，只有10%采用中文。外文包括英文、法文、日文等。英文占全部外文的90%。

四、开滦历史老档案的记载媒介

1901年后，开平煤矿采用西方先进的记账方式，产生了大账簿。开滦历史老档案中的羊皮大账簿、墨迹和实物档案等曾被开滦展出，跨越近百年时空的大账簿，令许多专家学者惊奇不已。开滦档案馆保存的1 661本大账簿，是1901年至1952年5月开滦的财务账，大多采用英文，分为六大类。这些大账簿有的采用精压牛皮或羊皮全封，烫有漂亮的金字，至今金光耀眼。里面的账面纸全部采用英国高级道格纸或铜版纸，账页中印有水印和隐形标记以防伪。这些账簿有的厚达10厘米，长80厘米，宽50厘米，最重的一本竟达30公斤。

五、开滦历史老档案存放的地点

开滦矿务局和滦州煤矿公司联合成立开滦矿务总局后，由于两矿以前都在天津设有总办事处机构，所以在天津和唐山都有档案资料存放。有文字记载的开滦档案馆成立于1927年，后来开滦矿务总局在唐山和天津总部分别设有档案科。另外，这些历史老档案中还有一部分关于秦皇岛开滦矿务局的档案，由于历史和地理位置原因，现藏于秦皇岛港近代档案室。

六、开滦历史老档案的保密和保管

为了管理好档案，旧开滦还聘请过美国档案专家斯诺。1931—1932年斯诺和一个叫罗旭初的高级档案管理人，带领一批档案人员，对档案进行了一系列的改革，以使档案管理适应近代资本主义企业发展。

开滦的历史老档案分为密卷和普通卷。密卷分为总经理特密卷、总经理密卷、总局密卷、矿区主管特密卷、矿区密卷；普通卷分为总局普通卷、矿区普通卷。开滦历史老档案用颜色区分密级。密卷为绿色且从右上角到左下角有一红色斜条带；普通卷中财务为黄色，船务为浅蓝色，其他卷为棕黄等颜色。

七、开滦历史老档案的保存与丢失

开滦集团公司现设有专门贮藏开滦近 10 万卷 144 年历史档案的开滦档案馆，其保管的历史档案，是目前全国工业企业中最丰富、最悠久、最完整的，为我国工业界档案之最。其中有中国共产党 1952 年正式代管开滦之前的历史老档案 41 507 卷，此外还有 4 534 张历史照片档案，以及一些实物档案。史学界一般将公司 1878 年成立至 1952 年之前这些旧开滦时期形成的档案称为历史老档案，历史老档案占目前开滦档案近一半。

开滦历史老档案历经数次劫难。

第一次劫难是 1901 年英国人骗占开平煤矿后。

从 1878 年建矿至 1900 年，开平矿务局一直采用明朝末年以来代代相传的"龙门账"记账法，其文件都是中国传统式的用毛笔写的流水账之类的记录。

开平煤矿被英商毕威克—墨林公司骗占后，英方代理人胡佛和德璀琳，在一个月内对开平所有产业进行了全面接管，包括所有的文书、契约、账簿。后这些档案大部分被存在天津麦加利银行。在英国人完成对开平产业的接收后，这批早期档案不知所终。目前在开滦档案馆中，所能见到的早期开平煤矿的档案，有的已经不是原始文件。1878 年至 1900 年的 22 年间，开滦的档案很少，很不完整。

第二次劫难在"文化大革命"期间。

由于旧开滦的办事总机构设在天津，所以开滦大量档案资料保存在天津玉皇阁。"文化大革命"开始后，滦矿办事处的房子被占，致使一部分档案丢失。

当时提出"深挖洞，广积粮"，为了备战需要，开滦档案又先后经历了在承德的一个山洞存放，在唐山东矿区 602 厂炸药库存放，在唐山矿井下、井上存放。在十多次的搬迁过程中档案丢失、损坏不少。

第三次劫难是唐山大地震。

地震中，存放档案的房屋全部震毁，成为一片废墟，档案纸片飘散满地。地震当天又下起了大雨，对档案的破坏严重。部分实物档案也震散在砖头瓦砾中，清代的"明黄"瓷碗（旧开滦时企业间互赠的礼品）被一些人拿到简易棚中当饭碗。一些百年前征地、修铁路、挑挖运煤河的珍贵图纸，原来都用特制的马口铁铁筒密封保存，地震中有些人竟将图纸抽出扔掉，而将铁筒插在地震棚中的灶台上当烟筒使用。地震中档案的破坏和实物档案的丢失无法估量。地震以后，档案的存放地搬家变换 7 次，造成不同程度的损坏和丢失。

第四次劫难是 1987 年库房漏水。

震后第 7 次搬家是在 1981 年，搬进新建的矿务局大楼地下室。但是，由于大楼结构原因，档案多次被水淹。最严重的一次是 1987 年，库房的水达半尺多深，档案箱全部泡在水中。虽经紧急抢救，仍有大批档案被水浸泡，损失相当严重。

尽管历经劫难，但开滦历史档案数量之多、跨越时空之悠久，仍然是目前全国所有企业中独一无二的，仍不失为一个文化传承的奇迹。

第四节　秦皇岛港藏"滦外档"的历史形成

1898 年 3 月，光绪皇帝钦批秦皇岛为自开口岸。秦皇岛港由开平矿务局出资建设，"试办码头，借资利运"，最初在秦皇岛附近的东盐务村成立开平矿务局秦皇岛经理处，负责港口经营管理。在百余年沧桑历程中，秦皇岛港和其创办者开滦煤矿一直生死与共，患难相随，命运相通，但在个别历史时期又有所差异。在秦皇岛港的经营发展过程中，先后经历了清朝政府、北洋军阀政府、国民党政府，以及英国人和日本人的统治、回归祖国等几度港权变更重大时期，使得秦港在这一时期形成、保藏了一大批珍贵的历史档案。尤其在 1912 年 1 月至 1941 年这 12 年期间，由于前述历史原因，秦皇岛港实际上由英商统治，形成了大量的英文档案。1941 年 12 月至 1945 年 8 月期间，日本帝国主义从英国殖民者手中接收了开滦与秦皇岛港，对港口实行军事管制，因此，在秦皇岛港形成了大量的日文档案。

目前，秦皇岛港近代档案室（1900—1952 年）保存着各类档案 2 782 卷，其中：文书档案 2 732 卷、科技档案 50 卷，另有历史照片档案 260 张、各种资料 380 册。因这批档案主要是在 1952 年之前旧开滦煤矿时期形成的，又多为英文和日文等外文档案，如在 1912 年至 1952 年的近代档案中 90%是外文卷，其中英文卷占 80%，法文卷和日文卷合占 10%，其余 10%是中文卷，所以一般称"秦港开滦外文档案"，简称"秦港滦外档"或者"滦外档"。这批档案构成了开滦历史老档案的一部分，只不过由于历史沿革和地理位置原因，关于秦皇岛开滦矿务局的档案现藏于秦皇岛港近代档案室，而关于开滦矿务总局的档案现藏于开滦集团公司的开滦档案室。

一、秦港"滦外档"的形成

秦皇岛在 1898 年成立开平矿务局秦皇岛经理处（秦皇岛港前身）之前就有了档案，据资料记载，当时秦皇岛港档案主要是一些中国传统式的用毛笔书写的流水账。1901 年，英国人攫取秦皇岛港，导致在 1897 年至 1901 年间秦皇岛港绝大部分档案不知所终。

1901 年，英国人接管秦皇岛港后，对港口实行了资本主义的经营管理方式，重新设立了会计账簿，将中国毛笔书写的四柱式的龙门账改为现代会计科目。秦皇岛港档案也从此进入外文时代。1912 年，开平煤矿与滦州煤矿联合后，成立了开滦矿务总局。开平矿务局秦皇岛经理处随之更名为秦皇岛开滦矿务局，档案采取中、英文并用的写法，即秦皇岛港档案是一式两份的。因此，现保存的近代档案中，从1902年以后，特别是成立秦皇岛开滦矿务局后形成的档案以外文为主。

1949年9月20日，华北人民政府下令，秦皇岛港一切行文档案、账册、报表、单据全部改用中文汉字。当年10月5日秦皇岛港按行文执行。1950年8月开始，近代人事档案归人事部门管理。1952年，港口由人民政府燃料工业部代管。1953年初秦皇岛港被中央交通部接管后，秦皇岛港近代档案进入了新的管理阶段。

二、秦港"滦外档"的保管

在秦皇岛港档案的保管过程中，历史上有文字记载的港口档案管理部门成立于1927年，由秦皇岛经理处秘书部门专人管理；技术档案由工程技术部门的"绘图房"兼职人员管理。20世纪30年代初期，秦皇岛港档案管理进行了一系列的改革，使之步入现代资本主义企业管理的轨道，从此，卷宗归档比较齐全，保管利用制度趋于健全。

新中国成立后，党和政府在对港口进行代管、接管的过程中，也接收了秦皇岛港的档案，1953年1月，交通部接管秦皇岛港后，文书档案由局长办公室专人管理，技术档案仍由局工程科设计室管理。但是由于受到政治因素、档案知识水平等多方面影响，部分珍贵的历史档案惨遭"淘汰"。

1955年，港口根据中央关于清理旧政权档案的通知精神，抽调一批人员成立了清档领导小组，进行了一次大规模的清档工作。此次清档历时3年，清理了港口的全部外文档案，共形成8 667卷。这次清档后，由于当时政治运动不断，其中有3 346卷所谓的敌伪档案和政治档案划归市公安部门。在历次运动中，外调内查人员对档案乱拆乱拼、随意抽走，又使秦皇岛港档案遭受了一次人为的损失，导致档案数量降至5 247卷。

20世纪70年代初期，为进行"备战"的准备，成立了秦皇岛港战备后方基地，设置了后方档案库，将港口档案迁到抚宁县平山乡秋子峪的"山洞"中秘密保存。直至1982年才从山洞中迁回老局办公楼二楼，后搬至六楼拆箱保管。此时的秦皇岛港近代档案已从20世纪五六十年代的5 247卷减至3 887卷，损失了1 360卷，损失率达25.9%。

1998年初，近代档案又搬运到三楼的两个房间，这批档案得以集中保管，正式存放。后于1999年至2001年的三年中，采取集中整理与日常整理并用的方式，全部重新编制了新目录，打印了新卷号，原卷一个不少，只是有些薄卷"合并同类项"，总计形成2 782卷新卷。

三、秦港"滦外档"的翻译、开发和利用

自1982年以来，秦皇岛港曾聘请7个翻译组织对秦皇岛港近代的这批外文档案进行翻译，共翻译英、日文档案160万字，开启了重新整理这批档案的序幕。尽管聘请和组织人员进行重点翻译和重新整理，但大部分外文案卷仍未翻译出来，影响了这些外文档案的进一步开发和利用。

第五节　耀华机器制造玻璃有限公司介绍

秦皇岛耀华玻璃厂（前身为耀华机器制造玻璃股份有限公司）位于河北省秦皇岛市，始建于1922年，是我国第一家大型玻璃制造企业，亚洲第一个用现代工业法生产玻璃的厂家，拥有亚洲第一条"弗克法"生产线，制造了中国第一块机制平板玻璃，也使秦皇岛成为"中国玻璃产业的摇篮"。2018年1月，耀华玻璃厂荣获中国工业遗产保护名录第一批名单。

耀华玻璃厂于1922年3月破土动工，1924年9月正式建成投产，年生产能力达到15万标准箱。耀华玻璃公司是我国最早使用佛克法专利技术、用机器连续生产玻璃的近代企业，使我国近代玻璃行业由传统手工业生产水平跨入使用先进技术设备进行大批量生产的行列，产品不仅畅销全国，而且还远销美国、日本、东南亚等国家和地区，到1936年已经成

为全国玻璃工业的龙头企业。从民国时期的耀华机器制造玻璃股份有限公司到如今的中国耀华玻璃集团，这一民族工业企业已走过近百年的发展历程，它是近代中国民族工业发展的缩影，是华北地区近代工业发展的典型代表之一。

从耀华创办到秦皇岛解放前夕，耀华经历了"中比合办""中日合办"和"官商合办"三个时期，前后长达 27 年之久。从创建之初至 1993 年，曾先后使用"耀华机器制造玻璃股份有限公司""耀华玻璃股份有限公司""公私合营耀华玻璃股份有限公司""秦皇岛耀华玻璃厂""秦皇岛耀华玻璃总厂"等名称。现名称为中国耀华玻璃集团有限公司。该公司在 1995 年度中国工业企业综合评价最优 500 家中名列第 35 位和建材行业第 1 名，在企业自身发展的同时，为中国玻璃工业的发展输送了大批技术、管理人才和专业技术，为国家经济建设、平板玻璃开辟国际市场作出了较大的贡献。1995 年 8 月 21 日在第五十届国际统计大会上，该公司被授予最高荣耀称号——"中国玻璃生产之王"。

一、耀华机器制造玻璃股份有限公司与滦州煤矿、秦皇岛经理处的关系

耀华机器制造玻璃股份有限公司（以下简称耀华玻璃公司）是中国近代第一家中外合资企业（与比利时合资），总公司设于天津，总工厂设于秦皇岛。其时天津属直隶（今河北），为省会所在。耀华玻璃公司和滦州煤矿都是周学熙创办的，耀华公司中方股金主要是滦州煤矿各股东由累计的"新实业开发基金"拨交。因此，很多开滦的股东亦是耀华股东，开滦矿务总局为耀华的创建解决了土地、设备、交通线、原燃料、销售等问题，1924 年 5 月耀华投产前与开滦矿务总局签订了耀华委托代管全部业务合同，开滦矿务总局接管耀华玻璃公司，由秦皇岛经理处经营管理。此后耀华玻璃公司的办事方式、市场开拓、产品销售都利用开滦矿务总局的资源，开滦成为耀华发展的强大后盾，对耀华的发展至关重要。

二、耀华公司外文档案的形成

耀华公司从创建伊始，由开滦矿务局长期代管，中英合办时期的开滦在代管耀华期间，便采用了当时先进的企业管理制度，在档案管理上仿照开滦，采用中英文分别记录模式，因此也保存了大量中外文（主要为英文和日文）档案，虽历经岁月，但这些珍贵档案总体状况依然良好。目前，这批档案绝大部分收藏于秦皇岛市档案馆、天津市档案馆、秦皇岛市玻璃博物馆（原耀华厂档案室）和秦皇岛港口博物馆（原秦皇岛港史志科档案室），其中部分中文档案已经过整理，计有三千多卷，更多的大量外文档案还处于未整理的封存状态，这些都是难得一见的珍贵历史宝藏。耀华档案体量丰富，其中完整保存了耀华玻璃公司从1922年创立到1946年重新改组之前，公司发展各个阶段的总计八十余次董事会的议事录，主要包括股东会议事录、股东常会议事录、董事会议事录、董监事联席会议事录等以及耀华玻璃的经销，充分见证了耀华在这一历史时段的发展历程。其中第四至二十次董事会议事录现藏于秦皇岛市档案馆，第二十一至四十二次董事会议事录现藏于秦岛市玻璃博物馆。而关于耀华玻璃经销的英文档案大都藏于秦皇岛港口博物馆。

第二章

秦皇岛港藏"滦外档"之耀华玻璃经销合同

第一节 开滦矿务总局耀华机器制造玻璃有限公司与同祥湧玻璃庄之合同（1934年）

MEMORANDUM

From: sales department, Tientsin　　To: Agent Chinwangtao

Time: 12th January 1934　　Serial Number: 18119

　　We now enclose herewith a copy of the Agreement made between the Administration and Tung Hsiang Yung for the sales of glass in Tientsin during 1934, for your information and retention.

译文：

备忘录

发信人：天津销售部　　　　收信人：秦皇岛事务部

时间：1934年1月12日　　　卷号：18119

　　现随函附上1934年开滦矿务总局耀华机器制造玻璃有限公司与同祥湧玻璃庄就在天津销售玻璃一事签订的协议副本一份，供你方参考并保留。

合同英文：

MEMORANDUM OF AGREEMENT made and entered into this 18th day of January 1934, at Tientsin, North China, between the Kailan Mining Administration, as General Managers of the Yao Hua Mechanical Glass Co.,Ltd., (hereinafter referred to as the Administration) of the one part and the Tung Hsiang Yung (hereinafter referred to as the Contractor) of the other part, WHEREBY it is mutually agreed:

1. That the Administration undertakes to employ Tung Hsiang Yung as their Contract for the sale of the products of the Yao Hua Mechanical Glass Company, Limited. of Chinwangtao, within the period of this Agreement, in the Tientsin Area, and in turn the Contractor undertakes not to be interested directly or indirectly in the sale and /or purchase of any articles or commodities competing with these products.

In the event of the Contractor being not interested directly or indirectly in the sale and/or purchase of any articles or commodities competing with the products of the Yao Hua Mechanical Glass Co.,Ltd., the Administration reserve the right to cancel forthwith this Contract, and withhold payment of any rebate outstanding.

2. That the Contractor shall do his best to promote the sales of Yao Hua Glass in Tientsin and undertakes to sell to all consumers and declare without discrimination. Should he for any reason be unwilling to transact business with an individual or individuals, he will report the circumstances to the Administration with full explanation, and the Administration reserve the right to undertake the business subject to Clause 7 of this Agreement.

3. That the Tientsin Area shall be understood to mean sales made at the Administration's godowns, Tientsin.

4. That the Contractor shall provide security against sums due to the Administration in the form of a cash deposit of Thirty Thousand Chinese

Standard Dollars (c.s.$30,000) whereon the Administration will credit the Contractor's account with interest calculated at 6% per annum.

5. That all orders for glass shall be sent to the Administration properly chopped by the Contractor's official shop and on forms to be supplied by the Administration.

6. That the administration agrees to grant the Contractor an initial rebate of 3.5% per case on all glass purchased by him. This rebate to be credited him monthly on rendition of accounts. Should the amount of glass purchased by the Contractor during the period of this Contract exceed 50,000 standards, additional rebates will be given as detailed hereunder:

a) <u>Over 50,000 but under 60,000 standards</u>

An additional rebate of one half per cent, making 4% in all, will be paid on the total quantity purchased.

b) <u>Over 60,000 but under 65,000</u>

An additional rebate of one per cent, making 4.5% in all, will be paid on the total quantity purchased.

c) <u>Over 65,000 standards but under 70,000</u>

An additional rebate of 1.5%, making 5% in all, will be paid on the total quantity purchased.

d) <u>Over 70,000</u>

An additional rebate of 2%, making 5.5% in all, will be paid on the total quantity purchased.

Such additional rebates will be paid, if earned, on the final settlement of the contractor's account in January 1935.

7. That the Administration reserve the right to sell glass in the Tientsin market but will not sell at less than the market prices without consultation with and the agreement of the Contractor but reserve the right to issue any free of charge as samples as they may consider necessary and to supply free

or at special rates such glass as may be required for their own use.

8. That the market ruling prices for the standard specification of the 4th Quality Single Thickness glass and other grades and thickness shall be fixed by the Administration as they deem fit from time to time; but the Administration agree that the price will not be increased without a fortnight's notice being given to the contractor.

9. That the Contractor will purchase 4th Quality single thickness glass in accordance with the standard specification, and should he require a greater proportion of large sizes than is allowed in such a specification, he shall pay for them at the market price ruling for such sizes.

The definition or a "Standard Specification" is as follows:-

60% of the specification up to 50 united inches

40% of the specification from 51 to 80 united inches

The united inch total is computed from the additions of length and width.

10. That for the purposes of the rebates set forth in Clause 6, the better qualities and heavier grades will be computed as follows:-

4th Quality

One case S'double of 100 sq. ft. shall count as 2 cases single

One case Double of 100 sq. ft. shall count as 2.5 cases single

One case Triple of 100 sq. ft. shall count as 3 cases single

One case Thick of 100 sq. ft. shall count as 4 cases single

One case E. Thick of 100 sq. ft. shall count as 5 cases single

2nd and 3rd Quality

One case S'double of 100 sq. ft. shall count as 3 cases single

One case Double of 100 sq. ft. shall count as 4 cases single

One case Triple of 100 sq. ft. shall count as 5 cases single

One case Thick of 100 sq. ft. shall count as 6 cases single

One case E. Thick of 100 sq. ft. shall count as 7.5 cases single

In 2nd and 3rd Quality Single Thickness, one case of 100 sq. ft. over 27 united inches shall count as 2 cases of single thickness 4th Quality and one case of 100 sq. ft. of small size 27 united inches or under as one case 4th Quality, Single Thickness.

11. That the Contractor agrees to pay in full on or before the 25th of every month for all glass supplied by the Administration during the preceding month (as an example: All glass supplied during the month of January must be paid for by the 25th of February).

12. That the Contractor shall supply to the Administration such information as they may require from time to time as to market conditions, and imports and selling prices of competitive glass in the Tientsin Area.

13. That this Agreement is made out in the English and Chinese languages and, in the event of any dispute arising as to its interpretation, the English version shall be binding on both parties.

14. That the Administration shall have the right to suspend the provisions of this Agreement so far as they concern the delivery of glass to the Contractor during such period or periods as the output of the Factory or the ability of the Administration to deliver is or may be affected by flood, war, internal rebellion, civil disturbances, strikes of workmen, shortage of railway cars, interruption of rail communication or any other unforeseen circumstances of whatsoever kind.

15. That this Agreement shall be considered to have come into force on the First day of January, 1936, and shall remain in full force end effect until the 31st day of December,1936, subject to cancellation by either party upon giving one month's notice in writing.

In witness whereof the hands of the parties hereunto:-

```
THE KAILAN MINING ADMINISTRATION( General Managers, The Yao
Hua Mechanical Glass Co., Ltd.)
Witness to the signature of: _____
                             CHIET HANAGERS .
Witness to the signature of: _____
                             TUNG HSIANG YUNG .
```

合同中文：

本合同于中华民国二十三年一月十八日在华北天津订立。此造为经理耀华机器制造玻璃有限公司营业事宜之开滦矿务总局（此后称总局），彼造为同祥湧玻璃庄（此后称分销人），兹将两造之认可之条件列左。

（一）总局承认在本合同期限之内委任同祥湧为天津区域推销秦皇岛耀华机器制造玻璃有限公司产品之分销人，同时分销人承认不直接或间接买卖与耀华玻璃公司产品对竞之货物。

分销人有直接或间接买卖与耀华玻璃公司产品对竞之货物情事，总局可立即取消本合同及停付未结清之回用。

（二）分销人应大力推广天津区域耀华玻璃之销路，并当一视同仁售给各用户及各商人，如对某某有不愿与之交易情事，应将事实详细向总局述明，总局依据各本合同第七条之规定有办理此项业务之权。

（三）所谓天津区域系指在天津总局货栈交货之各销数而言。

（四）分销人备中国国币三万元交付总局，作为对于各欠款之保证金。总局按年息六厘付息计入分销人账内。

（五）凡订购玻璃机订货单悉当填在总局发给之单据上，并于送交以前按分销人正式登记。

（六）总局对分销人购买之一切玻璃承诺每箱按 3.5%给予通常回用，并将该回用于每月结账之时收入分销人账内，分销人在本合同期限以内购买玻璃过单位数五万以上者当照左开情形加给回用。

A. 单位数超过五万而不足六万者，按所购买量加给回用 0.5%，即统共合成 4%。

B. 超过六万而不足六万五千者，按所购买量加给回用 1%，即统共合成 4.5%。

C. 超过六万五千而不足七万者，按所购买量加给回用 1.5%，即统共合成 5%。

D. 超过七万者，按所购买量加给回用 2%，即统共合成 5.5%。

（七）总局仍有在津市销售玻璃之权，惟未经商得分销人同意以前不得按较此市价低廉之价格出售，但总局认为必要时可以颁发免费之样品及免费或按特价供给其所自备之玻璃。

（八）通常尺寸四等单厚及其他种类与厚度之玻璃市价应由总局随时按其所宜而规定，但总局承认非在两星期前通知分销人外不许增价。

（九）分销人应按照通常尺寸购买四等单厚玻璃。遇需要比该尺寸数大之玻璃时，分销人应按尺寸照现行之市价付给价款。

兹将通常尺寸之意义解释列左。

大至五十联英寸为止之玻璃占百分之六十，

由五十联英寸起至八十联英寸止之玻璃占 40%。

联英寸之总数由长度与宽度两数相加而得。

（十）凡较佳及较重之玻璃当按左开办法计算第六条规定之回用。

四等玻璃

半双厚玻璃一百方英尺一箱者合作单厚玻璃两箱。

双厚玻璃一百方英尺一箱者合作单厚玻璃两箱半。

三厚玻璃一百方英尺一箱者合作单厚玻璃三箱。

厚玻璃一百方英尺一箱者合作单厚玻璃四箱。

加厚玻璃一百万英尺一箱者合作单厚玻璃五箱。

二等与三等玻璃

半双厚玻璃一百方英尺一箱者合作单厚玻璃三箱。

双厚玻璃一百方英尺一箱者合作单厚玻璃四箱。

三厚玻璃一百方英尺一箱者合作单厚玻璃五箱。

厚玻璃一百万英尺一箱者合作单厚玻璃六箱。

加厚玻璃一百万英尺一箱者合作单厚玻璃七箱半。

二等与三等之单厚玻璃其大小在二十七联英寸以上，每箱装 100 方英尺者，应作四等单厚玻璃两箱计算。若不足二十七联英寸之小块玻璃，每箱装 100 方英尺者则仍作四等单厚玻璃一箱计算。

（十一）每月由总局供给玻璃之价款，分销人承认于次月二十五日以前全数付清（例如：一月份所取之玻璃，其价款必须于二月二十五日以前付清）。

（十二）分销人应按总局所需，随时将津区竞销玻璃之市况及输入情形，以及出售价目等消息供给总局。

（十三）本合同用英汉文缮写，如有争执，两造应以英文为准。

（十四）遇工厂出品或总局能力上受水灾、战事、内乱、民众罢工、路局车辆缺乏或铁路交通断绝，以及其他一切意外情事之影响时，总局在此期内对于本合同各条件中关于装交分销人玻璃之规定，有停止履行之权。

（十五）本合同于民国二十三年一月六日发生效力，除经任何一造在一个月之前通知取消本合同外，其有效时期当迄同年十二月三十一日为止。

开滦矿务总局经理耀华机器制造玻璃有限公司营业事宜
在见人
分销人
在见人

第二节　开滦矿务总局耀华机器制造玻璃有限公司与同祥湧玻璃庄之合同（1936 年）

合同英文：

> MEMORANDUM OF AGREEMENT made and entered into this 1st day of January, 1936, at Tientsin, North China, between the Kailan Mining Administration, as General Managers of the Yao Hua Mechanical Glass Co.,Ltd., (hereinafter referred to as the Administration) of the one part and

Messrs. Tung Hsiang Yung (hereinafter referred to as the Contractor) of the other part, WHEREBY it is mutually agreed:-

1. That the Contractor shall have sole selling rights of Yao Hua Glass in the North China Area excluding the Metropolitan Area of Peiping and stations along the Peiping -Suiyuan Railway subject to the Administration retaining the right to quote for any wholesale business at market rates on a delivered basis.

2. That the Contractor shall not buy any competitive glass except that which cannot be supplied by the Administration.

3. That the Contractor will undertake to sell a minimum quantity of 60,000 standards during the period of the Agreement.

4. That the prices to be paid for the standard specification of 4th quality single thickness glass and for all other grades and thickness at all stations shall be determined from time to time by the Administration in accordance with market conditions but the Administration agrees that the price or prices of any grade or grades will not be increased without a fortnight's notice to the Contractor.

5. That the prices notified shall be understood to be free on car at railway stations along the railways within the area covered by this Agreement with the exception of Tientsin where they shall be understood to be ex the Administration's Tientsin godowns.

6. That the administration agrees to grant the Contractor an initial rebate or 35 cents per standard on all glass purchased by him up to the guaranteed minimum of 60,000 standards. Should the amount of glass purchased by the Contractor during the period of this Agreement exceed 60,000 standards additional rebates will be given as detailed hereunder:

a) <u>Over 60,000 standards but under 80,000 standards</u>

An additional rebate of 5 cents, making 40 cents per standard will be paid on the total quantity purchased.

b) <u>Over 80,000 standards but under 100,000 standards</u>

An additional rebate of 5 cents, making 45 cents per standard will be paid on the total quantity purchase.

c) <u>Over 100,000 standards</u>

An additional rebate of 5 cents, making 50 cents per standard will be paid on the total quantity purchased.

7. That the Administration agrees to advance the initial rebate by crediting it in the monthly settlement of accounts and that the additional rebates if earned will be paid on the final settlement of the Contractor's account at the termination of the Agreement. The contractor agrees, however, that should he fail to purchase the guaranteed minimum quality of 60,000 standards he will refund to the Administration the full amount of the initial rebate advanced to him by the Administration.

8. That the Contractor shall provide security against sums due to the Administration in the form of a cash deposit of Thirty Thousand Chinese Standard Dollars (c.s.$30,000) whereon the Administration will credit the Contractor's account with interest calculated at 6% per annum.

9. That the Contractor will purchase 4th Quality Single Thickness glass in accordance with the standard specification, and should he require a greater proportion of large sizes than is allowed in such a specification, he shall pay for them at the market price ruling for such sizes.

The definition or a "Standard Specification" is as follows: -

60% of the specification up to 50 united inches

40% of the specification from 51 to 80 united inches

The united inch total is computed from the additions of length and width.

10. That for the purposes of the rebates set forth in Clause 6, the better qualities and heavier grades will be computed as follows: -

4th Quality

One case S'double of 100 sq. ft. shall count as 2 cases single

One case Double of 100 sq. ft. shall count as 2.5 cases single

One case Triple of 100 sq. ft. shall count as 3 cases single

One case Thick of 100 sq. ft. shall count as 4 cases single

One case E. Thick of 100 sq. ft. shall count as 5 cases single

2nd and 3rd Quality

One case S'double of 100 sq. ft. shall count as 3 cases single

One case Double of 100 sq. ft. shall count as 4 cases single

One case Triple of 100 sq. ft. shall count as 5 cases single

One case Thick of 100 sq. ft. shall count as 6 cases single

One case E. Thick of 100 sq. ft. shall count as 7.5 cases single

In 2nd and 3rd Quality Single Thickness, one case of 100 sq. ft. over 27 united inches shall count as 2 cases of single thickness 4th Quality and one case of 100 sq. ft. of small size, 27 united inches or under as one case 4th Quality, Single Thickness.

11. That the Contractor agrees to pay in full on or before the 25th of every month for all glass supplied by the Administration during the preceding month (as an example: All glass supplied during the month of January must be paid for by the 25th of February).

12. That the Contractor shall supply to the Administration such information as it may require from time to time as to market conditions, and imports and selling prices of competitive glass in the Tientsin Area.

13. That this Agreement is made out in the English and Chinese languages and, in the event of any dispute arising as to its interpretation, the English version shall be binding on both parties.

14. That the Administration shall have the right to suspend the provisions of this Agreement so far as they concern the delivery of glass to

the Contractor during such period or periods as the output of the Factory or the ability of the Administration to deliver is or may be affected by flood, war, internal rebellion, civil disturbances, strikes of workmen, shortage of railway cars, interruption of rail communication or any other unforeseen circumstances of whatsoever kind.

  15. That this Agreement shall be considered to have come into force on the First day of January, 1936, and shall remain in full force and effect until the 31st day of December,1936, subject to cancellation by either party upon giving one month's notice in writing.

  In witness whereof the hands of the parties hereunto:-
THE KAILAN MINING ADMINISTRATION(General Managers, The Yao Hua Mechanical Glass Co., Ltd.)
 Witness to the signature of: _____
        CHIET HANAGERS .
 Witness to the signature of: _____
        TUNG HSIANG YUNG .

合同中文：

  本合同于中华民国二十五年一月一日在华北天津订立。此造为经理耀华机器制造玻璃有限公司营业事宜之开滦矿物总局（此后称总局），彼造为同祥湧玻璃庄（此后称分销人），兹将两造之认可之条件列左。

  （一）除北平市区及平绥铁路沿线各站外，分销人在华北一带有经理耀华玻璃之专销权，但总局对于任何批发营业有按送货到地行市开价之权。

  （二）分销人不得购买任何竞销玻璃，惟总局所不克供给者不在此例。

  （三）分销人应在本合同期内至少任销玻璃6万箱。

  （四）通常尺寸四等单厚及其他种类与厚度之玻璃在各站交卖之价目应

由总局随时按照市面情形规定，但总局承认无论任何一种或数种之玻璃价目非给予分销人两星期前之通知不得增加。

（五）除天津系在总局天津货栈货站交货外，所有通知之价目均系指本合同所载之区域内沿铁路各站车上交货而言。

（六）总局承认对于分销人购买之各种玻璃，遇其担保之数量至少六万箱时，每箱给予最初回用洋三角五分。倘分销人在本合同期限以内所购玻璃超过六万箱则当照左开办法加给回用。

A. <u>超过六万箱而不足八万箱者</u>

按照所购总量每箱加给回用洋五分，即每箱共计洋四角。

B. <u>超过八万箱而不足十万箱者</u>

按照所购总量每箱再加给回用洋五分，即每箱共计洋四角五分。

C. <u>超过十万箱者</u>

按所购总量每箱再加给回用洋五分，即每箱共计洋五角。

（七）总局同意最初之回用预先付给，于每月结账时收入账内。如有额外加给之回用，当于本合同期满与分销人最后清算时付给分销人，亦承诺如所购之玻璃未能达到其所担保之数量6万箱时，则总局预付之最初回用当由分销人悉数还于总局。

（八）分销人应预留国币三万元存于总局，作为欠总局价款之担保品，由总局收入分销人账上，按年息六厘计算。

（九）分销人应按照通常尺寸购买四等单厚玻璃。遇需要比该尺寸数大之玻璃时，分销人应按所要尺寸照现行之市价付款。

兹将通常尺寸之意义解释列左。

大至五十联英寸为止之玻璃占百分之六十，

由五十联英寸起至八十联英寸止之玻璃占百分之四十。

联英寸之总数系由长度与宽度两数相加而得。

（十）为核算第六条规定之回用计，凡成色较佳及分量较重之玻璃，当按左开办法计算。

四等玻璃

一百方英尺半双厚玻璃一箱作为单厚玻璃两箱。

一百方英尺双厚玻璃一箱作为单厚玻璃两箱半。

一百方英尺三厚玻璃一箱作为单厚玻璃三箱。

一百方英尺厚玻璃一箱作为单厚玻璃四箱。

一百方英尺加厚玻璃一箱作为单厚玻璃五箱。

二等与三等玻璃

一百方英尺半双厚玻璃一箱作为单厚玻璃三箱。

一百方英尺双厚玻璃一箱作为单厚玻璃四箱。

一百方英尺三厚玻璃一箱作为单厚玻璃五箱。

一百方英尺厚玻璃一箱作为单厚玻璃六箱。

一百方英尺加厚玻璃一箱作为单厚玻璃七箱半。

二等与三等之单厚玻璃，其大小在二十七联英寸以上，每箱装一百方英尺者，作为四等单厚玻璃两箱计算。若不足二十七联英寸之小块玻璃，每箱装100方英尺者则仍作四等单厚玻璃一箱计算。

（十一）分销人承认于次月二十五日以前将总局于上月内所供给玻璃之价款全数付清（例如：一月份所取之玻璃，其价款必须于二月二十五日以前付清）。

（十二）分销人应按总局所需，随时将津区内竞销玻璃之市况及输入情形，以及出售价目等消息供给总局。

（十三）本合同用英汉文缮写，如有争执，两造均应以英文为准。

（十四）遇工厂出品或总局对于装交玻璃与分销人能力上受水灾、战事、内乱、民众工人罢工、路局车辆缺乏或铁路交通断绝，以及其他一切意外情事之影响，总局在此期内对本合同各条件之规定，有停止履行之权。

（十五）本合同于民国二十五年一月一日发生效力，除经任何一造在一个月之前书面通知取消本合同外，其有效时期当至同年十二月三十一日为止。

开滦矿务总局经理耀华机器制造玻璃有限公司营业事宜

在见人

分销人　　　同祥湧

第三节　开滦矿务总局耀华机器制造玻璃有限公司与北平地区经销商之合同（1936年）

合同英文：

> MEMORANDUM OF AGREEMENT made and entered into this lst day of January, 1936, at Tientsin, North China, between the KAILAN MINING ADMINISTRATION, as General Managers of the YAO HUA MECHANICAL GLASS Co., Ltd., (hereinafter called the "Administration") of the one part and Messrs.
>
> Tian Yuan Tai（天源泰）
> Ching Shun Ho（庆顺和）
> Ching Yuan The（庆源德）
> Heng Yee Hou（恒义厚）
> Heng Yuan Hsing（恒元祥）
> Chien Hsing Hou（乾兴厚）
> Wen Hsing Yung（文祥湧）
> Shun Tai Yee（顺泰义）
>
> Glass Dealers of Peiping (hereinafter called the "Dealers") of the other part, whereby it is mutually agreed as follows:
>
> 1. The Dealers agree to purchase the whole of their Window Glass requirements in the metropolitan area of Peiping and Stations along the Peiping-Suiyuan Railway from the Administration, which are estimated at 20,000 standards per annum. Should, however, the Administration consider themselves unable to supply the entire requirements of the Dealers, they will advise them by letter to this effect and the Dealers shall be at liberty to purchase elsewhere.
>
> 2. The Dealers agree to order their requirements of glass in such quantities that the cases may be transported to Peiping and Stations along the

Peiping-Suiyuan Railway in full carloads.

3. Each of the Dealers agrees to lodge with the Administration a first glass shop guarantee to the value of $3,000.

4. The Dealers agree to pay in full after 35 days for all glass supplied by the Administration during the preceding month (as an example:- All glass supplied during the month of January must be paid for by the 5th March).

5. All orders for glass shall be sent to the Administration officially chopped with the seal of Messrs. Tien Yuan Tai and the Administration will hold this Dealer responsible for the collection of monies due on behalf of glass supplied to the dealers. The Dealers on their part will hand the Administration a letter, duly chopped with their official seal, stating that in the case of default by Messrs. Tien Yuan Tai, the Shop Guarantee submitted by them as stated in paragraph 3 of this Agreement may be used by the Administration.

6. The Administration agree not to sell 4th Quality, Single Thickness Glass F.O.C.Chienmen or Stations along the Peiping-Suiyuan Railway to any other purchasers in the Area covered by this Agreement except the dealers, but retain the right to sell better quality or heavier glass to any who may require it at 3% over the Standard F.O.C.prices.

7. The prices for 4th Quality Single Thickness glass of Standard specifications shall be fixed by the Administration and these prices will be notified to the Dealers. The prices shall be regulated by the market price of Yao Hua Glass in Tientsin.

8. For any requirements not of Standard Specification, the Dealers shall refer to the Administration for a special quotation. The definition of a "Standard Specification" as applied to this Agreement shall be 60% of the Specification up to 50 united inches and 40% of the specification from 51 to 80 unite inches. The united inch total is computed from the addition of the

length and width.

9. The Administration agrees to grant the Dealers an initial rebate of 3% off the Standard F.O.C. Peiping price per case of 4th Quality Single Thickness glass in the Standard Specification on all glass purchased during 1936 up to 20,000 Standards, this rebate to be credited monthly on rendition of accounts. Should the amount of glass purchased during 1936 exceed 20,000 Standards, additional rebates will be given as detailed hereunder:-

a) <u>Over 20,000 but under 22,500 standards</u>

An additional rebate of one half per cent, making 3.5% in all will be paid on the total quantity purchased during 1936.

b) <u>Over 22,500 but under 25,000 standards</u>

An additional rebate of one per cent, making 4% in all will be paid on the total quantity purchased during 1936.

c) <u>Over 25,000 standards but under 27,500 standards</u>

An additional rebate of one half per cent, making 4.5% in all will be paid on the total quantity purchased during 1936.

d) <u>Over 27,500 standards</u>

An additional rebate of one half per cent, making 5% in all will be paid on the total quantity purchased during 1936.

Such additional rebates will be credited, if earned, in the final settlement of account to be rendered in January 1937.

It is understood that, for the purpose of calculating the above rebates, purchases of the better qualities and heavier grades will be computed as follows.

4th Quality

One case S'double of 100 sq. ft. shall count as 2 cases 4th single

One case Double of 100 sq. ft. shall count as 2.5 cases single

One case Triple of 100 sq. ft. shall count as 3 cases single

One case Thick of 100 sq. ft. shall count as 4 cases single

One case E. Thick of 100 sq. ft. shall count as 5 cases single

2nd and 3rd Quality

One case S'double of 100 sq. ft. shall count as 3 cases single

One case Double of 100 sq. ft. shall count as 4 cases single

One case Triple of 100 sq. ft. shall count as 5 cases single

One case Thick of 100 sq. ft. shall count as 6 cases single

One case E. Thick of 100 sq. ft. shall count as 7.5 cases single

In 2nd and 3rd Quality, Single Thickness, one case of 100 sq. ft. over 27 united inches shall count as 2 cases of 4th Quality, single thickness, and one case of 100 sq. ft. of small size, 27 united inches or under as one case 4th Quality, Single Thickness.

10. That this Agreement is made out in the English and Chinese languages and, If any dispute arises, the English version shall be binding on both parties.

11. For any cause beyond the control of the Administration such as fire, flood, riots, war revolution, strikes, or any acts of God which might force the Administration to suspend the provisions of this Agreement, the Dealers shall have no claims on the Administration whatsoever.

12. That this Agreement shall be considered to have come into force on the First day of January, 1936, and shall remain in full force and effect until the 31st day of December,1936, subject to cancellation by either party upon giving one month's notice in writing.

IN WITNESS WHEREOF THE HANDS OF THE PARTIES HERETO:

The Kailan Mining Administration (General Managers, The Yao Hua Mechanical Glass Co., Ltd.)

Witness to the signature of: _____

CHIET HANAGERS.

Witness to the signature of: _____

TIAN YUAN TAI.

合同中文：

本合同于中华民国二十五年一月一日在华北天津订立。此造为经理耀华机器制造玻璃有限公司营业事宜之开滦矿务总局（此后称总局），彼造为北平天源泰、庆顺和、庆源德、恒义厚、恒元祥、乾兴厚、文祥涌、顺泰义玻璃庄（此后称经售人），兹将两造之认可之条件列左。

（一）经售人承认北平区域沿平绥路各站统共所需之窗户玻璃预计每年约2万箱悉向总局购买，但遇总局不克照经售人所需之全部供给时，应将此项情形函知经售人，俾其自由向他处购买。

（二）经售人承认订购之玻璃箱数，必能合整车发运至北平或延平绥路各站。

（三）经售人承认各兑价值三千元之一等铺保交与总局。

（四）每月由总局供给玻璃之价款，经售人承认于三十五日以后全数付清（例如一月间所取之玻璃，其价款必须于三月五日付清）。

（五）凡购用玻璃之订货单应由天源泰盖用正式戳记送交总局，总局即责成该经售人收集供给各经售人之玻璃价款。但各经售人应分别盖用本局正式戳记致函总局，声明天源泰如不履行合同，所有各经售人照本合同第三条规定所写之铺保，总局得令其负责。

（六）总局承认除供给各经售人外，不再将四等单厚玻璃在前门车站或沿平绥路各站车上交货，售与本合同所指区域内之其他购户，但有需要较佳或加厚之玻璃者，总局售与其价目应较车上交货之定价增加百分之三。

（七）通常尺寸四等单厚玻璃之价目应由总局规定，分别通知各经售人，此项价目当按天津耀华玻璃之市价整订。

（八）对于非通常尺寸之需求，经售人应向总局征询特别报价。适用于本合同时，通常尺寸定义解释为：

大至五十联英寸为止之玻璃占百分之六十，

由五十联英寸起至八十联英寸止之玻璃占百分之四十。

联英寸之数量系由长度与宽度两数相加而得。

（九）总局承认给予经售人于民国二十五年内购用四等单厚、通常尺寸玻璃两万箱者，其每箱之最初回扣按北平车站车上交货价目之百分之三。此项回扣于每月结账时计入账内，若民国二十五年内所购之玻璃超过二万箱时，其累加之回扣按照左开详细办法办理。

  A. 超过二万箱而不足二万二千五百箱者

加给回扣 0.5%，即按民国二十五年所购玻璃之全数核算，供给回扣 3.5%。

  B. 超过二万二千五百箱而不足二万五千箱者

再加给回扣 0.5%，即按民国二十五年所购玻璃之全数核算，供给回扣 4%。

  C. 超过二万五千箱而不足二万七千五百箱者

再加给回扣 0.5%，即按民国二十五年所购玻璃之全数核算，供给回扣 4.5%。

  D. 超过二万七千五百箱者

再加给回扣 0.5%，即按民国二十五年所购玻璃之全数核算，供给回扣 5%。

此项合同回扣当按民国二十六年一月总局给付之数计入账内。

凡成色较佳及分量较重之玻璃，当按左开办法计算。

为核算以上规定之回用计，凡成色较佳及分量较重之玻璃，当按左开办法计算。

四等玻璃

一百方英尺半双厚玻璃一箱应按单厚玻璃两箱核算。

一百方英尺双厚玻璃一箱应按单厚玻璃两箱半核算。

一百方英尺三厚玻璃一箱应按单厚玻璃三箱核算。

一百方英尺厚玻璃一箱应按单厚玻璃四箱核算。

一百方英尺加厚玻璃一箱应按单厚玻璃五箱核算。

二等与三等玻璃

一百方英尺半双厚玻璃一箱应按单厚玻璃三箱核算。

一百方英尺双厚玻璃一箱应按单厚玻璃四箱核算。

一百方英尺三厚玻璃一箱者应按单厚玻璃五箱核算。

一百方英尺厚玻璃一箱应按单厚玻璃六箱核算。

一百方英尺加厚玻璃一箱应按单厚玻璃七箱半核算。

二等与三等之单厚玻璃，其大小超过二十七联英寸者，则每箱一百方英尺当作为四等单厚玻璃两箱计算。若不足二十七联英寸之小块玻璃，每箱装 100 方英尺者则仍作为四等单厚玻璃一箱计算。

（十）本合同用英汉文缮写，如有争执，两造均应以英文为准。

（十一）如遇总局能力以外之事故发生，例如：火灾、水灾、暴动、战事、罢工以及天灾致总局无法履行本合同条件时，经售人不得向总局提出任何要求。

（十二）本合同于民国二十五年一月一日发生效力，除经任何一造在一个月之前书面通知取消本合同外，其有效时期当至同年十二月三十一日为止。

开滦矿务总局经理耀华机器制造玻璃有限公司营业事宜

在见人

分销人　　　同祥湧

第三章

开滦矿务总局耀华公司玻璃经销部门间备忘录

（共 107 份）

部门间备忘录一①
INTER-DEPARTMENTAL MEMORANDUM

To:　Agent　　　　　　　　Reference　18119
　　　Chinwangtao　　　　　Serial Number ....
　　　　　　　　　　　　　　Tientsin　Agency　Dec 4, 1934

Subject ....

　　With reference to the Sales Dept's memo to you No.18119 of 19th January, 1934 and the copy of the agreement between the Administration and Messrs. Tung Hsing Yung enclosed therein, this agreement expires on 31/12/34.

　　We shall be glad to learn whether you wish us to negotiate a renewal of this agreement, and if so, whether you desire my change in this wording.

E. J. Cowell
Tientsin Sales Office.

译文：

参考编号　18119
序号 ....
天津　　代理商　1934 年 12 月 4 日

---

① 关于同一事务的前后多份档案归类于同一序号备忘录下面，本章共有 107 份档案。

致：秦皇岛代理商

根据 1934 年 1 月 19 日销售部给你的第 18119 号备忘录，以及附上的总局与同祥湧玻璃庄的签订的合同副本，本合同于 1934 年 12 月 31 日到期。

贵公司是否希望我们就延长本协议进行谈判？如果希望，贵公司是否希望我修改本协议的措辞？

考威尔
天津销售处

18119

E. J. Cowell, ESq.,
TIENTSIN　　　　　　　　　　　　　Chinwangtao　　7th Dec, 34

Dear Cowell,

　　With reference to your letter 18119 of the 4th inst. on the subject of Messrs. Tung Hsiang Yung's agreement, I think that before we bind ourselves to any selling arrangement for 1935 we must carefully consider, (a) how we have fared during the past year under our agreement with Tung Hsiang Yung, and (b) the report and recommendations made by Messrs. Chen and Wang on the hinterland markets.

　　If you are satisfied that our best interests have been served by the 1934 arrangement, we must consider the facts that we desire, (a) to extend our sales in our "Home Markets" of North China to the elimination of all competition, and (b) that according to the recent survey there is a possibility of effecting an increase. However, to realise these increased sales it will be necessary to alter our selling methods to meet the recommendations of direct shipments, sub-agents and the carrying of stocks at the main centres.

　　I do not mean to infer that I agree with these three recommendations completely, but I am of the opinion that whilst working through Tung Hsiang Yung is sound and reliable, we will never increase our sales until he is persuaded out of his conservatism: I am sure that much interior business goes beyond us on account of his very conservative methods. However he is a very powerful force in the glass trade in North China and it is to our advantage to keep him working with us.

 I consider, therefore, your first plan should be to explain to Tung Hsiang Yung our ambition in North China and our ideas of expanding sales by direct rail shipments, and the maintenance of a closer contact with the distant markets. I suggest you have a talk with Mr. Sung and obtain his views, particularly on the question of direct shipments and the holding of stocks at the various large centres. If you think I would be of any help in your dealing I can run up.

Yours sincerely,
H. H. Faulker.

译文：

18119
秦皇岛 1934 年 12 月 7 日

致：天津的考威尔

亲爱的考威尔：

  关于您本月 4 日就同祥湧玻璃庄的协议问题的 18119 号来信，我想，在我们确定 1935 年的任何销售安排之前，我们必须仔细考虑（a）过去一年我们与同祥湧玻璃庄的协议进展如何；（b）陈、王两位先生就内陆市场所作的报告和建议。

  如果您认为 1934 年的协议符合我们的最大利益，我们必须考虑以下情况：（a）我们希望扩大我们在华北"本土市场"的销售，以消除所有竞争；（b）根据最近的调查，有可能实现销售增长。然而，为了实现销售额增长，有必要改变我们的销售方法，以满足直接发货、分代理和在主要中心储备库存的建议。

  我并不是说我完全同意这三个建议，但我的观点是，虽然通过同祥湧玻璃庄开展业务是合理可靠的，但是，除非说服他摆脱保守主义，否则我们的销售额永远不会增加：由于他极其保守的做法，我确信很多国内业务都不在我们手中。然而，他在华北地区的玻璃贸易中有非常强大的实力，让他继续与我们合作对我们有利。

因此，我认为，您的第一个计划应该是向同祥湧玻璃庄解释我们在华北的雄心壮志，以及我们通过铁路直接运输扩大销售的想法，并与远一些的市场保持更密切的联系。我建议您和宋先生谈谈，征求他的意见，特别是关于直接装运和在各大中心储藏存货的问题。若您觉得我能为您的交易助一臂之力，我愿效犬马之劳。

谨上
福克纳

部门间备忘录二
INTER-DEPARTMENTAL MEMORANDUM

To: Agent,　　　　　　　Reference　18119
CHINWANGTAO.　　　　Serial Number _____

<u>Tientsin</u>　Agency　<u>3 Jan., 1935</u>

We enclose a translation copy of Tung Hsiang Yung's letter dated 29/12/34 on the subject of the glass sales contract for 1935.

We consider their proposals somewhat vague but a step in the right direction and would suggest for your consideration, negotiation along the following lines:

1. Direct up-country business

A. Tung Hsiang Yung to accept full responsibility for custody of stocks, issues from stock and payment.

According to their own proposals, Tung Hsiang Yung will pay monthly for the quantities shipped to branch offices, but in order to obtain the maximum benefit from these agencies, it might be advisable to encourage the maintenance of stocks by giving longer credit terms. The glass could be considered as sold to Tung Hsiang Yung on delivery to their branch offices, and no further responsibility accepted by Yao Hua. But we think longer credit will result in larger stocks being carried and a greater likelihood of a response to canvassing in the surrounding districts.

B. If, after investigating details, we agree to accept for Yao Hua account the $7,000 or so overhead of up-country agencies, we consider the commission on up-country sales should be lower than proposed by Tung Hsiang Yung, say 5% for sales of 35,000 standards or under, rising by 0.5% per additional 5,000 standards to 6.5% per 5,000 standards or over.

2. Tientsin local sales.

We think an increase in commission for Tientsin sales should be dependent upon Tung Hsiang Yung being able to arrange for the Shoko dealers to cooperate with them and the amount of commission necessary to secure this cooperation. We presume 1.5% to 2% would be sufficient for this.

Possibly the best way to arrange the above would be to have two contracts, one for Tientsin and one for up-country, each with their own terms and guarantees.

We propose, without committing ourselves, to sound Tung Hsiang Yung along the above lines tomorrow, and we think it would be advisable for Mr. Faulkner to discuss these points with Mr. Sung of Tung Hsiang Yung on Saturday, 5th inst.

If it is convenient for Mr. Faulkner to be in Tientsin on Saturday as suggested, we shall be glad if you will wire us so that we can arrange a meeting with Mr. Sung.

E. J. Cowell
TIENTSIN SALES OFFICE.

译文：

参考编号　18119

序号

天津　　代理商　1935年1月3日

致：秦皇岛代理商

随函附上同祥湧玻璃庄于1934年12月29日就1935年玻璃销售合同问题所写的信的翻译本一份。

我们认为他们的建议有些模糊，但朝着正确的方向迈出了一步，并建议您考虑按照下列原则进行谈判：

1. 直接国内业务

a. 同祥湧玻璃庄承担保管存货、库存以及付款的全部责任。

根据他们自己的建议，同祥湧玻璃庄将按照运送给各办事处的数量按月付款，但为了从这些代理机构获得最大的利益，最好给予较长的信贷期限，以鼓励维持库存。运至同祥湧玻璃庄办事处的玻璃可视作已售予同祥湧玻璃庄，耀华不承担进一步的责任。但我们认为，较长的信贷期限将导致库存囤积更甚，经销商们更有可能在周边地区招徕生意时有所动摇。

b. 如果在调查细节后，我们同意耀华承担7 000美元左右的内陆代理费用，我们认为国内销售的佣金应低于同祥湧玻璃庄的建议，即销售35 000标准箱或以下的佣金为5%；每增加5 000标准箱，佣金提高0.5%；销量达50 000标准箱或以上，佣金6.5%封顶。

2. 天津本地销售

我们认为，天津销售佣金的增加应取决于同祥湧玻璃庄能否安排曙光玻璃经销商与他们合作，以及足够确保这种合作所需的佣金。我们推测1.5%到2%足矣。

安排上述事宜的最好办法应该是签订两份合同，一份给天津，一份给内陆，各附条款和保证书。

我们建议明天按照上述思路来探听同祥湧玻璃庄的口风，但不作任何承诺。我们认为福克纳先生最好在本月5日星期六与同祥湧玻璃庄的宋先生讨论这些问题。

如福克纳先生方便按照安排于星期六来天津，请电告我们，我们很乐意安排他与宋先生会晤。

考威尔

天津销售处

29th Dec., 1934

Since we entered into a contract with your Administration for 1934, the sales was rather good. It was because of our ability to compete with the Shoko glass and control the market price. Although our own personal interests are sacrificed, we must conquer the market and achieve good name for you. When you consider the real conditions of the recent two years, you will know all about it. Last week we had been summoned to a meeting with Mr. Faulkner and you to discuss the best method of pushing our sales during the next year. After receiving your instructions, we had thought over carefully for several days to work out a method of pushing sales. Since our minds are shallow, our opinions may not be the best. If it does not meet with your approval, please give us a directions so as to get the best results of co-operation. And I believe you and Mr. Faulkner will concur with me. Our opinions are as follows:

1. Our firm may establish branch offices or agencies in Shansi, Kalgan, Chengchow of Honan and Tsinan of Shantung. Goods will be shipped to them by you by direct rail shipments for our accounts. We will settle the accounts monthly together with the payments due on local sales. But the annual overhead charges as fire insurance, godown charges and other expenses for their branch offices shall be for your account. The total amount is about $7,000 yearly (Shansi, $2,000; Chengchow, $2,000; Shantung and Kalgan, $1,500 each).

2. On account of sharp competition with the Shoko glass, our profits are entirely sacrificed in these recent two years. If no adequate commission is allowed, we cannot carry on the struggle. We, therefore, request you to increase our commission. If the annual sales are below 50,000 cases, 5% commission shall be allowed; If it is above 50,000 to $55,000 cases, 5.5% shall be allowed; If it is above 55,000 to 60,000 cases, 6% shall be allowed;

> if it is above 60,000 to 65,000 cases, 6.5% shall be allowed. If the sales reach 100,000 cases, 10% shall be allowed. For other bonuses in addition to monthly payments, the commission shall be allowed in accordance with the rates for 50,000 cases as per the actual sales. If the sales exceed 50,000 cases, the total amount of extra commission shall be settled at the end of year.
>
>   The essentials of our opinion are as above. You will oblige us by giving directions.
>
> Yours faithfully,
Tung Hsiang Yung.

译文：

1934 年 12 月 29 日

  自我方在 1934 年与贵总局签合同以来，销售情况相当好。这是因为我们有能力与曙光玻璃竞争，并控制市场价格。虽然我方牺牲了自己的个人利益，但我方必须赢得市场，为贵方赢得好名声。考虑到这两年的实际情况，您就会知道实情了。上周，我方应邀与福克纳先生和您开会，讨论明年推动我们的销量的最佳方法。在收到贵方指示后，我们仔细考虑了几天，想出了推动销量的方法。我们见识浅薄，所以我方意见可能未必尽善尽美。如果您不同意，请给我们指示，以达到最好的合作效果。我相信你和福克纳先生会同意我的看法。我们的意见如下：

  1. 我公司可在山西、张家口、河南郑州、山东济南等地设立分公司或代理机构。货物将由贵方通过铁路直接运给他们，费用由我方承担。我们将按月与当地销售的应付款项一起结账。但其销售办事处每年的间接费用，如火灾保险、仓库费和其他费用应由贵方负担。总金额约为每年 7 000 元（山西，2 000 元；郑州，2 000 元；山东和张家口各 1 500 元）。

  2. 由于与曙光玻璃的激烈竞争，近两年我们的利润亏损殆尽。如果不能获得足够的佣金，我们很难继续下去。因此，我们请求贵方提高佣金。

如果年销售量低于 5 万箱，佣金应为 5%；超过 5 万至 5.5 万箱，佣金为 5.5%；超过 5.5 万至 6 万箱，佣金为 6%；超过 6 万至 6.5 万箱，佣金为 6.5%。如果销量达到 10 万箱，佣金应为 10%。对于除按月支付外的其他奖金，根据实际销售情况，按 5 万箱费率给予提成。如果销售量超过 50 000 箱，额外佣金的总额将在年底结清。

我们意见的要点如下。请您给我们指示。

谨上

同祥湧玻璃庄

部门间备忘录三
INTER-DEPARTMENTAL MEMORANDUM

To: Agent, CHINWANGTAO.	Reference 18119
	Serial Number
	Tientsin Agency 28th, January, 1935

SUBJECT: PEIPING GLASS SALES ARRANGEMENTS

We have today had an interview with a representative of Peiping Tien Yuan Tai Glass Dealer, the leader of the combine of 8 dealers through whom we sell in Peiping. According to him, the Mitsubishi people are making strong efforts to interest some of the Peiping dealers in selling Shoko glass, offering to quote the same price for Shoko as Yaohua glass and in addition to give a rebate of 5% to the dealers. An independent investigation carried out by us confirms that attempts are being made to put Shoko glass on the Peiping market, but we are unable to confirm whether the rebates offered for this business are as stated by the Peiping dealer. The attitude of Tien Yuan Tai was that he was not asking for a price reduction or for a rebate, but he considered that unless we did something we must face the possibility of some of our dealers going over to Shoko. We therefore consider that we should take immediate steps to prevent this happening.

His idea is that we should keep our price unchanged, but should give Peiping dealers a commission of 5% on their sales. He maintained that this would suffice to keep the combine together, and that as soon as the Shoko overtures have been definitely rejected, we could recoup ourselves by increasing the Peiping price.

Without committing ourselves we suggested that if any rebate was granted, it should be on a sliding scale basis and in accordance with quantity sold in a similar manner as that of Tientsin, but Tien Yuan Tai considered that would not be satisfactory.

We believe that, on the whole, the position as outlined by Tien Yuan Tai is correct and that it would probably pay us to keep the combine in being and Shoko glass off the market even if we have to give some kind of rebate. Once Shoko Glass is sold in quantity on the market, it will be difficult to revert to the former conditions and undoubtedly by price cutting, etc. We should lose considerably. We therefore recommend a) that we offer a flat 3% commission to Peiping dealers or b) that we offer them a rebate increasing up to 5% in accordance with quantities sold.

Neither of these suggestions appear to meet Tien Yuan Tai's requirements in full, but no doubt there is some leeway for bargaining and we would suggest one of the alternatives as a start, probably a).

The representative of Tien Yuan Tai is remaining in Tientsin until tomorrow afternoon, and we shall, therefore, be obliged if you will phone us (30024) either before 10 tomorrow morning or after 2 p.m. as the undersigned will be out after 10 a.m. tomorrow morning.

Tien Yuan Tai also raised the question of direct shipments and indicated that the Peiping dealers would like to obtain glass on a direct shipment basis

> along the Peiping Suiyuan railway, to which we replied that the matter would be referred to you. We believe, however, that it should be possible to reserve this Area to the Peiping dealers without much difficulty from the Tientsin dealer Tung Hsiang Yung.
>
> E. J. Cowell
TIENTSIN SALES OFFICE.

译文：

参考编号 __18119__

序号 _____

<u>天津</u>　　<u>代理商</u>　　<u>1935 年 1 月 28 日</u>

致：秦皇岛代理商

主题：北平玻璃销售安排

　　我们今天采访了北平天源泰玻璃经销商的代表，他是我们在北平负责销售的 8 家经销商联合组织的负责人。据他说，三菱公司的人正在大力吸引北平的一些经销商销售曙光玻璃，条件是曙光玻璃的报价与耀华玻璃持平，此外还可以给经销商 5% 的佣金。我们进行的独立调查证实，有人正试图将曙光玻璃投放到北平市场。但我们无法确认为这项业务提供的返利是否如北平经销商所言。天源泰的态度是他并不要求我们降价或给佣金，但他认为，除非我们采取行动，否则我们必须面对一些经销商转向曙光玻璃的可能性。因此，我们认为应该立即采取措施，防止这种情况发生。

　　他的想法是，我们应该保持我们的价格不变，但应该给北平的经销商们提供 5% 的销售佣金。他坚持认为，这些将足以使经销商联合组织团结一心，而且，一旦曙光玻璃的提议被明确拒绝，我们就可以通过提高北平的价格来收回成本。

我们建议，在不作出承诺的条件下，如果给予任何返利，应该以递增佣金为基础，以类似天津的做法，根据销售数量返利，但天源泰认为这不会令人满意。

我们认为，总体而言，天源泰的观点是正确的，即使我们不得不给予某种形式的返利，只要能够保住经销商联合组织，让曙光玻璃退出市场，这就很有可能会给我们带来好处。一旦曙光玻璃在市场上大量销售，就很难恢复到以前的局面，而且无疑要通过降价等方式来收拾局面。我们应该会有很大的损失。因此，我们建议：a）我们向北平的经销商提供统一的3%的佣金，或者b）我们根据销售数量将给他们的返利增加至5%。

在我看来，这两个建议都不完全符合天源泰的要求，但无疑还有一些讨价还价的余地，我们建议从其中一个方案开始，可能是a）。

天源泰的代表将在天津停留到明天下午。因此，如果您能在明天上午10点前或下午2点后给我们（30024）打电话，我们将不胜感激，因为签字人将在明天上午10点后外出。

天源泰还提出了直接运输的问题，并表示北平的经销商希望在北平绥远铁路沿线以直接运输的方式获得玻璃，对此我们回答说，此事将呈报您。不过，我们认为，从天津经销商同祥湧那里把这一地区留给北平经销商应该是没有太大困难的。

考威尔
天津销售处

TO BE TRANSLATED INTO CHINESE.

Tientsin, 31st January, 1935
Ref. 18151.

CONFIDENTIAL.

Tien Yuan Tai Glass Dealer,
PEIPING.

Dear Sirs,

    In confirmation of our conversation of Tuesday last, we have pleasure in advising that we are prepared for the calendar year 1935 to give a rebate on sales of glass by you and your fellow dealers in Peiping as follows:

An initial rebate of 3% off the standard f. o. c. Peiping price per case of 4th quality Single Thickness glass in the Standard Specification, will be allowed on all glass purchased during 1935 up to 20,000 standards, this rebate to be credited monthly on rendition of accounts. Should the amount of the glass purchased by our Peiping dealers during 1935 exceed 20,000 standards, additional rebates will be given as detailed hereunder:

a). Over 20,000, but under 22,500 standards.

An additional rebate of one half per cent, making $3\frac{1}{2}$ % in all will be paid on the total quantity purchased during 1935.

b). Over 22,500, but under 25,000 standards.

An additional rebate of one half per cent, making 4% in all will be paid on the total quantity purchased during 1935.

c). Over 25,000 but under 27,500 standards.

An additional rebate of one half per cent, making $4\frac{1}{2}$ % in all will be paid on the total quantity purchased during 1935.

d). 27,500 standards and over.

An additional rebate of one half per cent, making 5% in all will be paid on the total quantity purchased during 1935.

Such additional rebates will be credited, if earned, in the final settlement of account to be rendered in January 1936.

It is understood that for the purpose of calculating the above rebates purchases of the better quantities and heavier grade will be commuted as follows:-

4th Quality

One case	S'double	of 100 sq. ft. shall count as	2	cases	Single
" "	Double	" " " " " "	$2\frac{1}{2}$	"	"
" "	Triple	" " " " " "	3	"	"
" "	Thick	" " " " " "	4	"	"
" "	E. Thick	" " " " " "	5	"	"

2nd and 3rd Quality

One case	S'double	of 100 sq. ft. shall count as	3	cases	Single
" "	Double	" " " " " "	4	"	"
" "	Triple	" " " " " "	5	"	"
" "	Thick	" " " " " "	6	"	"
" "	E. Thick	" " " " " "	$7\frac{1}{2}$	"	"

In 2nd and 3rd quality Single Thickness, one case of 100 sq. ft. over 27 united inches shall count as 2 cases of Single Thickness 4th quality and one case of 100 sq. ft. of small size under 27 united inches as one case 4th quality, Single Thickness.

With regard to the possibility of direct shipments from Chinwangtao to points along the Peiping Suiyuan Railway, we are communicating with Chinwangtao, and will advise you later.

We shall be obliged if you will in due course confirm the above terms when we shall instruct our Accounts Department to commence crediting your account accordingly.

Yours faithfully,
TIENTSIN SALES OFFICE.

Copy to: -Agent Chinwangtao.

译文：

待译成中文

天津，1935 年 1 月 31 日

编号 18151

机密文件

致：北平的天源泰玻璃经销商

亲爱的先生们：

兹确认我们上周二的谈话，我们很高兴地通知您，我们准备在公历 1935 年对您和您在北平的同行经销商的玻璃销售给予如下回扣：

1935 年期间购买的所有玻璃数量在 20 000 标准箱以内，则每箱标准规格的四等单厚玻璃的初始折扣为北平标准离岸价的 3%，该折扣将按月记入经销商账内。如果我们的北平经销商在 1935 年购买的玻璃数量超过 20 000 标准箱，将按以下详细规定给予额外回扣：

A）超过 20 000 标准箱但低于 22 500 标准箱。

在 1935 年购买总数量应得回扣基础上再额外支付 0.5% 的回扣，即总计 $3\frac{1}{2}$% 回扣。

B）超过 22 500 标准箱但低于 25 000 标准箱。

在 1935 年购买总数量应得回扣基础上再额外支付 0.5% 的回扣，即总计 4% 回扣。

C）超过 25 000 标准箱但低于 27 500 标准箱。

在 1935 年购买总数量应得回扣基础上再额外支付 0.5% 的回扣，即总计 $4\frac{1}{2}$% 回扣。

D）达到或超过 27 500 标准箱。

在 1935 年购买总数量应得回扣基础上再额外支付 0.5% 的回扣，即总计 5% 回扣。

如果获得了这些额外的回扣，将在 1936 年 1 月进行的最终结算中记入经销商账户。

为了计算上述基础采购量，质量较好、品级较厚的玻璃采购量将折算如下：

四等质量

一百平方英尺半双厚玻璃一箱应按单厚玻璃两箱核算。

一百平方英尺双厚玻璃一箱应按单厚玻璃两箱半核算。

一百平方英尺三厚玻璃一箱应按单厚玻璃三箱核算。

一百平方英尺厚玻璃一箱应按单厚玻璃四箱核算。

一百平方英尺加厚玻璃一箱应按单厚玻璃五箱核算。

二等与三等玻璃

一百平方英尺半双厚玻璃一箱应按单厚玻璃三箱核算。

一百平方英尺双厚玻璃一箱应按单厚玻璃四箱核算。

一百平方英尺三厚玻璃一箱应按单厚玻璃五箱核算。

一百平方英尺厚玻璃一箱应按单厚玻璃六箱核算。

一百平方英尺加厚玻璃一箱应按单厚玻璃七箱半核算。

二等和三等之单厚玻璃，其大小在二十七联英寸以上，每箱装 100 平方英尺者，应按四等单厚玻璃两箱计算。若不足二十七联英寸之小块玻璃，每箱装 100 平方英尺者，则仍按四等单厚玻璃一箱计算。

关于从秦皇岛直接装运至京绥铁路沿线各点的可能性，我们正在与秦皇岛方面进行沟通，稍后会通知您。

如果您能在适当时候确认上述条款，我们将不胜感激，届时我们将责成我们的会计部门开始相应地记入您的账户。

谨上

天津销售部

抄送：秦皇岛代理

部门间备忘录四
INTER-DEPARTMENTAL MEMORANDUM

To: H. H. Faulker, Esq.,   Reference   2563

CHINWANGTAO   Serial Number

                                Tientsin   Agency   1st Feb, 1935

Subject

Dear Faulkner,

    Referring to your official Memo. of the 30th ultimo advising that you have opened a new file M-18504: "Recording of Agreements and Selling Arrangements in the Tientsin and Peiping Areas":

    You will see in the complete list of glass files, of which the Chinwangtao Agency has a copy, that we already have two presumably suitable files (No. 18066 and No. 18119). These files refer respectively to glass sales agreements for the Tientsin area and selling arrangements with Tientsin glass dealer. Peking is by implication included in the term "Tientsin Area".

    Would you, besides asking your filing office to bring your file in line with these, tell them to refer to list of existing files before allocating new titles and numbers? Better still, perhaps (and when practicable) get them to apply to us for a number and title!

                                                        Yours sincerely,

                                                        E. J. Cowell.

译文：

参考编号　M-18003
序号　　　……………
天津　　代理处　1935年2月1日

致：秦皇岛的福克纳先生

主题　……………………………………………………………………

尊敬的福克纳：

　　您在上月30日的官方备忘录中提及，您已新建一份编号M-18504的档案文件，题目为："天津和北平地区协议和销售安排的记录"：

　　您可以在完整的玻璃档案列表中看到，我们已经有两份可能合适的档案文件（编号18066和18119），秦皇岛经销处藏有这些文件的一份副本。这些文件分别涉及天津地区的玻璃销售协议和与天津玻璃经销商的销售安排。北京相应地包含在"天津地区"这一表述的范围内。

　　请要求您的档案室将您的文件与上述文件保持一致。除此之外，可否请您告诉他们在分配新的标题和编号之前参考现有文件的列表？更好的是，也许（在可行的情况下）让他们向我们申请一个编号和标题！

　　　　　　　　　　　　　　　　　　　　　　　　　　　谨上
　　　　　　　　　　　　　　　　　　　　　　　　　　　考威尔

M-18504

G.H.A. Snow, Esq.,
　　　TIENTSIN　　　　　　　　　Chinwangtao　　　7th Feb., 35

Dear snow,

　　With reference to your note of the 1st instant, we have File 18119 here, but 18066 was left behind in Tientsin with Tientsin Glass Sales.

　　Our idea in opening M-18504 was to have a file for confidential documents as 18119 is an open file.

　　If you wish us to make any change, will you let me know in future? In future we will always refer to you before opening new files.

　　　　　　　　　　　　　　　　　　　　　　　　　Yours sincerely,
　　　　　　　　　　　　　　　　　　　　　　　　　H.H.Faulker.

译文：

编号 M-18504

秦皇岛　　　1935年2月7日

致：天津的斯诺先生

亲爱的斯诺，

　　关于您本月1日的留言，我们这里有18119号文件，但是18066号文件被天津玻璃销售公司留在了天津。

　　我们建立 M-18504 号文件的想法是有一个机密文件的文档，因为18119号文件是一个公开的文件。

　　如果您希望我们有任何更改，请让我知道，好吗？今后，我们在建立新文件前一定会参考您的意见。

谨上

福克纳

部门间备忘录五
INTER-DEPARTMENTAL MEMORANDUM

To: Agent Chinwangtao	Reference 2563
	Serial Number
	Tientsin Agency 11th Feb, 1935

Subject ……………………………………………………

Dear Faulkner,

　　Many thanks for your memorandum of the 7th instant. Please don't think that I am making a mountain out of this small molehill. The fact is that I hold always on to the hope that one day soon I shall have a sufficient and well enough trained staff to institute identical filing and reference arrangements throughout the administration. The intention is that this will be rendered possible-and all information throughout the Administration rendered accessible to all-by a plan (already laid down) whereunder all the essential detail work, except actual registration of correspondence, will be done in the Head Office.

The task that will have to be faced when this is set going will be very much reduced if Shanghai and Chinwangtao Files are kept as much in line with ours as possible. Shanghai, I am afraid, is not too good; but Chinwangtao is. Hence our anxiety to keep details straight.

So much by way of explanation of what must seem to you a minor matter. As regards such details in future I (or Miss Marsh) will write direct to Miss Donohue or whoever is in charge of your files. This has already been arranged between Chilton and myself-some time ago. As regards your 18504 in particular. We do not mind your using the number, but we dislike your title, which clashed with 18066 and 18119.

If practicable at your end the simplest solution would be to suppress 18504 and make 18119 an "M" File. There is no reason why any open file should not be labeled "M" (temporarily or permanently) but never make two with the same title and never use a number twice (in case a file is at any time suppressed)

Should you prefer to retain 18504, then give it a title such as will avoid any confusion with 18119. I do not know the exact matter of the contents so cannot definitely suggest one. Perhaps "Rec. Policy & procedure covering sales of Glass in Tientsin and Peiping" would do-but, as I say, better just make your 18119 an "M" file if practicable.

Yours sincerely

译文：

参考编号 2563
序号
天津　　代理处　　1935年2月11日

致：秦皇岛代理商

主题　　　　18504号文件

亲爱的福克纳：

　　非常感谢您提供的本月7日的备忘录。请不要以为我在小题大做。事实上，我始终希望，在不久的将来我会拥有足够多的、训练有素的员工，在总局内部建立统一的文件归档和查阅系统。希望能够通过一项计划（已制定）来实现这一点，这项计划将令所有人都能够访问总局的全部信息。根据该计划，除实际的通信登记外，所有重要的细节工作都将在总局办公室完成。

　　如果上海和秦皇岛档案尽可能与我们的档案保持一致，那么当这项工作开始时，所面临的任务将大大减少。恐怕上海在这方面做得不太好；但秦皇岛做得很好。因此，我们渴望保持细节清晰明了。

　　以上解释在您看来肯定只是一件小事。关于今后工作的细节，我（或马什小姐）将直接写信给多诺霍小姐或负责您档案的任何人。这件事齐尔顿和我早些时间已经安排好了。关于您的18504号备忘录，我们不介意您使用这个序号，但我们不喜欢您的标题，因为它与18066号和18119号产生了冲突。

　　如果您那端可行的话，最简单的解决方案是取消18504号序号，改为18119号，并将其作为"M"档案保存。任何公开的文件都应该标记为"M"（临时性或永久性），但两份档案不能使用相同的标题，也不要重复使用同一个数字（以防文件在任何时候被删除）。

　　如果你想保留18504的编号，那么就给它加上一个标题，以避免与18119号文档产生混淆。我不知道里面的具体内容，所以不能肯定地提出建议。也许"记录天津和北平玻璃销售文件、政策和程序"可以作为标题——但正如我所说，如果可行的话，最好把18119号文档作为"M"档案。

谨上

部门间备忘录六

M-18504

Tientsin Sales Office
TIENTSIN

      Chinwangtao   11th Feb., 35

<u>1935 Glass Sales Agreement</u>

CONFIDENTIAL.

With reference to your negotiations regarding the above, we shall be glad to hear how the matter now stands.

          H.H.Faulker
          for AGENT.

译文：

M-18504
秦皇岛　1935 年 2 月 11 日

致：天津销售处
关于你方就上述事项进行的谈判，我们很乐意听到事情的进展情况。

福克纳

INTER-DEPARTMENTAL MEMORANDUM

To: Agent Chinwangtao	Reference 18119
	Serial Number ....
	Tientsin Agency 12th Feb, 1935

Subject ....1935 Glass Sales Agreement..

  With reference to your memo M-18504 of the 11th February, 1935, we regret that no progress has been made in regard to the above agreement. Mr. Sung, senior of Tung HsingYung has been quite seriously ill for the last few weeks. While we understand he is now convalescing, we have been unable to make any definite arrangements with his son who was reluctant to discuss matters without reference to his father.

  Since Mr. Sung, senior, is likely to be shortly able to take an interest in business matter, we propose to resume negotiations at first with his son and as soon as possible with Mr. Sung himself.

E. J. Cowell
TIENTSIN SALES OFFICE.

译文：

参考编号 ....18119....

序号 ....

天津　代理处　1935 年 2 月 12 日

致：秦皇岛代理商

主题　　　1935 年玻璃销售协议

关于你方 1935 年 2 月 11 日 M-18504 号备忘录，我们很遗憾上述协议尚未取得任何进展。同祥湧玻璃庄的宋先生最近几周病得很重。虽然我们知道他现在正在康复，但我们无法与他的儿子一起作出任何明确的安排，因为他的儿子不愿在不提及他父亲的情况下讨论问题。

  鉴于老宋先生不久就会开始经营业务，我们建议先与他的儿子然后尽快与宋先生本人恢复谈判。

考威尔
天津销售处

部门间备忘录七
INTER-DEPARTMENTAL MEMORANDUM

To: H.H. Faulkner, Esq., CHINWANGTAO	Reference 18119
	Serial Number
	Tientsin Agency 13th Feb, 1935

CONFIDENTIAL.

Subject ....

  With reference to your memo 18119 of 11th February, Mr Kuo of Hua Sheng Tung approached us early last year with a somewhat similar request for a sole contract, or failing that, privileged credit terms.

  He offered a bank Guarantee of $10,000 and a Shop Guarantee, the former of which was accepted and the latter rejected, and we agreed to sell to him at market rates with credit up to the amount of his guarantee. This was done because it was not considered policy to antagonise Mr. Kuo unnecessarily.

  Later, Tung Hsiang Yung complained of this arrangement saying that we should restrict credit sales to themselves and that by selling to Hua Sheng Tung even at market price rates, the latter was enabled to disturb the market by selling Yao Hua Glass at fancy prices. We suggested to Hua sheng Tung that they should obtain supplies through Tung Hsiang Yung who could let them have the glass cheaper than we could owing to our sales arrangements, but Hua Sheng Tung refused, so we dropped the matter.

Tung Hsiang Yung was informed that for political reasons, we would continue the arrangement with Hua Sheng Tung until it was obvious sales to this firm were detrimental to Yao Hua interests, and as a matter of fact Hua Sheng Tung took no glass after last March.

Under the circumstances and in view of Hua Sheng Tung's venture in Soviet Glass last year, we propose, subject to your approval, to reply to Mr. Kuo's letter, stating that we will always sell to him at market rates and for cash, but that our 1935 sales arrangements do not permit us to grant him any sole sales contract, nor to extend credit terms to him.

E. J. Cowell.

译文：

参考编号 __18119__

序号 _____

天津　　代理处　　1935 年 2 月 13 日

致：秦皇岛的福克纳先生

机密文件

主题 _____

关于您 2 月 11 日编号 18119 的备忘录，华盛堂的郭先生去年年初曾与我方联系，向我们提出了类似的要求，要求签订独家合同，如果签不了独家合同，也要签特权信贷条款。

他提供了一份一万美元的银行担保和一份商店担保，前者被接受，后者被拒绝。我们同意以市场价格与他交易，并根据他的担保金额提供信贷。做出这个决定，是因为与郭先生进行非必要的对抗并非明智之举。

后来，同祥湧对此颇有怨言，认为我们应该只向他们提供信用销售服务，并且认为不应以市场价格和华盛堂交易，因为后者会据此高价出售耀华玻璃，从而扰乱市场。我们向华盛堂建议，受我们的销售政策所限，他们应该通过同祥湧获得货源供应，同祥湧可以以比我们更便宜的价格向他们出售玻璃，但华盛堂拒绝了，所以我们放弃了这件事。

同祥湧被告知，出于政治原因，我们将继续与华盛堂达成协议，直到向这家公司的销售明显损害了耀华的利益。事实上，华盛堂在去年3月之后就再没有购买过玻璃了。

在这种情况下，考虑到华盛堂去年在苏联玻璃公司的投资，我们建议回复郭先生的来信，声明我们将始终以市场价格和现金向他出售，但我们1935年的销售安排不允许我们授予他任何独家销售合同，也不允许我们向他提供信贷条款，但须经贵方批准。

考威尔
天津销售部

M-18119

Tientsin Sales Office
TIENTSIN　　　　　　　　　Chinwangtao　　　　15th Feb., 35

CONFIDENTIAL.

With reference to your memo 18119 of the 13th instant, we agree with your proposals regarding Messrs. Hua Sheng Tung.

H.H.Faulker
for AGENT.

译文：

M-18119

秦皇岛　1935 年 2 月 15 日

致：天津销售处

关于你方本月 13 日第 18119 号备忘录，我们同意你方关于华盛堂公司的建议。

福克纳

部门间备忘录八

INTER-DEPARTMENTAL MEMORANDUM

To: Agent,	Reference 18119
CHINWANGTAO	Serial Number
	<u>Tientsin</u>　Agency　<u>15th Feb, 1935</u>

Subject　　1935 GLASS SAIES AGREEMENT.

We have had an interview with Mr. Sung, Junior, who said that his father would probably be well enough to discuss the Agreement next week.

Meanwhile he indicated that they could not accept the rebates proposed by you and insisted upon the terms mentioned in Tung Hsiang Yung's letter of 29th December, 1934, i.e. $7,000 overhead for upcountry branches to be found by Yao Hua and rebates mounting from 5% on sales of 50,000 cases to 10% on sales of 100,000 cases, these rebates to be expressed in cents per case if desired.

We did not discuss this, saying we preferred to wait until Mr. Sung, Senior, was available, but we stated that we considered the rebates offered by us more than generous. We believe, however, it will be necessary to increase the proposed initial rebate slightly since after giving away the equivalent of 2.5% to intermediary dealers, Tung Hsiang Yung are left with very little return on the first 50,000 cases they sell. Of course they stand to make a lot on subsequent sales, but one can understand their reluctance to commit themselves to too small an initial margin.

Please let us know whether you wish us to hold firm on the rebates already offered and our refusal to be responsible for the $7,000 upcountry overhead, or whether we are authorised to meet Tung Hsiang Yung in any way on these points.

Naturally we shall not give anything away that can be avoided and all arrangements will be submitted to you for approval.

E. J. Cowell
TIENTSIN SALES OFFICE.

译文：

参考编号 18119

序号

天津　代理处　1935 年 2 月 15 日

致：秦皇岛代理商

主题　1935 年玻璃销售协议

我们已经和小宋先生面谈，他说他的父亲下周身体可能会痊愈，能和我们谈谈协议的事情了。

与此同时，他表示他们不能接受贵方提出的回扣，并坚持 1934 年 12 月 29 日同祥湧的信中提出的条件，即耀华要支付给内陆销售分公司 7 000 美元的日常管理费用，回扣从销售 5 万箱的 5%增加到 10 万箱的 10%，如果愿意，这些回扣可以以美分/箱表示。

我们没有讨论这个问题，说我们宁愿等到老宋先生有空，但我们表示，我们认为我们提供的回扣很慷慨了。然而，我们认为有必要略微提高拟议的初始回扣，因为在向中间经销商赠送相当于 2.5%的回扣后，同祥湧在销售的前 5 万箱中只剩下很少的回报了。当然，他们会在后续销售中赚很多，但可以理解他们不愿承诺最初的比较少的利润。

请告知我方是否贵方希望我方坚持已提供的返利，并且拒绝对 7 000 美元的境内管理费用负责？是否授权我方以任何方式就这些问题与同祥湧会面？

当然，我们不会泄漏任何可以避免的事情，所有的安排都将提交给贵方批准。

考威尔
天津经销处

M-18119

Tientsin Sales Office
TIENTSIN

Chinwangtao   16th Feb., 35

<u>1935 Glass Sales Agreement</u>

CONFIDENTIAL

Reference your 18119 of the 15th instant please advise when Mr. Sung, Senior, is well enough to talk over the Agreement and undersigned will visit Tientsin to assist you in the negotiations.

H. H. Faulker
for AGENT.

译文：

M-18119
秦皇岛　1935年2月16日

致：天津销售处

参阅您本月15日的18119号信，告知老宋先生何时可以商谈本协议，本协议的签署人将访问天津协助您洽谈。

福克纳

部门间备忘录九
INTER-DEPARTMENTAL MEMORANDUM

To:	Agent, CHINWANGTAO	Reference 18151
		Serial Number _____
		Tientsin Agency　15th Feb, 1935

Subject　PEIPING GLASS DEALERS.

The Peiping Glass Dealers have just confirmed their acceptance of the scale of rebates offered in our letter No. 18151 to them of the 31st January, a copy of which was forwarded to you.

We have, therefore, advised the Accounts Department of the arrangements for 1935 and have asked them to credit Peiping dealers with the rebates as from 1/1/35.

E. J. Cowell
TIENTSIN SALES OFFICE.

译文：

参考编号　18151
序号　_____
天津　代理处　1935年2月15日

致：秦皇岛代理商

主题 _____北平玻璃经销商_____

  北平玻璃经销商刚刚确认接受我公司1月31日给他们的第18151号信中提出的折扣幅度，确认接受的副本已转寄你方。

  因此，我们已将1935年的安排通知财务处，并请他们从1935年1月1日起将回扣存入北平商人账内。

考威尔

天津经销处

部门间备忘录十

INTER-DEPARTMENTAL MEMORANDUM

To: Agent, CHINWANGTAO	Reference __18055__ Serial Number _____ <u>Tientsin</u> Agency <u>12th March, 1935</u>

Subject _____

  We are instructed to forward to you, for favour of your comment, enclosed copy of a letter, with enclosure, received from the Secretary of the Yao Hua Mechanical Glass Co., Limited, written on behalf of Mr Li Shu Chih, Director.

GENERAL DEPARTMENT.

Encl:-2

译文：

参考编号 __18055__

序号 _____

<u>天津</u> 代理处 <u>1935年3月12日</u>

致：秦皇岛代理商

  兹奉指示寄给您耀华机械玻璃有限公司秘书处代表董事李书齐先生所写的一封信，以征求你方意见。

总务处

附件：2

COPY

THE YAO HUA MRCHANICAT GIASS CO.,LTD.

Tientsin, 6th March, 1935.

No.148

The Chief Managers,

Kailan Mining Administration.

Tientsin.

Dear Sirs,

    Mr. Li Shu Chih, one of the Company's Directors, handed me a memorandum under date of the 4th instant which he told me was received from a certain shareholder who mas very interested in the welfare of the Company. The original memorandum is enclosed herewith together with an English translation for your consideration.

    Mr.Li also asked me to inform you that according to this anonymous shareholder, Messrs. Hua Sheng Tung mentioned in the memorandum were now selling Shoko glass and that the sales of Shoko glass in Tientsin were entirely under their control. If we can give a contract to them, they mill cease to sell Shoko glass and sell ours instead. In this way, they will be able to increase our price by $0.40 to begin with since Shoko glass will be unable to compete with us any more.

Yours faithfully,

THE YAO HUA MECHANICAI GLASS CO.,LTD.

Secretary (sgd.) C. C. Kuo

Enclos:

1 memorandum with English translation.

Copy to:-

Agent Chinwangtao

译文：

耀华机械玻璃制造有限公司

天津（1935年3月6日）

No.148

致：天津开滦矿物总局的各位首席经理：

亲爱的先生们，

  公司董事之一李书齐先生于本月4日向我递交了一份备忘录，他告诉我这封备忘录来自一位对公司福利非常关心的股东。随函附上备忘录原件及英文翻译件，以供参考。

  李先生还请我通知您，据这位匿名股东了解，备忘录中提到的华盛堂公司现在销售曙光玻璃，并且曙光玻璃在天津的销售完全在他们的控制之中。如果我们能与他们签订合同，他们就会停止销售曙光玻璃，转而销售我们的玻璃。这样一来，他们就可以把我们的价格提高0.40美元，因为曙光玻璃将无法再与我们竞争。

谨启

耀华机械玻璃制造有限公司

秘书处　　郭先生

附件：

1份备忘录及英文翻译。

抄送：

秦皇岛代理商

Copy

<u>Translation of a Memorandum</u>

The followings are the actual conditions of the Yao Hua company's contractor Messrs. Tung Hsiang Yung:-

1. They have recently reduced their scope of business by cutting down several salesmen.

2. Since the scope business was reduced, glass sales have been greatly affected. Those reliable local dealers who have business transactions with the said contractor can only sell about 200 cases per month whereas small dealers can sell not more than a hundred. It is estimated that the total amount of sale the said contractor is now able to make each month is only about 1,000 cases, i.e. only 10,000 or over cases per annum.

3. In the past three years, glass sales made by Messrs. Tung Hsiang Yung have gradually diminished. On the other hand, those dealing in Shoko glass have increased their sales by leaps and bounds. The reason is that the said Tung Hsiang Yung refuse to associate with the local dealers with the result that they have been completely isolated. There is no wonder that Yao Hua glass has been seriously affected by the Shoko glass competition.

4. At present, the only firm that has a great influence over glass sales in North China is Messrs. Hua Sheng Tung. Their promised characteristics may be stated as follows:

a. They have carried on glass business exclusively for many years and have therefore had business relations with a large number of glass dealers in the northern provinces.

b. In Tientsin alone, they have altogether four branches.

c. They have the ability to associate with the local dealer which is lacking on the part of Messrs. Tung Hsiang Yung.

d. The said Hua Sheng Tung have sufficient capital in carrying on their business.

译文：
一份备忘录译本

耀华公司承包商同祥湧玻璃庄的实际情况如下：

1. 他们最近裁减了几名推销员，从而缩小了业务范围。

2. 由于业务范围缩小，玻璃销售受到了很大影响。那些和上述承包商有业务往来的可靠的本地经销商每月只能卖出约 200 箱，而小经销商只能卖出不超过 100 箱。据估计，该承包商现在每个月的总销售额仅为 1 000 箱左右，即每年仅为 10 000 箱或以上。

3. 在过去三年中，同祥湧玻璃庄的玻璃销售额逐渐减少。另一方面，他们对曙光玻璃的销售额大幅增长。原因是同祥湧拒绝与当地经销商联合，结果他们被完全孤立。难怪耀华玻璃受到了曙光玻璃销售竞争的严重影响。

4. 目前，华北地区唯一一家对玻璃销售有很大影响的公司是华盛堂。该公司能够保证以下几点：

    a. 多年来，他们专门从事玻璃业务，因此与北方省份的大量玻璃经销商建立了业务关系。

    b. 仅在天津，他们就有四个分支机构。

    c. 他们有能力与当地经销商合作，而这一点正是同祥湧缺乏的。

    d. 上述华盛堂公司在开展业务时有充足的资金保证。

部门间备忘录十一
INTER-DEPARTMENTAL MEMORANDUM

To: Agent,   Reference 18119
     CHINWANGTAO   Serial Number
                                         Tientsin Agency 15th March, 1935

Subject   TIENTSIN GLASS SAIES ARRANGEMENTS.

We return herewith the General Department's letter 18055 of 12th inst, and enclosures (2) which were handed to us by Mr. Faulkner for our comments.

In connection with the memorandum on the subject of the ability of our present dealer Tung Hsiang Yung to sell glass, it is apparent that the writer of the memorandum has been misinformed, as will be apparent from the following:

1) It is stated that Tung Hsiang Yung can only sell about 10,000 cases of glass this year.

Tung Hsiang Yung has guaranteed to sell a minimum of 60,000 standards during 1935, his sales record to-date being:-

January	1,100 standards,
February	2,070 "
March (up to the 15th)	5,073 "
Total	8,249 standards

January and February are always poor months, but the improvement that usually commences in March has taken place and there is no reason to believe that sales will be other than normal throughout the year.

2) It is stated that sales of Yao Hua in Tientsin have declined during the past three years.

We give below the sales of Yao Hua for 1932/34, from which it will be seen that sales have progressively increased. Furthermore, 1934 sales constitute a record since the opening of the Factory.

1934	1933	1932
68,318.5 standards	63,871 standards	62,561 standards

3) It is stated that sales of Shoko Glass have increased by "leaps and bounds". Sales of Shoko increased by 1,200 standards during 1934, but the information at our disposal shows that this was primarily due to the attractive prices quoted and the better condition of the glass market, rather than to any lack of energy on the part of our dealer.

With regard to Hua Sheng Tung, it is true this concern was a considerable business in Shoko Glass, but it is hardly correct to state that they control Sales of this Glass. They are some of a combine of 8 dealers selling this glass and they were actually out of the market for some months last year owing to a lawsuit between themselves and the other Shoko dealers who claimed they had infringed their agreement by importing Soviet Glass without the cognisance of the rest of the combine. Hua Sheng Tung lost the case and had to pay the costs and compensation before being readmitted into the combine.

We have no idea what quantity of Yao Hua Glass Hua Sheng Tung could sell if appointed our contractor, but we consider it highly unlikely that this action would result in a cessation of Shoko sales, since this obviously cannot be arranged without the agreement of the Japanese themselves. The defection of a Shoko dealer or dealers would only result in others being appointed.

Immediately it is interesting to note that although we give Hua Sheng Tung the opportunity in 1934 of purchasing from it on credit up to the amount of his guarantee ($10,000), they only took 2,000 cases, and subsequently imported Soviet Glass which they sold at price necessitating our price reduction of $1.00 per case.

In conclusion, while we hold no brief for Tung Hsiang Yung, it is only fair to state that we have found them energetic and reliable. We have a cash guarantee of $30,000 and have convinced no difficulty in regard to their accounts which are always paid at due date.

Enclos:- (1)

译文：

参考编号　18119

序号

天津　代理处　1935 年 3 月 15 日

致：秦皇岛代理商

主题　　天津玻璃销售安排

兹回复总务部于本月 12 日发出的 18055 号信函，并附上此前由福克纳先生转交给我们并需要我们给出意见的两份附件。

关于我们目前的经销商同祥湧销售玻璃能力的备忘录，很明显，备忘录的撰写者得到了错误的信息，这可以从以下内容明显看出：

1）据称，同祥湧玻璃庄今年只能卖出约 1 万箱玻璃。

同祥湧玻璃庄已保证在 1935 年期间销售至少 6 万标准件，他迄今为止的销售记录是：

1 月	1 100 标准件
2 月	2 070 标准件
3 月（截至 15 日）	5 073 标准件
合计	8 249 标准件

1 月和 2 月一直是销售不景气的月份，但通常从 3 月开始好转已经出现，没有理由相信全年的销售情况会不正常。

2）据称，耀华在天津的销售额在过去三年中有所下降。

下面我们给出了 1932 至 1934 年期间耀华的销售额，从中可以看出，销售额逐渐增加。此外，1934 年的销售额创下了工厂开业以来的最高纪录。

1934	1933	1932
68 318.5 标准件	63 871 标准件	62 561 标准件

3）据称，曙光玻璃的销量"突飞猛进"。1934 年，曙光玻璃的销售额增加了 1 200 标准件，但我们掌握的信息表明，这主要是由于报价吸引人，以及玻璃市场状况较好，而不是因为我们的经销商没有尽力。

关于华盛堂，确实我们担心它与曙光玻璃有大量销售业务，但说他们控制了整个曙光玻璃的销售是不正确的。他们只是和其他 7 家销售商联合起来组成一个商会销售曙光玻璃，去年他们实际上已经退出了市场几个月，由于他们和其他曙光玻璃经销商之间的诉讼，其他经销商声称华盛堂违反了他们的协议，在没有其他经销商的许可的情况下进口了苏联玻璃。华盛堂败诉，在交了赔偿金之后才被重新纳入商会。

如果指定华盛堂为我们的销售承包商，我们不知道耀华玻璃能卖出去多少，但我们认为这一行为不太可能导致曙光玻璃销售的停止，因为没有日本人自己的同意，这显然是无法安排的。一个或几个曙光玻璃经销商的退出只会导致其他人被任命。

有趣的是，尽管我们在 1934 年给了华盛堂一个机会，可以赊购他的担保金额（10 000 美元），但他们只接受了 2 000 箱，随后他们进口了苏联玻璃并销售，这使得我们不得不每箱降价 1 美元。

总而言之，虽然我们不为同祥湧辩护，但公平地说，我们发现他们公司有活力，可靠。我们有 3 万美元的现金担保，并相信他们在到期日付款方面没有任何困难。

考威尔

天津销售部

部门间备忘录十二
INTER-DEPARTMENTAL MEMORANDUM

To:	Agent.,	Reference	2563
	CHINWANGTAO	Serial Number	
		Tientsin Agency	19th Mar, 1935

Subject ....1935 Glass Sales Arrangement..................................

We enclose here with draft of the Agreement with Messrs. Tung Hsiang Yung covering 1935 glass sales. We believe that it covers all the points arranged by Mr. Faulkner in Tientsin, but we shall be glad to have your comments before arranging for the official signatures.

You will note that there is no provision in the contract for the procedure regarding possible upcountry sales, but this can be arranged by an exchange of letters when the position in this respect is clarified. Should it later appear desirable to have a clause protecting us as regards glass to be shipped upcountry for Tung Hsiang Yung to hold as stocks, this can be arranged by making the necessary addition to the contract.

E. J. Cowell
TIENTSIN SALES OFFICE.

译文：

参考编号 ...2563...
序号 ....
天津　代理处　1935年3月19日

致：秦皇岛代理商

主题 ....1935 玻璃销售安排.....................

兹随函附上与同祥湧签订的1935年玻璃销售协议草案。我们相信它包含了福克纳先生在天津安排的所有事项，但在安排正式签字之前，我们乐意听取您的意见。

您将注意到，合同中没有关于可能在内陆销售的手续的规定，但在这方面的立场明确后，可以通过信函交流来安排。如果以后需要加入一条保护我方的条款，关于将玻璃运往内陆给同祥湧作为库存持有，这可以通过对合同进行必要的补充来安排。

考威尔
天津销售部

18119

Tientsin Sales Office
TIENTSIN

　　　　　　　　　　　　Chinwangtao　　20th March, 35

<u>1935 Glass Sales Agreements</u>
CONFIDENTIAL.

With reference to your 18119 of the 19th instant we have studied the draft Agreement and believe with you that all the points have been covered.

With regard to the question of the up-country sales we agree that the details of this business can be covered by an exchange of letters.

H. H. Faulker
for AGENT.

译文：

18119
秦皇岛　1935年3月20日

致：天津销售处

关于你方本月19日来函18119号的询盘，我们已研究了协议草案，相信所有问题都已涉及。

关于内陆销售的问题，我们同意交易的细节可以通过书信交流来解决。

福克纳

18119.

E.J.Cowell, Esq.,

TIENTSIN.   Chinwangtao, 3rd April, 35

UP-COUNTRY GLASS SALES.
CONEIDENTIAL.

Dear Cowell,

With reference to your letter No.18120 of the 27th ultimo, we give below the costs of direct shipments by rail to the various interior centres:-

To	Freight per ton	Freight per case Single Thickness
Tsinanfu	$16.50	$1.10
Taiyuanfu	$33.30	$2.10
Shihehiachwang	$23.51	$1.50
Chengchow	$29.98	$1.90
Kaifeng	$28.85	$1.80

N.B. Unloading charges at all stations for buyer's account. Transhipment charges at Shihchiachwang for Taiyuanfu cargo for buyer's account. Orders should be placed for quantities not under a 20-ton car load.

With regard to quotations for direct deliveries, if we take the present return to factory from Tientsin sales and add the above freight, and commissions, we get the following for single thickness in standard specifications:-

Tsinanfu	$7.20
Taiyuanfu	$8.20
Shihchiachwang	$7.60
Chengchow	$8.00
Kaifeng	$7.90

However before giving these prices to Messrs.Tung Hsing Yung We suggest you obtain some idea of the costs of delivering to these points by the present via Tientsin method for both shoko and our own glass.

> As you are aware our policy is to endeavour to increase sales in the interior by making our glass cheap enough to reach the real hinterland and replace paper, but we want to make sure that this will be realized and not that we will be merely assisting the dealer to increase his or his sub-agents' profits.
>
> However, you know the position better than we do, and the above prices can be used as the minimum rates, if you can improve upon them so much the better.
>
> Yours sincerely

译文：

18119

秦皇岛 1935 年 4 月 3 日

致：天津的考威尔先生

内陆玻璃销售

机密文件

亲爱的考威尔先生，

关于贵公司 27 日第 18120 号最后通牒，现将铁路直达内地各中心的运费开列如下：

运往	每吨运费	每箱单厚玻璃运费
济南府	$16.50	$1.10
太原府	$33.30	$2.10
石家庄	$23.51	$1.50
郑州	$29.98	$1.90
开封	$28.85	$1.80

注意：所有卸货站的卸货费由买方负担。石家庄到太原府的玻璃转运费用由买方承担。订购的数量不能低于 20 吨的汽车载重。

关于直接交货的报价，如果我们把现在天津销售的回厂单，加上上面的运费和佣金，我们得到标准规格单厚玻璃的报价如下：

济南府	$7.20
太原府	$8.20
石家庄	$7.60
郑州	$8.00
开封	$7.90

不过，在把这些价格告诉同祥湧玻璃庄之前，我们建议你先了解一下经由天津的曙光玻璃和我们自己的耀华玻璃目前交货到这些地点的成本。

如你所知，我们的政策是努力提高内地的销售量，使我们的玻璃产品足够便宜，以到达真正的内陆地区，取代纸张，但我们要确保这一点能够实现，而不仅仅是帮助经销商增加他或他的子代理商的利润。

但是你比我们更了解现状，以上价格可以作为最低价格。如果你能改进它们，那就更好了。

谨启

部门间备忘录十三
INTER-DEPARTMENTAL MEMORANDUM

To:	H. H. Faulker, Esq.,	Reference	18119
	CHINWANGTAO	Serial Number	
		Tientsin Agency	5th April, 1935

Subject   UPCOUNTRY GLASS SALES.

With reference to your letter 18119 of the 3rd of April, I am arranging to obtain the information you require from Messrs. Tung Hsiang Yung. With reference to the freight you have quoted to upcountry stations, however, are those rates under Railway Risk Regulations? I inquire because when we made out some months ago and estimate of the cost of the freight charges from Chinwangtao to upcountry stations, the rates quoted us by the Railway were some 10% higher than those you have given, and it therefore struck me that perhaps the latter are not Railway Risk rates, which presumably the Railway would charge if we made any shipments.

Yours faithfully,
E. J. Cowell.

译文：

参考编号 18119
序号
天津　代理处　1935年4月5日

致：秦皇岛的福克纳先生

主题　　内陆玻璃销售

关于您 4 月 3 日的编号为 18119 的来信，我正安排从同祥湧公司获取您所需要的信息。然而，关于向内陆车站运货您所报的运费，这些费率是根据铁路风险条例规定的吗？我之所以询问您，是因为几个月前，当我们计算从秦皇岛到内陆车站的运费成本时，铁路公司给我们的报价比贵方的报价高出 10%，因此我突然想到，后者可能没包含铁路风险费，如果我们装运货物，铁路公司将会收取这一费用的。

谨上

考威尔

18119

E.J.Cowell, Esq.,
　　TIENTSIN.　　　　　　　　　　　　　　　Chinwangtao, 6th April, 35

CONEIDENTIAL.

Dear Cowell,

　　with reference to your letter 18119 of yesterday's date regarding the Freight Rates from Chinwangtao to upcountry stations, I confirm that these rates include Railway Risk charges.

　　In this connection, I send you herewith a copy of statement showing details of the above rates, received from the Station Master at Chinwangtao.

　　　　　　　　　　　　　　　　　　　　　　　Yours sincerely

译文：

18119

秦皇岛 1935 年 4 月 3 日

致：天津的考威尔先生

机密文件

亲爱的考威尔先生，

关于你昨天 18119 信中谈及从秦皇岛到内陆站的运费的问题，我确认这些运费已包括铁路风险费用。

关于这一点，我随函附上一份从秦皇岛站长处收到的上述费率的详细说明。

谨启

COPY		
From C.W.T to Tsinan	Car load rate per ton being	$16.50
From C.W.T to Taiyuan	Car load rate per ton being	$33.30
From C.W.T to Shihchiachwang	Car load rate per ton being	$23.51
From C.W.T to Chengchow	Car load rate per ton being	$22.98 Via TCS
From C.W.T to Chengchow	Car load rate per ton being	$36.27 Via F.T.
From C.W.T to Kaifeng	Car load rate per ton being	$38.15 Via F.T.
From C.W.T to Kaifeng	Car load rate per ton being	$28.85 Via TCS

Remarks:-

1. Railway risk charges are included.

2. "Charges for Tran-shipment" for glasses to Tai-yuan will be collected by Cheng-Tai Railway at Shih-Chia-Chwang.

3. Loading and unloading charges are not included and the unloading charge is to be collected by the destination station.

4. "Via Feng-Tai" or "Via Tientsin central" should be clearly inserted in the consignor's note by the consignor.

译文：

从秦皇岛到济南	每吨运费为	$16.50	
从秦皇岛到太原	每吨运费为	$33.30	
从秦皇岛到石家庄	每吨运费为	$23.51	
从秦皇岛到郑州	每吨运费为	$22.98	经由天津港中心
从秦皇岛到郑州	每吨运费为	$36.27	经由丰台
从秦皇岛到开封	每吨运费为	$38.15	经由丰台
从秦皇岛到开封	每吨运费为	$28.85	经由天津港中心

补充：

1. 铁路风险费用已被包含。
2. 到太原的"转运费"将由郑太铁路在石家庄收取。
3. 不包括装卸费用，卸货费用由目的站收取。
4. 发货人在发货通知单上应注明"经丰台"或"经天津中心"。

部门间备忘录十四
INTER-DEPARTMENTAL MEMORANDUM

To: H.H. Faulkner, Esq.,   Reference 18119
       CHINWANGTAO.   Serial Number ____

<u>Tientsin</u> Agency <u>9th May, 1935</u>

SUBJECT: <u>UPCOUNTRY GLASS SALES</u>

Dear Faulkner,

    I must apologize for the delay in replying to your letter 18119 of 3rd April, but Tung Hsiang Yung was rather slow in providing the information of inland dealers' current selling prices.

    I now enclose a statement showing the F.O.C. to Tung Hsiang Yung and Shoko dealers costs of glass at inland centres as compared with the proposed direct shipment costs given by you and the reported selling prices at inland towns.

You will note that there is no particular advantage in the direct shipment method at the prices proposed by you. Of course Tung Hsiang Yung does not himself sell at the inland towns from Tientsin at present, his sales being made F.O.B. or F.O.C. Tientsin, but for the purpose of comparison it has been necessary to set out the figures as we have done.

It is true, of course, that even if there is no price advantage to Tung Hsiang Yung in the direct shipment method, it is more convenient and should interest him purely from the point of expanding his sales, but I think that unless there is also a certain advantage in price, he will be inclined to continue in his present methods, particularly since he would have to spend a certain amount in keeping agents, etc. at the main inland centres.

Please, therefore, let me know whether there is any possibility of reducing your through shipment prices or whether we should advise Tung Hsiang Yung in accordance with the prices in your letter under reply.

I am, of course, unable to vouch for the accuracy of the selling prices at inland towns quoted by Tung Hsiang Yung, but in comparison with the costs we have compiled, they appear to be reasonably accurate. It would appear, however, quite certain that we could not improve upon the direct prices quoted by you without prohibiting this type of sale.

Yours sincerely,

Enclos: - (1).

译文：

参考编号　18119
序号
天津　　代理处　1935年5月9日

致：秦皇岛的福克纳先生

主题：内陆玻璃销售

亲爱的福克纳：

对于您4月3日18119的来信，迟复为歉。因为同祥湧玻璃庄在提供内陆经销商当前的销售价格信息时相当迟缓。

现随函附上一份报表，说明给同祥湧玻璃庄的离岸价和给内陆中心的曙光玻璃公司经销商的成本价，以和贵方提出的直接运输成本及报告记载的内陆城镇售价作比较。

您会注意到，按贵方提出的价格，直运方式并没有什么特别的好处。当然，同祥湧玻璃庄目前并没有在天津的内陆城镇销售，他是按离岸价或天津备品价进行销售的，但为了比较起见，有必要像我们这样列明数据。

当然，即使直运方式对同祥湧玻璃庄没有价格优势，这种方式也更方便，而且仅从扩大销售的角度考虑，他应该也会感兴趣。但我想，除非在价格上也有一定的优势，否则他会倾向于继续采用目前的方式，在他必须花费一定的费用在主要的内陆中心留住代理商等的情况下尤为如此。

因此，请告知是否有可能降低贵方的全程运费价格，或者我们是否应该按照贵方回复的信中的价格通知同祥湧玻璃庄。

当然，我不能保证同祥湧玻璃庄所报的内陆城镇售价的准确性，但与我们编制的成本相比，它们似乎是合理准确的。然而，很显然，在不禁止此类销售的情况下，我方无法在贵方直接报价的基础上再提高价格。

谨上

附注：（1）。

部门间备忘录十五

INTER-DEPARTMENTAL MEMORANDUM

To: Agent,　　　　　　　　　　Reference __18119__

　　CHINWANGTAO,　　　　　Serial Number

　　　　　　　　　　　　　　__Tientsin__ Agency __13th June, 1935__

SUBJECT: __UPCOUNTRY PRICES__

　　With reference to our letters to Messrs. Tung Hsiang Yung dated 16/5/35, quoting prices for upcountry sales, Messrs. Tung Hsiang Yung have informed us that they are now investigating the various markets with a view to arranging direct shipment business. They have stated that the prices we have quoted work out at approximately the same as for shipments via Tientsin, but we have pointed out to them that even if the prices for direct shipment are no cheaper, the advantage of this method of sale should alone serve to stimulate business to our mutual benefits.

　　They have informed us, however, that while from preliminary advices, our prices along the Peiping-Hankow Railway appear satisfactory, our prices for sales in Honan are likely to be unfavorable in comparison with the price at which shipments from Shanghai can be sold in these districts, since it is reported that Yao Hua prices at Shanghai have recently been reduced 50 cents per case.

　　We shall be grateful, therefore, if you will advise us whether prices now ruling at Shanghai are such as to compete with those you have given us, in order that we may advise Tung Hsiang Yung of the position.

　　　　　　　　　　　　　　　　　　　　　　　　E. J. Cowell

　　　　　　　　　　　　　　　　　　　　　　　　Tianjin Sales Office.

译文：

参考编号　18119

序号　

天津　　代理处　　1935年6月13日

致：秦皇岛代理商

主题：内陆玻璃销售

　　关于我方1935年5月16日致同祥湧公司的信中有关内陆销售的报价，同祥湧玻璃庄通知我方，他们正在调查各市场，以期安排直运业务。他们称我方所报价格与经天津装运的价格大致相同，但我方已向他们指出，即使直接装运的价格不便宜，但单凭这种销售方式的优势，就应能促进业务的发展，使双方都受益。

　　不过，他们通知我方，虽然根据初步意见，我方的北平—汉口铁路沿线价格似乎令人满意，但与上海来货在这些地区的销售价格相比，我方在河南的销售价格可能不占优势。因为据报道，最近上海的耀华玻璃价格每箱降低了50美分。

　　因此，如贵方能告知上海现行价格与贵公司所报价格相比是否有竞争优势，以便我方将有关情况通知同祥湧公司，则甚为感激。

考威尔

天津销售部

<u>TO BE TRANSIATED INTO CHINESE.</u>

Tientsin, 16th May, 1935
Ref. 18119.

Messrs. Tung Hsiang Yung,
TIENTSIN

Dear Sirs,

With reference to your recent request for quotation for glass shipped direct to inland towns, we have pleasure in quoting you our prices for 4th Quality Single Thickness glass delivered in railway cars at the following stations:-

Shihchiachwang	$7.95	per	case	7.60
Chengchow	8.35	"	"	8.00
Kaifeng	8.25	"	"	7.90
Tsinanfu	7.55	"	"	7.20
Taiyuanfu	8.55	"	"	8.20

The above prices are subject to deduction of the usual commission as laid down in your current contract. It is understood, however, that all charges in connection with unloading and shunting etc., at all stations are for buyers' account. Orders should be placed for quantities not less than a 20-ton carload.

As we are anxious to extend our business in the interior, we hope that by delivering in railway cars direct to dealers at the above stations, our sales through you will increase, and consequently yield greater returns to you, especially when you establish direct contact with the interior dealers.

We shall be glad to learn, in due course, how these prices work.

Your faithfully,
E. J. Cowell
TIENTSIN SALES OFFICE.

Copy to:- A.T.
      Mr. Chiu
      Ag. Cwt.

译文：

　　　　　　　　　待译成中文
　　　　　　　　　天津，1935 年 5 月 16 日
　　　　　　　　　　编号：18119

致：天津的同祥湧玻璃庄

亲爱的先生们：

关于贵方最近对直运至内陆各城镇的玻璃的报价要求，我们很高兴向贵方报出在以下车站用火车车厢运送的四等单厚玻璃的价格：

石家庄	$7.95	每箱	7.60
郑州	8.35	每箱	8.00
开封	8.25	每箱	7.90
济南府	7.55	每箱	7.20
太原府	8.55	每箱	8.20

上述价格都要扣除当前合同中规定的常规佣金。然而，所有车站与卸货和调车等相关的所有费用均由买方承担。订单数量应不少于 20 吨车厢荷载量。

由于我们急于扩大我们在内陆的业务，我们希望通过铁路车厢在上述车站直接向经销商交付货物，通过您这一销售渠道的销售额会增加，从而为您带来更大的回报，特别是当您与内陆经销商建立直接联系时。

我们将很高兴在适当的时候了解这些价格是否可行。

　　　　　　　　　　　　　　　您的诚挚的朋友，
　　　　　　　　　　　　　　　　考威尔
　　　　　　　　　　　　　　　　天津销售部

抄送：秦皇岛代理处邱先生

18119

E.J.Cowell, Esq.,
TIENTSIN.

Chinwangtao, 6th April, 35

UP-COUNTRY SALES

With reference to your letter 18119 of the 13th instant, unless I hear from you that it is unsuitable, I intend to proceed to Tientsin on Monday mid-day to have a talk with you and Tung Hsing Yung on this up-country business.

Yours sincerely.

译文：

18119

秦皇岛 1935年4月6日

致：天津的考威尔先生

内陆销售

关于您本月13日第18119号来信，除非接到您的来信认为不合适，否则我打算于星期一中午动身前往天津，与您和同祥涌就此事谈一谈。

谨启

部门间备忘录十六

18119

E.J.Cowell, Esq.,
TIENTSIN.

Chinwangtao, 10th July, 35

UP-COUNTRY SALES
CONFIDENTIAL.

During the writer's visit to Tientsin last month, Mr. Sung of Messrs. Tunf Hsing Yung promised to give us a definite plan of his proposals for the extension of up-country sales and his views on the establishment of interior depots within two weeks. It is now three weeks since this promise was given and we would like to know when we may expect to hear further in this connection.

It is only a matter of six weeks or so before the opening of the autumn buying seasons, and we feel that further procrastination is undesirable if our plans are to be carried through this year.

for Agent.

译文：

18119

秦皇岛 1935 年 7 月 10 日

致：天津的考威尔先生

内陆销售

机密文件

笔者上月访问天津时，同祥湧玻璃庄的宋先生答应在两星期内给我们提出他关于扩大内地销售的建议和关于设立内地仓库的意见。自从作出这一承诺以来，现在已经有三个星期了，我们想知道我们什么时候可以得到这方面的进一步消息。

再过六个星期左右就是秋季采购季节了，我们认为，如果我们的计划今年预计实施，再拖延下去是不可取的。

福克纳

INTER-DEPARTMENTAL MEMORANDUM

To: Agent,　　　　　　　　　Reference ...18119 X...
　　CHINWANGTAO,　　　　　Serial Number ....
　　　　　　　　　　　　　　Tientsin Agency 12th July, 1935

SUBJECT: ....

　　With reference to your letter No. 18119 of the 10th inst., the following are summaries of letters from his dealers left with us yesterday evening by Mr Sung of Messrs Tung Hsing Yung, in which are set force their views regarding prices for upcounty glass sales:

　1. Yi Sheng Chang - Kaifeng

　　Prices quoted to them by Tung Hsing Yung

　　　　Per case large size　　　$8.45
　　　　Per case small size　　　 8.05

　　To this point it is stated that shipments from Shanghai can be offered at $7.12 per case regardless of size, and dealers prefer to ship to this point by boat.

　2. Teh Yuan Yai - Tsinanfu

　　Prices quoted to them by Tung Hsing Yung

　　　　Per case large size　　　$7.75
　　　　Per case small size　　　 7.05

　　Shipped from Tsingtao to Tsinanfu

　　　　Per case large size　　　$7.50
　　　　Per case small size　　　 7.10

　　In this case it is stated that if our prices could be reduced to $7.45 delivered to their godowns in Tsinanfu, they might be prepared to place an initial order for one carload.

　3. Kwang Tai Hsing-Chengchow

　　Prices quoted to them by Tung Hsing Yung

　　　　Per case large size　　　$8.55
　　　　Per case small size　　　 8.15

Information has been received from this dealer that the cost of f.o.c Chengchow shipped via Shanghai would be $7.27 per case (cost in Shanghai $6.00 plus freight $1.27). In this instance it has been intimated to us that only if our price could be reduced to Shanghai level will business be possible.

4. <u>Teh Sheng Heng - Taiyuanfu</u>

Apparently no quotation was given to this dealer by Tung Hsing Yung but a comparison is made with Shoko glass as under:

Price of Shoko Glass per case	$6.20
Freight by boat and rail	1.35
	$7.55
Yao Hua Glass per case	$6.40
Freight	1.50
	$7.90

The difference in the freight rate is said to be due to the fact that whereas Shoko Glass can be shipped at 350 cases per carload, shipment of Yao Hua Glass can only be effected at 320 cases per carload.

The above letters are summarized as per table hereunder:

	Gross F.O.C Price to T.H.Y	Price F.O.C. quoted by T.H.Y to dealers		Competitive prices of Y.H.& other glasses quoted to dealers from other sources
Shihchiachwang	$7.95			
Chengchow	$8.35	L. $8.55) S. $8.15)	av.$8.31	Y.H. $7.27 f.o.c. S'hai
Kaifeng	$8.25	L. $8.45) S. $8.05)	av.$8.21	Y.H. $7.12 f.o.c. S'hai
Tsinanfu	$7.25	L. $7.75) S. $7.35)	av.$7.51	Y.H. $7.26 del'd. Tsinan via Tsingtao
Taiyuanfu	$8.55			Shoko $7.55

Mr Sung has requested us to obtain for him f.o.c. prices at Shihchiachwang and Taiyuanfu and reports that in the latter town competition from Shoko glass is at the moment very keen.

We trust that the above information will be of value to you. In connection with the summary of prices given above you will understand that the prices mentioned are those quoted in letters from Tung Hsing Yung's dealers and that these may be only approximate or even entirely inaccurate. We have no means of checking these figures here but doubtless you will be able to check their correctness or otherwise.

G. H. Fawcett
TIENTSIN SALES OFFICE.

译文：

参考编号　18119X
序号　
天津　代理处　1935 年 7 月 12 日

致：秦皇岛代理商

主题：

关于贵公司本月 10 日第 18119 号信，以下是同祥湧玻璃庄的宋先生昨天晚上留下的他的经销商来信的摘要。在这篇文章中，他们对北部内陆玻璃销售价格的看法是：

1. 义昌盛—开封

　　同祥湧玻璃庄给他们的报价是：每箱大玻璃　　$8.45
　　　　　　　　　　　　　　　　　　每箱小玻璃　　$8.05

在这一点上，据说从上海发货，无论大小，每箱 7.12 美元，经销商更喜欢用船运到这里。

2. 德源泰—济南府

同祥湧玻璃庄给他们的报价是：每箱大玻璃　　$7.75

每箱小玻璃　　$7.25

从青岛船运至济南：每箱大玻璃　　$7.50

每箱小玻璃　　$7.10

在这种情况下，据说如果我们的价格可以降低到 7.45 美元，送货到他们在天津的仓库，他们可能会准备一车厢的第一批订单。

3. 康泰箱—郑州

同祥湧玻璃庄给他们的报价是：每箱大玻璃　　$8.55

每箱小玻璃　　$8.15

从该经销商处获悉，经由上海的郑州离岸价为每箱 7.27 美元（上海成本价为 6.00 美元 + 1.27 美元的运费）。在这种情况下，对方已向我们暗示，只有我们的价格降至上海的水平，才有可能成交。

4. 德盛恒—太原府

显然，同祥湧玻璃庄没有给这个经销商报价，但与曙光玻璃进行了比较，如下：

曙光玻璃每箱$6.20 + 船或铁路运费$1.35，合计每箱$7.55

耀华玻璃每箱$6.40 + 船或铁路运费$1.50，合计每箱$7.90

运费的差异据说是由于曙光玻璃每车厢可装运 350 箱，而耀华玻璃每车只能装运 320 箱。

上述信件摘要如下表所示：

	给同祥涌的总离岸价	同祥涌给经销商的离岸价	其他货源报给经销商的耀华玻璃及其他玻璃的具有竞争力的价格
1. 石家庄	$7.95		
2. 郑州	$8.35	大玻璃$8.35 小玻璃$8.15	均价：$8.31 耀华上海离岸价$7.27
3. 开封	$8.25	大玻璃$8.45 小玻璃$8.05	均价：$8.21 耀华上海离岸价$7.12
4. 济南府	$7.25	大玻璃$7.75 小玻璃$7.35	均价：$8.51 经由天津的耀华价$7.26
5. 太原府	$8.55		曙光玻璃价格$7.55

宋先生要求我们为他索取石家庄和太原府的离岸价，并报告说，在太原府，目前与曙光玻璃的竞争非常激烈。

我们相信上述信息对贵方将有价值。关于以上所提供的价格总结，贵公司应明白所述价格乃同祥涌经销商信中所报的价格，而这些价格可能只是近似值，甚至可能完全不准确。我们没有办法在这里检查这些数字，但毫无疑问，你将能够检查它们的正确性或错误。

福西特
天津销售处

部门间备忘录十七
INTER-DEPARTMENTAL MEMORANDUM

To: Agent,　　　　　　　　Reference ....18119 X....
　　CHINWANGTAO,　　　Serial Number ....

　　　　　　　　　　　　　Tientsin　Agency　17th July, 1935

SUBJECT: ....UPCOUNTRY GLASS BUSINESS.................

With further reference to your letter No.18119 of the 10th of July, and further to our letter No.18119 of the 12th of July, we send you herewith translation of a letter dated 13th of July from Tung Hsiang Yung in connection with up country business, and shall be glad if in due course you will advise us in what manner you wish us to reply.

　　　　　　　　　　　　　　　　　　　G.H. Fawcett
　　　　　　　　　　　　　　　　TIENTSIN SALES OFFICE.

Enclos:-(1).

译文：

　　　　　　　　　　　　　　参考编号 ....18119....
　　　　　　　　　　　　　　序号　　　............
　　　　　　　　　　　　　　天津　代理处　1935年7月17日

致：秦皇岛代理商

主题：..............内陆玻璃业务..............

关于贵公司7月10日第18119号来信和我公司7月12日第18119号信，现寄上同祥湧玻璃庄7月13日关于贵公司业务的来信翻译件，如能及时告知希望以何种方式答复，我们将不胜感激。

　　　　　　　　　　　　　　　　　　　福西特
　　　　　　　　　　　　　　　　　　天津销售处

附件：（1）。

Copy
Translation

13th July, 1935

Tientsin Sales Office,
K.M.A.,
Tientsin

Dear Sis,

With reference to sales of glass in the upcountry districts, please be advised that we have sent out representatives to various districts to push the sales.

Now, we are in receipt of letters from those dealers who have most of your goods, saying that the prices fixed by you are higher than the selling price ruling at the sport. The reason is that the price of Shoko Glass is cheaper and the price of your glass shipped from Shanghai to the districts is also cheaper than that shipped from Tientsin.

We are hereby asking you to devise way and means without delay so as to compete with the Shoko Glass, as it would otherwise not only affect the sales of your goods, but we shall also sustain a heavy loss.

You faithfully,

(Chopped) Tung Hsing Yung.

译文：

1935 年 7 月 13 日

致：开滦矿物总局天津经销处，

敬启者：

关于内陆地区玻璃的销售情况，我们已派代表到各个地区进行推销，请知悉。

现在，我们收到了那些拥有贵方大部分货物的经销商的来信，他们说贵方所定的价格高于本地区规定的售价。原因是曙光玻璃的价格比较便宜，贵方从上海到各区的玻璃价格也比从天津到各区的便宜。

我们在此要求你们尽快设计出与曙光玻璃竞争的方法，否则不仅会影响你们的销售，我们也将蒙受重大损失。

谨启

（商号）同祥涌

18119

G.H. Fawcett, Esq.,
TIENTSIN   Chinwangtao   18th July, 35

UP-COUNTRY GLASS SALES

Dear Fawcett,

With reference to your letter 18119-X of the 17th instant, I will be in Tientsin early next week and will discuss all details of this business with you then.

Yours sincerely,

H. H. Faulker.

译文：

18119

秦皇岛　1935 年 7 月 18 日

致：天津的福西特先生

内陆玻璃销售

亲爱的福西特先生，

关于您本月 17 日 18119-X 的来信，我将于下周初到达天津，届时将与您讨论此事的所有细节。

谨上

福克纳

部门间备忘录十八
INTER-DEPARTMENTAL MEMORANDUM

To: H. H. Faulker, Esq.,   Reference 18119
         CHINWANGTAO   Serial Number
                                                  Tientsin Agency 19th July, 1935

Subject   UPCOUNTRY GLASS SALES.

Dear Faulkner,

    From conversations with Cowell and referring to your letter to him, No. 18119 of 3rd April last, his letter to Tung Hsiang Yung dated 16th May, and to your letter, 18119-A of 16th inst., there is some doubt in our minds as to whether the price quoted in your letters of 3rd April and 16th July are gross (i.e. prices which include the dealers' rebate of 35 cents per case as per contract) or net (i.e. prices from which the dealers' commission of 35 cents has already been deducted).

    Cowell himself, according to his letter to Tung Hsiang Yung of 16th May, assumed that they were net (since he added 35 cents to them), but we now both think this was a mistake and that they are intended to be gross. If this is so, it would seem that they should, in almost all cases, be competitive. I am now going into this and shall get hold of Mr. Sung as soon as possible after receipt of your reply.

                                          Yours sincerely,
                                             G. H. Fawcett.

译文：

参考编号　18119

序号

天津　　代理处　　1935年7月19日

致：秦皇岛的福克纳先生

主题　　　　内陆玻璃销售

尊敬的福克纳：

根据与考威尔的谈话，并参照您上次4月3日寄给考威尔的编号为18119的信，考威尔5月16日寄给同祥湧的信以及本月16日考威尔寄给您的编号为18119-A的信，我们有一点疑问，贵方4月3日和7月16日信函中所报价格是毛价（即包括根据合同经销商应得的每箱35美分回扣的价格）还是净价（即已扣除经销商佣金35美分的价格）呢？

根据5月16日考威尔本人给同祥湧的信，他认为这是净价（因为他给这些报价加了35美分），但我们现在都认为这是一个错误，这应该是毛价。如果事实是这样的话，这些报价在几乎所有情况下都应该具有竞争力。我现在正在着手调查此事，在收到您的答复后，我会尽快与宋先生取得联系。

谨上

福西特

18119

G.H. Fawcett, Esq.,

　　TIENTSIN　　　　　　　　Chinwangtao　　　　20th July, 35

Dear Fawcett,

　　With reference to your letter 18119 of the 19th instant, the prices given in my letter No.18119 of 3rd April last were the minimum prices we are prepared to accept for direct shipment business, and as clearly stated, commissions were included.

　　　　　　　　　　　　　　　　　　Yours sincerely,

　　　　　　　　　　　　　　　　　　H. H. Faulker.

译文：

18119

秦皇岛　1935年7月20日

致：天津的福西特先生

内陆玻璃销售

亲爱的福西特，

关于您本月19日18119的来信，我方去年4月3日第18119号信所报价格是我方可以接受的直运业务的最低价格，而且明确地说，佣金已包括在内了。

谨上

福克纳

部门间备忘录十九
INTER-DEPARTMENTAL MEMORANDUM

To: H.H.Faulkner, Esq., CHINWANGTAO,	Reference　X-18119
	Serial Number
	Tientsin　Agency　1st Aug, 1935

SUBJECT:

CONFIDENTIAL.

Dear Faulkner,

　　With reference to your official letter 18119 of 16th of July and your D/o letters 18119 of 18th and 20th of July Fawcett, nothing has so far been definitely arranged with Tung Hsiang Yung.

　　Fawcett, who was dealing with the matter, has been in hospital for over a week and I was waiting for your visit to Tientsin as promised in your letter to Fawcett of July the 18th.

　　Time is getting on, however, and I do not think we can delay this matter much longer.

　　Tung Hsiang Yung will not, I am afraid, produce any comprehensive scheme to sell upcountry, but are waiting for our prices to be reduced to levels which they consider more reasonable than those previously advised. In view of your letter of July the 20th, stating that the prices given by you on April the 3rd last include commissions. I think that by reducing to these levels, we will be able to interest Tung Hsiang Yung.

Unless I hear from you to the contrary, therefore, I shall quote Tung Hsiang Yung next week these minimum prices from which his commission will be deducted, and try to get him to get a move on.

I shall be in Chinwangtao over the week end, so that if you wish to discuss this matter I shall be available.

Yours sincerely,
G. H. Fawcett.

译文：

参考编号　X-18119

序号

天津　　代理处　　1935 年 8 月 1 日

致：秦皇岛的福克纳先生

主题：　　　　　内陆玻璃销售

机密文件

尊敬的福克纳先生：

关于您 7 月 16 日的编号为 18119 的公函和福西特先生 7 月 18 日和 20 日的就同意内容的两封信，到目前为止，和同祥湧玻璃庄之间还未有任何明确的安排。

负责处理此事的福西特先生已经住院一个多星期了，您于 7 月 18 日给福西特的信中承诺要访问天津，我一直在等待您的到来。

时间过得很快，我觉得我们不能一拖再拖了。

恐怕同祥湧玻璃庄不会制定任何国内销售的全面计划，而是等待我们的报价降至他们认为比先前建议的价格更合理的水平。考虑到您 7 月 20

日的信中说贵公司上次在4月3日给出的报价是包括回扣的，我认为只要我们把价格降至这个水平，我们就能引起同祥湧玻璃庄的兴趣。

因此，除非我收到您反对的答复，否则我下周就把这些扣除佣金的最低价格报给同祥湧，并设法让他加快行动。

这个周末我将在秦皇岛，因此如果您想讨论此事，我随时奉陪。

谨上
福西特

部门间备忘录二十

INTER-DEPARTMENTAL MEMORANDUM

To: H.H.Faulkner, Esq.,   Reference   X-18119

CHINWANGTAO,   Serial Number

                            Tientsin   Agency   10th Aug, 1935

SUBJECT   UPCOUNTRY GLASS SALES

    We enclose copy of our letter No.18119-X of 9/8/35 to Messrs. Tung Hsiang Yung giving the revised prices for upcountry sales.

    You will note that with the exception of Tsinanfu, where it seems possible to obtain a higher return, we have reduced to the limits authorised by you, and we trust business will now materialise.

    We have recently called Tung Hsiang Yung's attention to their rather poor sales in the last month or so and enclose a copy of their reply.

    The new prices for Kaifeng and Chengchow should remove the danger of undue competition from Shanghai, but we are now looking into our Tientsin prices for the heavier grades of 4th quality.

    You will remember that at the time of our last two reductions in 4th Single no change was made in the prices of the heavier grades, and it now appears that in certain popular sizes our prices are considerably higher than those of competing qualities. It appears to us that without making a general reduction in the prices of heavy grades, we might be able to stimulate business in certain sizes by reductions in those sizes alone.

    We shall refer to this again shortly when we have gone more fully into the matter.

G.H. Fawcett
TIENTSIN SALES OFFICE.

译文：

参考编号　X- 18119

序号　....................

天津　　代理处　1935 年 8 月 10 日

致：秦皇岛的福克纳先生

主题：..............内地玻璃销售..................

    兹随函附上我方 1935 年 8 月 9 日致同祥湧玻璃庄的第 18119-X 号信的副本，信中给出内地销售的修正价格。

    你会注意到，除了济南这个似乎有可能获得更高的回报的地方外，我方已减少到你方授权的限度，相信交易将会达成。

    我方最近已请同祥湧玻璃庄注意他们在过去一个月左右相当糟糕的销售情况，并附上他们的答复副本。

    开封和郑州的新价格应该可以消除来自上海的不正当竞争的危险，但我们现在正在考虑天津的 4 等加重玻璃的价格。

    你应该记得，在我们最近两次减少四等单玻璃的价格时，较重等级的价格并没有改变，现在看来，在某些流行的尺寸中，我们的价格比竞争质量的价格要高得多。在我们看来，即使不全面降低重玻璃的价格，我们也可能仅通过降低某些品级的价格来刺激这些品级的业务。

    当我们更加充分研究这一问题之后，我们会再次商量。

考威尔
天津经销处

TO BE TRANSLATED INTO CHINESE

Tientsin, 9th August, 1935.

Ref.X18119

Messrs, Tung Hasiang Yung,

TIENTSIN.

Dear sirs,

UPCOUNTRY GLASS SALES

With reference to our letter 18119 of 16th May, 1935 quoting prices for direct shipments of glass to inland towns and your subsequent report that our prices were not competitive, the Agent Chinwangtao has informed us that he can not reconcile the pieces at which Yao Hua Glass, shipped from Shanghai, is reported by you as being sold in Kaifeng and Chengchow.

According to information in our possession as to freight and charges from Shanghai to these towns, Yao Hua Glass cannot possibly be sold at prices as low as mentioned by you.

Nevertheless we are most anxious to initiate direct shipments to the interior and we have therefore gone carefully into the comparative costs of our own and competitive glass at the various towns and have pleasure in revising our prices as follows:

Shihchiachwang	$7.60	per case of 4th quality, Single Thickness Glass Standard Specification	
Taiyuanfu	$8.20	"	- do-
Tsinanfu	$7.40	"	- do-
Chengchow	$8.00	"	- do-
Kaifeng	$7.90	"	- do-

The above pieces are all gross, i.e. your commission will be deducted there from in accordance with the terms of your contract. All charges in connection with unloading, shunting, etc. are for buyer's account and orders

> should be placed for quantities not less than a 20-ton carload.
>   We trust that the above substantial reductions will enable you to secure business and push sales vigorously, and we now await your orders.
>
>   　　　　　　　　　　　　Yours faithfully,
>   　　　　　　　　　　　　　E. J. Cowell
>   　　　　　　　　　　TIENTSIN SAILES OFFICE.
>
> Copy to:- A.T.
> 　　　　Ag. CWT

译文：

　　　　　　　　　　　　　　　　　天津，1935年8月9日
　　　　　　　　　　　　　　　　　编号：X18119

致：天津的同祥涌玻璃庄

敬启者：

内陆玻璃销售

　　对于我方在1935年5月16日第18119号函件对直接运往内陆城镇玻璃的报价，以及贵方随后关于我方价格没有竞争力的报告，秦皇岛的代理通知我们，他无法协调你们报告的从上海运来的耀华玻璃在开封和郑州的销售价格。

　　根据我们掌握的从上海到这些城市的运费和费用信息，耀华玻璃不可能以你们提到的那么低的价格出售。

　　尽管如此，我们还是非常希望能直接向内地发货，因此我们仔细比较了我们自己的玻璃和竞争对手的玻璃在各个城镇的成本，并很高兴地将我们的价格修改如下：

　　　　石家庄　　　　$7.60 美元　　　箱四等单厚玻璃标准规格
　　　　太原府　　　　$8.20 美元　　　箱四等单厚玻璃标准规格
　　　　济南府　　　　$7.40 美元　　　箱四等单厚玻璃标准规格
　　　　郑州市　　　　$8.00 美元　　　箱四等单厚玻璃标准规格
　　　　开封市　　　　$7.90 美元　　　箱四等单厚玻璃标准规格

以上均为毛重，根据合同条款，你的佣金将从中扣除。所有与卸货、中转等有关的费用均由买方承担，订单数量应不少于20吨的车厢装载量。

我们相信，上述大幅削减将有助于你方获得业务并推动销售大力发展，我们期待你们的订单。

谨启
考威尔
天津销售处

抄送：总局
秦皇岛代理商

Copy

Updated 1935.

Tientsin Sales office,

K.M.A.

TIENTSIN.

Dear sirs,

With reference to the recent visit of your representative in connection with the enquiry upon the stagnation of our glass business, we have to point out the following:

During recent years business of every description has been suffering extreme adversities, which is hard to enumerate. On account of the bankrupty of the rural districts, all businesses have faced financial difficulties. Such general business depression not only prevails in North China, but also in all parts in this country and even in the whole world, and all, in general, are under the threatening of economic pressure either directly or indirectly. This is providential and beyond human control.

We are, however, rather satisfied with our present total annual sales results so far as the present adverse business condition is concerned. But the business of this year has been prosperous. Kalgan has been put under the control of Peiping, most of the Shantung ports under Tsingtao, the interior of Honan has been affected by Shanghai, and the district of Tientsin by Shoko Glass.

In view of the above difficulties we have encountered, our sales have been handicapped. What has made us most note-worthy is that the prices of glass in all the other places are cheaper than those ruling at Tientsin.

As your Administration are not lacking enlightened people, you should have understood the situation.

During the last two years the monthly figures of our sales, of course, vary to some extent, but if the yearly figures are taken into account, the difference would almost be un-noticed.

On account of the instructions and encouragement of your representative, we will do our utmost to stimulate our sales in order to develop the business and make good the reputation.

Yours faithfully
(neither signature nor chop)

译文：

更新于 1935 年

致：开滦矿物总局天津经销处

敬启者：

关于贵方代表最近就我方玻璃业务停滞问题而来访一事，我们必须指出以下几点：

近几年来，各种类型的企业都在遭受极端的逆境，难以一一列举。由于农村地区的破产，所有的企业都遇到了财政困难。这种普遍的商业萧条不仅发生在华北地区，而且在全国乃至全世界都普遍存在，总体上所有的人都直接或间接地受到经济压力的威胁。这是天意，非人力所能控制。

然而，就目前不利的商业情况而言，我们对目前的全年总销售业绩还是相当满意的。但今年的生意很兴隆。张家口的业务归属于北平，山东大部分港口的业务归属于青岛，河南的内陆业务被上海所控制，天津地区业务被曙光玻璃所控制。

　　鉴于我们所遇到的上述困难，我们的销售受到了阻碍。最值得我们注意的是，所有其他地方的玻璃价格都比天津的价格便宜。

　　总局不乏开明之士，你们应该了解这种情况。

　　在过去两年中，我们每月的销售额当然有一定程度的差异，但如果考虑到每年销售额，这种差异几乎不会被注意到。

　　在贵公司代表的指导和鼓励下，我们将尽最大努力来促进我们的销售，以发展业务和提高声誉。

谨启
（有签名也没有印章）

18119-X

Tientsin Sales Office,
　　TIENTSIN　　　　　　　Chinwangtao　　12th August, 35

<u>UP-COUNTRY GLASS SALES</u>

CONFIDENTIAL.

　　We thank you for your letter 18119-X of the 10th instant advising the latest developments with regard to the pushing of sales in the interior, and we look forward to some early action on the party of Messrs. Tung Hsiang Yung.

　　With regard to your remarks regarding heavy glass prices, please bear in mind that we do not wish to lose any of this business, and if you consider a revision necessary, please put forward your ideas as soon as possible so as to meet the Autumn buying season.

H. H. Faulker
for Agent.

译文：

18119-X

秦皇岛　1935 年 8 月 12 日

致：天津销售处

     内陆玻璃销售

  感谢您 10 日第 18119-X 号来信，告知我们在内地推销的最新进展，我们期待同祥湧玻璃庄尽早采取行动。

  贵方关于玻璃价格高昂的意见，请记住，我们不希望失去这笔生意，如果贵方认为有必要修改，请尽快提出您的意见，以便赶上秋季采购季节。

              福克纳

部门间备忘录二十一
INTER-DEPARTMENTAL MEMORANDUM

To: Agent, CHINWANGTAO	Reference X-18119
	Serial Number
	Tientsin Agency 15th Aug, 1935

SUBJECT:　　SALES OF HEAVY GLASS.

  We have investigated the market for the above glass and find that our present prices for Extra Thick are rather too high to compete with imported glass, particularly in view of the current favorable exchange rate for importers. A statement of comparative prices is enclosed for your reference.

  On the other hand there appears to be nothing to justify a general reduction on all sizes and thicknesses, as except for the few sizes in which imported glass is popular there appears to be no demand for heavy grades.

  We therefore suggest that our price for Extra Thick glass in Tientsin be reduced in the following six sizes:-

EXTRA THICKK	YAO HUA CURRENT PRICE	PROPOSED PRICE	VITREA CURRENT PRICE
24×18	$34.00	$24.00	$28.00
30×20	34.00	29.00	34.00
36×24	34.00	29.00	39.00
44×28	39.00	32.00	39.00
52×36	45.00	36.00	46.00
60×40	52.00	42.00	51.00

We do not propose to make a similar reduction in Peiping unless Peiping dealers demand it and are able to show prospects of increased business at reduced prices. It will be made clear the reduction is temporary and that prices may be increased if exchange goes against importers. Please let us have your comments on our proposal in due course.

We have also investigated the sale of small mirrors made from glass corresponding to our double thickness 8"*6". Considerable quantities are imported from Japan already silvered and we thought a reduction in our prices might enable the local product to compete, but our information shows that this is not practical.

The landed cost of the Japanese 8"*6"double thickness mirrors is $2.05 per dozen, the cost of locally made mirrors of the same size being $2.35 per dozen. There being 300 sheets in a case of 8"*6" double, the cost of a case of Yao Hua Glass of this size and thickness in terms of the finished mirrors is $58.75 per 300 mirrors against the $51.25 for the Japanese article.

we understand there is little prospect of a reduction in the local cost of labor, silvering etc., so that to compete with the Japanese mirrors the difference of $7.5 per case would have to be met almost wholly by a reduction in our price. Since the latter is now $15.00 per case we assume that a 50% reduction is out of the question.

Apart therefore from the possibility of promoting sales in a few sizes of

> extra thick glass by a price reduction, we do not think much can be done to stimulate sales of heavy glass.
>
> Yours faithfully,
> TIENTSIN SALES OFFICE.
>
> Enclos:- (1)

译文：

参考编号　18119

序号　_____

天津　　代理处　1935 年 8 月 15 日

致：秦皇岛代理商

主题　　厚玻璃销售

我们对上述玻璃的市场进行了调查，发现我们目前特厚玻璃的价格太高，无法与进口玻璃竞争，特别是考虑到目前对进口商有利的汇率。随函附上一份比较价格表供你方参考。

另一方面，似乎没有什么理由要对所有尺寸和厚度进行普遍削减，因为进口玻璃只有少数尺寸受欢迎，市场似乎没有对厚玻璃的需求。

因此，我们建议将天津以下六种尺寸特厚玻璃进行价格下调：

特厚	耀华现价	建议价	维特利亚现价
24 × 18	$34.00	$24.00	$28.00
30 × 20	34.00	29.00	34.00
36 × 24	34.00	29.00	39.00
44 × 28	39.00	32.00	39.00
52 × 36	45.00	36.00	46.00
60 × 40	52.00	42.00	51.00

我们不建议在北平进行类似的降价操作，除非北平经销商提出要求，并且能够呈现价格下调带来的销售业务增长的前景。必须明确的是，降价是暂时的，如果汇率不利于进口商，价格可能会上涨。请在适当的时候对

我们的建议提出意见。

我们还调查了用相当于我们的 8"*6"规格的双厚玻璃制成的小镜子的销售情况。大量从日本进口的产品已经镀银,我们曾认为降低我们的价格可能会使本地产品具有竞争力,但我们的信息表明这是不切实际的。

日本 8"*6"规格的双厚玻璃的小镜子的落地成本为每打 2.05 美元。本地制造相同尺寸镜子的成本为每打 2.35 美元。一箱 8"*6"规格的双厚玻璃有 300 片,用一箱这种尺寸和厚度耀华玻璃制作的成品镜子成本为每 300 块镜子 58.75 美元,而日本商品的对应成本为 51.25 美元。

我们明白,降低当地劳动力、镀银等成本的希望不大。因此,为了与日本镜子竞争,每箱 7.5 美元的差价几乎必须全部通过降低我们的价格来弥补。由于后者现在是每箱 15.00 美元,我们认为降价 50%是不可能的。

因此,除了有可能通过降价来促进几种尺寸的特厚玻璃的销售外,我们认为没有其他什么措施能够刺激厚玻璃的销量。

谨上
考威尔
天津经销处

附录:(1)

PRICES OF YAO HUA AND VITREA GLASS (EXTRA THICK)		
YAO HUA CURRENT PRICE PER SHEET	VITREA CURRENT PRICE PER SHEET	PROPOSED PRICE FOR YAO HUA PER SHEET
$1.03	$0.85-$0.90	$0.73
1.44	1.40	1.21
2.00	2.30	1.70
3.25	3.30	2.67
5.62	5.70	4.50
8.66	8.50	7.00

The rather heavy reductions proposed are necessary to overcome tage of superior quality possessed by imported glass.

译文：

耀华玻璃与维特利亚玻璃价格对比（加厚）

耀华玻璃目前每片价格	维特利亚玻璃目前每片价格	建议耀华玻璃每片价格
$1.03	$0.85 ~ $0.90	$0.73
1.44	1.40	1.21
2.00	2.30	1.70
3.25	3.30	2.67
5.62	5.70	4.50
8.66	8.50	7.00

为了应对进口玻璃质量上乘的情况，提出耀华玻璃相当大幅度的降价是必要的。

部门间备忘录二十二
INTER-DEPARTMENTAL MEMORANDUM

To: Agent,   Reference X18119

CHINWANGTAO   Serial Number

Tientsin Agency 28th Aug, 1935

SUBJECT: EXTRA THICK GLASS

We enclose copy of our letter of today's date to Tung Hsing Yung, together with copy of our Sales Note No. TS.57, covering their order for 30 cases Extra Thick Glass, 4th Quality.

After due investigation we have concluded that a 10% reduction in price would not be sufficient, and have deemed it advisable to adhere to the prices is proposed in our letter to you No. X18119 of 15th instant.

                 G.H.Fawcett

             TIENTSIN SALES OFFICE.

Enclos:- (1)

译文：

参考编号　X18119
序号　　　………………
天津　　代理处　1935年8月28日

致：秦皇岛代理商

主题　　加厚玻璃

兹随函附上本公司今日致同祥湧公司的信的副本，及本公司TS.57号销售单据的副本，涉及他们订购的30箱四等的特厚玻璃。

经过适当的调查，我方认为降价10%是不够的，并认为保持我方本月15号发给您的X18119号信中所建议的价格为宜。

福西特
天津销售处

附件：（1）

TO BE TRANSLATED INTO CHINESE.

Tientsin, 28th August, 1935
X18119

Messrs. Tung Hsiang Yung,
TIENTSIN.

Dear Sirs,

　　We thank you for your initial trial order for 30 cases of 4th Quality Extra Thick Glass, which we accept at our recently reduced prices and for which we enclose, by way of confirmation, our Sales Note No.TS.57.

　　We trust that, at those prices, you will be enabled to extend your business in these sizes of 4th Quality Extra Thick Glass and we await the results of this order with interest.

Yours faithfully,
TIENTSIN SALES OFFICE.

Enclos:- (1)
Copy to:- Agent, CWT.

译文：

待译成中文

1935 年 8 月 28 日，天津

X18119

致：天津的同祥湧玻璃庄

敬启者：

谢谢你方 30 箱四等特厚玻璃的试订，我们最近已降价接受订单，现随函附上 TS.57 号销售说明作为确认。

我们相信，在这些价格下，你们将能够扩大这些尺寸的四等特厚玻璃的业务，我们对等待这个订单的结果抱有兴趣。

福西特

天津销售处

附件：（1）

抄送：秦皇岛代理商

部门间备忘录二十三
INTER-DEPARTMENTAL MEMORANDUM

To: Agent, CHINWANGTAO	Reference 18119
	Serial Number ....
	Tientsin Agency 10th Sept, 1935

SUBJECT: ....

We enclose herewith for your information translation-copy of a letter dated the 6th instant which we have received from Glass Contractor Tung Hsiang Yung together with translation-copies of the three enclosures attached there-to.

In view of the fact that prices for upcountry glass sales have recently been revised we do not think that any particular reply to Tung Hsiang Yung's letter is at present called for, but shall be glad to receive your advice regarding this matter should you consider any further action on our part is necessary.

G. H. Fawcett

TIENTSIN SALES OFFICE.

Enclo:

译文：

参考编号 ...18119...

序号 ....

天津　　代理处　　1935 年 9 月 10 日

致：秦皇岛代理商

主题 ....

兹随函附上玻璃分销商同祥湧 6 日来函的翻译件及所附三份附件的翻译件，以供参考。

鉴于最近内地玻璃销售价格有所调整，我们认为目前不需要对同祥湧的来信作出特别答复，但如果贵方认为我方有必要采取进一步行动，我们将很高兴收到贵方关于此事的建议。

福西特

天津经销处

附件：

Translation

Tientsin, 6th September, 1935

The Tientsin Sales Office, K.M.A.

Dear Sirs,

It is now nearly 10 years since we became a sales contractor for the products of your Glass works, and we believe that you must have kept a record of the particulars in the past ready for reference. Unexpectedly, your glass was out of stock this spring for a long time and customers ordered glasses from other works, so that we suffered a considerable loss, which we have written you for your note.

The greatest reason for the slackness of your glass sales might not have been noted by you. The price of your products in Tientsin is higher than those in other ports. The price for 30% (of large size) and 70% (of small sized) glass per case is respectively $6.00 in Shanghai, $6.10 in Chefoo and $6.00 in Tsingdao, which is lower than that in Tientsin. Even the price in Peiping which is nearest to Tientsin is lower than that in Tientsin. Besides, the Japanese "Chang Kuang" glass has flooded the Tientsin market. Customers are all complaining and considering our store dishonest. We can no longer remain silent under this condition, for we have always done our best in extending sales ever since we first became your sales contractor and we have received good comment from your Office and the customers. We believe that your Manager can adjust the prices of glass to reach a uniformity. We cannot understand why the price is higher in Tientsin alone but lower in any other port. The demand for glass in Tientsin has been increasing during the last year or two. The great blow received this year makes us feel uncertain about its future development. We especially write this to you stating every particular for your improvement and readjustment to get back what has been lost and to relieve the business depression we are suffering. We are ready to do our best in extending the sales, which is to your advantage. It is sincerely requested that you will accept our suggestion and act after deliberative consideration.

Yours faithfully,
Tung Hsiang Yung.

(Enclosed: 3 letters.)

译文：

天津，1935 年 9 月 6 日

致：开滦矿物总局天津销售部，

亲爱的先生们，

我们成为贵公司玻璃产品的销售承包商已近 10 年，我们相信贵公司过去一定有详细记录，以备参考。没想到的是，您的玻璃在今年春天很长一段时间缺货，客户从其他工厂订购了玻璃，因此我们遭受了相当大的损失，这一点我们此前已向您致信。

您可能没有注意到贵公司玻璃销售疲软的最大原因。贵公司产品在天津的价格比在其他港口的价格高。每箱装有 30%（大尺寸）和 70%（小尺寸）玻璃的价格在上海为 6.00 美元，在烟台和青岛分别为 6.10 美元和 6.00 美元，都低于天津。就连离天津最近的北平，价格也比天津低。此外，日本"昌光"玻璃大量涌入天津市场。顾客们都在抱怨，认为我们的商店不诚实。在这种情况下，我们不能再保持沉默，因为自从我们成为贵方的销售承包商以来，我们一直在尽最大努力扩大销售，并得到了贵公司和客户的好评。我们相信贵公司经理可以调整玻璃的价格使之统一，我们无法理解为什么仅天津一个港口的价格较高，而其他港口的价格却较低。

在过去的一两年里，天津市场对玻璃的需求持续增加。今年受到的巨大打击使我们对其未来发展感到不确定。我们特意给您去信，说明每一点细节，希望贵方进行改进和调整以弥补已经遭受的损失，并缓解我们正遭遇的商业萧条的局面。我们准备尽全力增加销售额，这对贵公司来说是有利的。真诚地请求您接受我们的建议，并在经过深思熟虑后采取行动。

谨启

同祥湧

（随函附上：3 封信）

Translation.

Chengchou, 15th August, 1935

Tung Hsiang Yung.

Dear Sirs,

We have received your letter and noted its contents. The price for glass moved by rail through consignment from Chinwangtao to the Chengchou Station for delivery is $8.00 par case. The large size glass sells at $6.70 and small size glass at $6.30 per case in Tientsin. The price is still higher than that in Shanghai. The boats by which the 400 cases of glass were shipped this spring are still staying under the bridge at Wei Hui, Honan, due to the flood. Business here is in a depressed condition. The price quoted for 40% [large size] and 60% [small size] glass in Shanghai is $6.00 per case. For every 20 tons of glass shipped to Chengchou, the freight is $43.54. The handling charges and delivery charges in Shanghai are at most $1.60 per case. There is a great difference between this Shanghai price and the Tientsin price. We must lose money to sell the goods shipped from Tientsin on Chao Sheng Kuan's boats, which have already arrived here. We can have some order made, only if the prices in Tientsin and Shanghai become the same.

Yours faithfully,

Kuang Tai Hsiang.

TJC

译文：

翻译

郑州，1935 年 8 月 15 日

致：同祥涌.

尊敬的先生们：

我们已收到您的来信，并注意到信中的内容。通过铁路托运将玻璃从秦皇岛运送至郑州站，每箱价格为 8.00 美元。在天津，大尺寸玻璃的售价为每箱 6.70 美元，小尺寸玻璃的每箱售价为 6.30 美元。这个价格仍然高于上海的售价。由于洪水的原因，今年春天运送 400 箱玻璃的船只目前仍停留在河南卫辉桥下。这里的生意不景气。上海每箱装有 40%（大尺寸）玻璃和 60%（小尺寸）玻璃的报价为每箱 6.00 美元。每运送 20 吨玻璃到郑州，运费为 43.54 美元。上海的手续费和送货费最多为每箱 1.60 美元。上海的价格和天津的价格有很大的差别。朝胜关的船从天津运来的货物已经到了这里，我们必须赔钱把这些货物卖掉。只有天津和上海的价格保持一致，我们才有可能接到订单。

谨上，

康泰祥

天津分销商

Translation.

Tsinan, 15th August, 1935

Tung Hsiang Yung.

Dear Sirs,

We have received your letter and noted its contents. You informed us of the fact that 20 tons of 40% large size and 60% small size glass shipped from Chinwangtao to the South Station, Tsinan, will be charged at $7.40 per case, which is 30 cents higher than that from Tsingtao. We shall have a price of $7.10 per case if we order glass from Tsingtao to be delivered at our store, Tsinan. In order to sell in Tsinan, we must secure a price lower than that in Tsingtao. Otherwise, the Tsingtao price shall give a bad influence over our sales. Besides, we should like to inform you that the prices for "Chang Kuang" glass and Yao Hua glass are the same at present.

Yours faithfully,

Teh Yuan Taig.

TJC

译文：

天津，1935 年 8 月 15 日

致：同祥涌，

尊敬的先生们：

我们已收到您的信，并注意到信中的内容。您告知我们，20 吨每箱装有 40% 的大尺寸和 60% 的小尺寸玻璃从秦皇岛运往济南南站，每箱将收取 7.40 美元，比从青岛运来的高出 30 美分。如果我们从青岛订购玻璃运至我们位于济南的商店交货，则每箱价格为 7.10 美元。为了在济南进行销售，我们必须确保价格低于青岛。否则，青岛的价格将对我们的销售产生不利影响。此外，我们想告知您，"昌光"玻璃和耀华玻璃目前的价格是一样的。

谨上，

德源泰

天津分销商

Translation.

Tsinan, 15th August, 1935

Tung Hsiang Yung.

Dear Sirs,

We acknowledge receipt of your letter. At present, the price for the large size glass is $6.70 and that for small size, $6.30. Including the handling charges and freight, the prices will be respectively, $7.70 and $7.30. But the prices in Tsingtao are $6.80 for large size glass and $6.40 for small size and the delivery charge for cartload glass at our store is $0.60 per case. In comparison with the Tientsin price, there is a difference of $0.30 per case. We are not in a favourable condition to have glass shipped from Tientsin. Please consider the case and give us a reply.

Yours faithfully,

Kuang Chu Cheng.

TJC

译文：

天津，1935 年 8 月 15 日

致：同祥湧，

尊敬的先生们：

  我们已确认收到您的来信。目前，大尺寸玻璃的价格为 6.70 美元，小尺寸玻璃的售价为 6.30 美元。包括装卸费和运费在内，价格分别为 7.70 美元和 7.30 美元。但青岛的大尺寸玻璃价格为 6.80 美元，小尺寸玻璃为 6.40 美元，我们店里一车玻璃的运费是每箱 0.60 美元。与天津价格相比，每箱相差 0.30 美元。我们从天津装运玻璃没有有利条件。请考虑这个问题并给我们一个答复。

谨上，
康珠正

天津分销商

M-18119.

Tientsin Sales Office,
  TIENTSIN.   Chinwangtao 12th Sept., 35

<u>UP-COUNTRY SALES.</u>
CONFIDENTIAL.

  With reference to your letter 18119 of the 10 th instant, we would like to know whether Glass Contractor Tung Hsieng Yung's letter is a reply to your letter X-18119 of the 9th August or whether it is a general complaint.

  We consider the prices you have quoted Tung Hsiang Yung for direct delivery are competitive, but if you think otherwise we are prepared to meet all competition, as we do not wish to miss any business in the north.

for AGENT.

译文：

M-18119.

秦皇岛　　1935年9月12日

致：天津经销商处

<u>内陆销售</u>

关于贵方本月10日第18119号来信，我们想知道玻璃销售商同祥湧的信是对贵方8月9日X-18119号来信的答复，还是一般的投诉。

我们认为贵方对同祥湧公司直接运输的报价很有竞争力，但如果你方不这样认为的话，我们已准备好迎接所有的竞争，因为我们不想错过在北方的任何一笔生意。

代理商

部门间备忘录二十四

INTER-DEPARTMENTAL MEMORANDUM

To:　Agent,　　　　　　　　Reference　X-18119
　　　CHINWANGTAO　　　　Serial Number _____
　　　　　　　　　　　　　　Tientsin　Agency　30th Sept, 1935

Subject　　　UP-COUNTRY GLASS SALES.

With reference to your letter M-18119 of 12th inst., Messrs. Tung Hsiang Yung's letter of Sept. 6th was primarily a reply to our X-18119 of 9th August regarding up-country prices.

It was also intended as a substantiation of their recent requests for a reduction in Tientsin prices, and to this extent may be considered a general complaint.

We have already advised you, in connection with our budget estimates, that we do not consider a reduction in Tientsin prices would be useful at present, but that we recommend a reduction in prices for direct shipment up-country.

E. J. Cowell

TIENTSIN SALES OFFICE.

译文：

参考编号　X-18119

序号　................

天津　　代理处　　1935年9月30日

致：秦皇岛代理商

主题　...............内陆玻璃销售.................

关于贵公司本月12日的M-18119号信件中的疑问，我方的回复是：同祥湧玻璃庄9月6日的信件主要是对我方8月9日的X-18119号信件中内陆销售报价的回复。

这也是为了证明他们最近要求天津降价的理由，从这个意义上说，也可以看作是一般投诉。

关于预算，我们已通知贵方，目前降低天津的价格并无益处，但我们建议降低内陆直运的价格。

考威尔
天津销售部

部门间备忘录二十五
INTER-DEPARTMENTAL MEMORANDUM

To:	Agent,	Reference	18119
	CHINWANGTAO	Serial Number	....
		Tientsin Agency	4th Oct, 1935

Subject　............UP-COUNTRY GLASS SALES.................

With reference to your letter M-18119 of 1st October, We give below our proposed revised rates for f. o. c. shipments of 4th Single:-

STATION	PRESENT RATES F.O.C.	PROPOSED RATES F.O.C.
Taiyuanfu	$8.20	$7.80
Yutsu	7.90	7.70
Shihchiachwang	7.60	7.30
Tsinanfu	7.40	7.00
Chengchow	8.00	7.50
Kaifeng	7.90	7.40

All the above prices to be subject to deduction of Tung Hsiang Yung's contract rebates.

You will note that the new prices are all just slightly lower than the competitive rates recently reported by Tung Hsiang Yung, and, if approved, should, we believe, lead to good business. The price for Yu Tsu just quoted by you at $7.90 is reduced to $7.70 because Tung Hsiang Yung state that they do not anticipate much business at $7.90. Apparently there is a transhipment to the Cheng Tai Railway en route which involves a fairly long cartage between stations and inland dealers are insisting upon a 20¢ price reduction to cover possible breakage intransit.

If you decide to authorise the above prices, please wire us as we wish to put them into force without delay.

E. J. Cowell
TIENTSIN SALES OFFICE.

译文：

参考编号 __18119__

序号 _____

天津　代理处　1935 年 10 月 4 日

致：秦皇岛代理商

主题 _____内陆玻璃销售_____

关于您 10 月 1 日的 M-18119 号信函，现将四等单厚玻离岸价的修改建议列下：

站名	目前的离岸价	建议离岸价
太原府	$8.20	$7.80
榆次	$7.90	$7.70
石家庄	$7.60	$7.30
济南府	$7.40	$7.00
郑州	$8.00	$7.50
开封	$7.90	$7.40

以上所有价格均须扣除同祥湧的合同返利。

您会注意到，新的价格都只是略微低于同祥湧最近报告的有竞争力的价格，如果得到批准，我们相信应该会带来好的生意。您对榆次的报价是 7.90 美元，现在已降至 7.70 美元，因为同祥湧表示，如果按照 7.90 美元的价格，他们预计生意不会很多。显然，途中有一批货要转运到成泰铁路，车站之间的运输距离相当长，内陆经销商坚持要降价 20 美分，以弥补运输途中可能出现的破损。

如果贵方决定批准上述价格，请电告我们，因为我方希望尽快生效。

考威尔
天津销售部

M-18119.

Tientsin Sales Office,
TIENTSIN.   Chinwangtao   1st Oct., 35

GLASS SALES
CONFIDENTIAL.

We have read with interest the remarks contained in your letter M-18537 of 28.9.35 on the present sales position and agree with the opinions you have expressed.

With regard to your letter X-18119 of yesterday's date, we agree to your recommendation to decrease prices for the direct shipment f.o.c. rates you now propose we should offer Tung Hsiang Yung.

for AGENT.

译文：

M-18119.

秦皇岛　1935年10月1日

致：天津经销商处

　　　　玻璃销售
　　　　机密文件

　　我方已阅读贵公司35年9月28日M-18537号来函，对其中关于目前销售状况的评论很感兴趣，并同意贵方所表达的意见。

　　此外，关于贵公司昨日的X-18119号信函，我们同意贵方的建议：在保持您建议我们给予同祥湧玻璃庄的离岸价格基础上，降低直运价格。

　　　　　　　　　　　　　　　　代理商

部门间备忘录二十六
INTER-DEPARTMENTAL MEMORANDUM

To: Agent, CHINWANGTAO	Reference 18119 Serial Number .... Tientsin Agency 7th Oct, 1935

Subject .... UP-COUNTRY GLASS SALES. ....

With reference to your telegram No. 95 of 5th October, the new prices have been put into effect as per our letter of today's date to Tung Hsing Yung, a copy of which is enclosed herewith.

　　　　　　　　　　　　E. J. Cowell
　　　　　　　　TIENTSIN SALES OFFICE.

Enclos:- (1)

译文：

参考编号 __18119__

序号 ....

天津　　代理处　　1935年10月7日

致：秦皇岛代理商

主题　_____内陆玻璃销售_____

关于你方10月5日第95号电报，根据我们今日致同祥湧的信，新价格已开始实施，随函附上信的副本。

考威尔
天津销售部

附件：1

TO BE TRANSLATED INTO CHINESE.

Tientsin, 7th October, 1935

Ref. 18119.

Messrs. Tung Hsiang Yung,
<u>TIENTSIN</u>.

Dear Sirs,

UP COUNTRY CIASS SALES.

With reference to our letter X-18119 of 9/8/35 on the above subject and your various letters stating that our prices for direct shipments to inland stations were not competitive, we are still unable to reconcile the various competitive prices quoted by you.

Nevertheless, since the Autumn season has already commenced and your sales are dull, we revise our prices as under, effective from to-day:-

Taiyuanfu	$7.80	F. o .c. per case 4th Quality Single thickness glass Standard Specification.
Yutsu	$7.70	-do- -do-
Shihchiachwang	$7.30	-do- -do-
Tsinanfu	$7.00	-do- -do-
Chengchow	$7.50	-do- -do-
Kaifeng	$7.40	-do- -do-

The above prices are all gross, i.e. your commission will be deducted therefrom in accordance with the terms of your contracts. All charges in connection with unloading, shunting, etc. are for your account, and orders should be placed for quantities not less than a 20-ton carload.

We trust that you will now place substantial orders at the above prices and that your sales will show a material improvement.

Yours faithfully,
E. J. Cowell
TIENTST SALES OFFICE.

译文：

待译成中文

天津，1935 年 10 月 7 日

编号 18119

致：天津的同祥湧玻璃庄

亲爱的先生们：

内陆玻璃销售

关于我们 35 年 8 月 9 日 X-18119 号信中提到的上述问题，以及贵方多次来信指出我方直运至内陆各站的价格没有竞争力，我们仍然无法接受贵方多次报出的有竞争力的价格。

然而，由于秋季已经开始，而贵方销售情况不佳，我们将我们的价格修改如下，从今天起生效。

太原府	$7.80	每箱四等单厚标准规格玻璃的离岸价
榆次	$7.70	同上
石家庄	$7.30	同上
济南府	$7.00	同上
郑州	$7.50	同上
开封	$7.40	同上

以上价格均为毛价，也就是说，根据你们的合同条款，您的佣金将从中扣除。所有与卸货、转车等有关的费用均由贵方负担，而且订单数量不应少于 20 吨车。

我们相信，贵方会按上述价格大量订购，贵方的销售将有实质性的增长。

谨上
考威尔
天津销售部

部门间备忘录二十七

INTER-DEPARTMENTAL MEMORANDUM

To: Agent,　　　　　　　Reference　X-18119
　　CHINWANGTAO　　Serial Number ....
　　　　　　　　　　　　Tientsin　Agency　24th Oct, 1935

Subject ....

　　With reference to your letter M-18119 of 23rd of October, we enclose copy of our letter of to-day's date to Messrs. Tung Hsiang Yung, giving them the necessary fortnight's notice of our intention to increase prices.

　　We shall do our best to restrict supplies during the next two weeks, and for this purpose we have intimated verbally to Messrs. Tung Hsiang Yung that we will only accept such orders from them as are covered by actual orders from their customers. In order further to ensure that Tung Hsiang Yung do not endeavour to lay in large stocks of glass at our present rates, we have verbally advised them that it is by no means absolutely sure that our prices will be raised and that we are merely considering the possibility of doing so at present.

E. J. Cowell
TIENTSIN SALES OFFICE.

译文：

参考编号　X-18119

序号　　　

天津　　代理处　　1935年10月24日

致：秦皇岛代理商

主题　　　

关于贵方10月23日的M-18119号来信，我们随信附上我们今天致同祥湧玻璃庄的信的副本，提前两星期通知他们，我们打算涨价。

在今后两周内，我公司将尽力控制供货，为此，我们已经口头通知同祥湧玻璃庄，我们将只接受他们客户实际订单范围内的订单。为了进一步确保同祥湧玻璃庄不试图以我们现在的价格大量囤积玻璃，我们已经口头通知他们，我们的价格绝非确定会提高，我们只是在考虑可能会提高。

考威尔

天津销售部

TO BE TRANSLATED INTO CHINESE

Tientsin, 24th October, 1935

Ref. X-18119.

Messrs. Tung Hsiang Yung,
TIENTSIN.

Dear Sirs,

In as much as we are considering the possibility of an increase in the price of glass in the areas covered by your agreement, we hereby give you the fortnight's notice called under Clauses 4 of your contract. This notice shall be considered to commence as from today.

Yours faithfully,

E. J. Cowell.

Copy to:-Ag.Cwt

译文：

待译成中文

天津，1935 年 10 月 24 日

编号：X-18119

致：天津的同祥湧玻璃庄

敬启者：

鉴于我方正在考虑你方协议所涉地区玻璃价格上涨的可能性，特此根据你方合同第 4 条，提前两周通知你方。本通知自即日起生效。

谨启

考威尔

天津销售处

抄送：秦皇岛代理商

M-18119.

Tientsin Sales Office,
TIENTSIN.

Chinwangtao 31st Oct, 35

GLASS

CONFIDENTIAL.

With reference to your letter X-18119 of 24th instant, addressed to Messrs. Tung Hsiang Yung, I shall be obliged if you would inform Tung Hsiang Yung that prices of glass in areas covered by our Agreement will be increased by $0.10 per unit as from and including November 8th.

It is considered possible that a further increase will be effected under Clause 4 of Tung Hsiang Yung's Contract but until such time as Shanghai prices are adjusted to our satisfaction we do not propose to further their increase North China prices.

Chilton

AGENT.

译文：

M-18119.

秦皇岛　　1935 年 10 月 31 日

致：天津经销商处

玻璃

关于您本月 24 日致同祥湧玻璃庄的 X-18119 信，如能告知同祥湧玻璃庄，本协议所涉地区的玻璃价格自 11 月 8 日起，每单位涨价 0.10 美元，我将不胜感激。

我们认为根据同祥湧合同第 4 条有可能实施进一步的价格上涨，但在上海的玻璃价格调整到令我们满意之前，我们不建议提高华北的玻璃价格。

齐尔顿

部门间备忘录二十八

INTER-DEPARTMENTAL MEMORANDUM

To: Agent, 　　CHINWANGTAO	Reference　X-18119 Serial Number　_____ Tientsin　Agency　2nd Nov, 1935

SUBJECT　　　　　　GLASS

　　With reference to your letter X-18119 of 31st October, we enclose a copy of a letter of today's date to Messr. Tung Hsing Yung informing them of increase in prices.

H. H. Faulkner
TIENTSIN SALES OFFICE.

Enclos:-(1)

译文：

参考编号　　X-18119

序号　　　　................

天津　　代理处　　1935年11月2日

致：秦皇岛代理商

关于你方10月31日X-18119号信，兹附上今日致同祥湧玻璃庄的信副本一份，通知他们涨价。

福克纳

天津销售处

附件：（1）

TO BE TRANSLATED INTO CHINESE.

Tientsin, 1st Nov, 1935

Ref. 18119.

Messrs. Tung Hsiang Yung,
<u>TIENTSIN</u>.

Dear Sirs,

　　Confirming our notice to you, ref. No.X-18119 of the 24th Oct., 1935, we hereby inform you that the prices of glass in the areas covered by your Agreement will be increased by $0.10 (cents ten) per unit as from and including Nov. 8th, 1935. This increase also applies to "up-country" glass sales covered by our letter X-18119 of the 7th October, 1935.

Yours faithfully,

G. H. Fawcett

TIENTSIN SALES OFFICE.

Copy to: -A.T.

　　　　　Ag.,CWT

　　　　　Mr.Chiu

译文：

待译成中文

天津，1935 年 11 月 1 日
编号 18119

致：天津的同祥湧玻璃庄

敬启者：

兹确认我公司 1935 年 10 月 24 日的 X-18119 号通知，自 1935 年 11 月 8 日起，本协议所涉地区玻璃的单价将上涨 0.10 美元（10 美分）。这一增长也适用于我公司 1935 年 10 月 7 日第 18119 号信所涉及的"内陆"玻璃销售。

谨上
天津销售部

抄送给：总局
　　　　秦皇岛经销商
　　　　邱先生

部门间备忘录二十九
INTER-DEPARTMENTAL MEMORANDUM

To: H.H. Faulkner, Esq., CHINWANGTAO.	Reference X- 18119
	Serial Number
	Tientsin Agency 7th Nov, 1935

URGENT

Dear Faulkner,

　　After your departure today, I had some trouble with Tung Hsiang Yung over the question of his outstanding orders. These orders totaled 4,228 cases of 4th Single ex-yard, Tientsin, and 320 cases for Yu Tze, none of which have been passed by me as yet.

Tung Hsiang Yung claimed that since these orders are genuine orders from customers we should pass them as the price increase is not due to commence until tomorrow the 8th. I informed him that he was advised of the possibility of a price increase and also that we would only accept business at a normal rate, but he maintained that unless we pass all these orders his reputation will be ruined and his business will cease.

I think the real position is that since we advised him on November the 1st that prices would be increased 10 cents per unit on the strength of the Agent, Chinwangtao's letter, No.18119 of October 31st, he collected all the orders he could and took a chance on our passing them. If we refused to accept the orders he would only have lost 10 cents per case which could be met from his commission, but now that we have raised the price $1.10 per case, he is unable to cover the increase. I would like to recommend that we hold out for the thousand cases as arranged, but I feel that our letter to Tung Hsiang Yung regarding the 10 cent price increase rather weakens our position. I hinted to Tung Hsiang Yung that I might pass, say 2,000 cases if necessary, but he maintained that it was the question of all or nothing. Under the circumstances, I shall be glad if you will wire me on receipt of this letter whether we may pass all Tung Hsiang Yung's outstanding orders, i.e. 4,548 cases, or if not, what proportion of this quantity you are prepared to accept at the old price.

It is understood, of course, that whatever quantity you decide to accept, there will be no question of any additional orders not yet in our hands being accepted at the old price.

E. J. Cowell

Yours sincerely

译文：

参考编号 __X-18119__

序号 _____

__天津__ 代理处 __1935 年 11 月 7 日__

致：秦皇岛的福克纳先生

急件

亲爱的福克纳：

您今天离开后，我和同祥湧就他未完成的订单问题发生了一些争执。这些订单中包括天津码头交货的 4 等单厚玻璃 4 228 箱，榆次交货的 320 箱，这些我都还未同意。

同祥湧声称，由于这些订单是客户的真实订单，我们应该同意，因为明天 8 号才会开始涨价。我告诉他，我方已经通知他价格可能会上涨，而且我方只会以正常的价格接受交易，但他坚持认为，除非我方批准所有这些订单，否则他的声誉将会受损，他的生意将会终结。

我认为真实情况是自从我们根据 10 月 31 日秦皇岛代理商的 18119 号信件，在 11 月 1 日通知他每件价格将提高 10 美分后，他尽可能地收集了所有的订单，想碰运气让我们同意成交。如果我们拒绝接受订单，他每箱只会损失 10 美分，这可以从他的佣金中支付，但现在我们每箱提价 1.10 美元，他无法弥补这部分涨价。我建议我们坚持按既定安排处理这几千箱玻璃，但我觉得我们给同祥湧的那封关于涨价 10 美分的信让我们的地位削弱了不少。我向同祥湧暗示，如果有必要，我可能会同意成交 2 000 箱，但他坚持认为，这是一个要么全部同意，要么全盘否决的问题。在此情况下，如您在收到本函后电告我方是否可接受同祥湧所有未完成的订单，即 4 548 箱；如不能，请告知贵方准备按原价接受多少比例的订单，则不胜感激。

当然，你我双方都理解，无论贵方决定接受多少数量，只要是我方尚未收到的额外订单，我方都不会以原价格接受。

考威尔

谨上

18119.

E.J.Cowell, Esq.,
TIENTSIN.

Chinwangtao　8th Nov, 35

Dear Cowell,

　　With reference to your letter X-18119 of the 7th instant, I have wired you to accept Tung Hsiang Yung's orders for 4,548 cases.

　　I consulted with Mr. Chilton on this point and in our opinion we considered this the best policy to adopt having regard to the future of our sales in Tientsin, and our desire to strengthen his hand against the Shoko. You should, however, point out that this is an exceptional favour we are granting, and I suggest you give him a time limit to take delivery.

　　I will leave it to you now to effect the increases after these orders are completed, and I hope you will have no further complications.

　　　　　　　　　　　　　　　　　　　　　　　　Yours sincerely

译文：

18119.

秦皇岛　1935年11月8日

致：天津的考威尔先生

尊敬的考威尔先生，

　　关于贵方本月7日的X-18119号信函，我已电告贵方接受同祥湧玻璃庄的4 548箱的玻璃订单。

　　在这一点，我和齐尔顿先生商量过，我们认为，考虑到我们在天津市场的未来，以及我们想要加强他的力量来让他对抗曙光玻璃，这是我们能采取的最好的办法了。然而，你应该明确说明，这是我们给予他的特殊恩惠，并且我建议您给他一个提货的期限。

　　现在完成这些订单后，将由贵方来决定实施涨价，希望不会再出现麻烦。

　　　　　　　　　　　　　　　　　　　　　　　　谨启

　　　　　　　　　　　　　　　　　　　　　　　　福克纳

　　　　　　　　　　　　　　　　　　　　　　　　天津销售处

部门间备忘录三十

INTER-DEPARTMENTAL MEMORANDUM

To: Agent,
CHINWANGTAO.

Reference（编号） 18119
Serial Number （序号）

Tientsin Agency 8th Nov, 1935

SUBJECT GLASS PRICES.

With reference to the price increase in Tientsin and Peiping, we forward for your approval revised price lists. These will not be distributed until you have signified your approval either by letter or wire.

You will note that heavy grades have been increased 20%, but as verbally advised this may prove too high as much as the prices of heavy grades were left unchanged when the last reduction was made.

We propose at present to leave the prices of heavy grades as per our revised price list, but to investigate the market and inform you later if they appear to be unduly high.

In accordance with your wire of today's date we have to-day passed Tung Hsiang Yung's orders for 4,548 cases at the old prices, and also orders totalling 1,358 cases received from Peiping dealers this morning.

The latter orders appear to be reasonable and in any case our letter advising the price increase had not been received in Peiping at time of despatch of these orders, so we have no grounds for refusing to accept them.

E. J. Cowell
TIENTSIN SALES OFFICE.

Enclos: (3)

译文：

参考编号　X-18119
序号
天津　　代理处　　1935年11月8日

致：秦皇岛代理商

主题：玻璃价格

  关于天津和北平的涨价，现寄去修改后的价目表，望批准。在您以信件或电报表示批准之后，这些文件才将会被分发下去。
  您会注意到重品级玻璃价格上涨了20%，但根据口头建议，这可能太高了，因为重品级玻璃的价格在上次降价时保持不变。
  目前我方建议按修改后的价目表保留重品级的价格，但在市场调查后，如发现价格过高，将通知贵方。
  根据贵方今日电报，我们已于今日收到同祥湧玻璃庄按原价订购4 548箱的订单，并于今晨收到北平经销商的订单，共1 358箱。
  后几批订货似乎还是合理的，而且在发出这几批订货时，北平方面还没有收到我们通知涨价的信，因此我们没有理由拒绝。

考威尔
天津销售处

附件：（3）

8th November, 1935

YAO HUA MECHANICAL GLASS CO., LTD.

The following are the F.O.C. up-country prices for Tientsin and Peiping Areas for 4th Quality Single Thickness Glass Standard Specification (In Tientsin Dollars).

Tientsin Area

Tsinanfu	$8.10
Kaifeng	8.50
Chengchow	8.60
Paotingfu	8.00
Shihchiachwang	8.40
YuTze	8.80
Taiyuanfu	8.90

Peiping Area

Kalgan	$8.20
TaTung	8.60
Fengchen	8.70
Suiyuan	9.00
Potou	9.20

Copy to:
    Ag. CWT
    A. T.
    File
    Mr Cowell
    Mr Chiu

译文：

1935 年 12 月 8 日

耀华机器制造玻璃有限公司

以下是标准规格的四等单厚玻璃在天津、北平地区国内价格（以天津货币单位计算）

<u>天津地区</u>

济南府	$8.10
开封	8.50
郑州	8.60
保定府	8.00
石家庄	8.40
榆次	8.80
太原府	8.90

<u>北平地区</u>

张家口	$8.20
大同	8.60
丰镇	8.70
绥远	9.00
包头	9.20

抄送：

总局秦皇岛代理处

考威尔

邱先生

TO BE TRANSLATED INTO CHINESE.

Tientsin, 7th November, 1935

X-18119

Messrs. Tung Hsiang Yung,

TIENTSIN

Dear Sirs,

Confirming our conversation with your Mr. Sung today, we have to advise the price of Yao Hua 4th Quality Single Thickness Glass in the Standard Specification will be increased to $7.70 per unit Ex-Yard, Tientsin as from November, 8th, 1935.

The price of Heavy Grades will be increased approximately 20% and prices will be quoted on application. Prices for direct shipments by rail to upcountry stations will all be increased by $1.10 per unit of 4th Quality Single Thickness Standard Specification.

New price lists will be supplied to you shortly.

Yours faithfully,

E. J. Cowell

TIENTSIN SALES OFFICE.

Copy to:- A.T.

Ag. CWT

TSS(Stat).

译文：

　　　　　　　待译成中文
　　　　　　　　天津　　1935年11月7日
　　　　　　　　　　　X-18119

致：天津的同祥湧先生，

敬启者，

　　确认今天与贵方宋先生的谈话，我们不得不通知，自1935年11月8日起，耀华标准规格的四等单厚玻璃的价格将提高到天津码头交货价每件7.70美元。

　　厚玻璃的价格将上涨约20%，价格将在申请时报出。通过铁路直运到内陆各车站的每件四等单厚标准规格玻璃的价格将全部上涨1.10美元。

　　新的价目表将稍后会提供给您。

　　　　　　　　　　　　　　　　　　谨启，
　　　　　　　　　　　　　　　　　　考威尔
　　　　　　　　　　　　　　　　　　天津销售部

抄送：　秦皇岛代理处
　　　　天津仓储站

TO BE TRANSLATED INTO CHINESE.

Tientsin, 30th December, 1935

Ref. 18003

Messrs. Tung Hsing Yung,

TIENTSIN.

Dear Sirs,

In order to compete with Vitrea and secure all the heavy grades glass business in your area, we wish to inform you that our heavy glass prices will not be increased by 20% as stated in our letter No.18119 of 7th November but the old prices remain in force from today. We also give you a few attractive prices for our 4th quality, E. Thick Glass as follows:-

Sizes	Each Case Containing	Price per Case
18"*12"	300 sq.ft.	$73.40
20"*14"	-do-	$73.90
20"*15"	-do-	$94.10
24"*16"	-do-	$95.60
26"*18"	-do-	$94.10

Yours faithfully,

Chilton

TIENTSIN SALES OFFICE.

Copy to:-

Ag. CWT

A.T. T.S.

Mr. Chiu

译文：

　　　　　　　待译成中文
　　　　　　　天津　　1935年12月30日
　　　　　　　　　　编号：18003

致：天津的同祥湧玻璃庄，
敬启者，
　　为了与维特利亚竞争并确保你方地区的所有重玻璃业务，我们在此通知你方，我们的重玻璃价格不会如我们11月7日第18119号信中所述的那样上涨20%，但从今天起旧价格仍然有效。我们也给你一些四等玻璃有吸引力的价格，我们的四等加厚玻璃信息如下：

尺寸	每箱装	每箱价格
18"*12"	300 sq.ft.	$73.40
20"*14"	同上	$73.90
20"*15"	同上	$94.10
24"*16"	同上	$95.60
26"*18"	同上	$94.10

　　　　　　　　　　　　谨启
　　　　　　　　　　　齐尔顿
　　　　　　　　　　天津销售处

抄送：总局秦皇岛代理处
　　　邱先生

TO BE TRANSLATED INTO CHINESE.

Tientsin, 7th November, 1935

18151

Messrs. Tien Yuan Tai Glass Dealer,

PEIPING.

Dear Sirs,

Please note that in conformity with our price increases in all markets, the price of Yao Hua 4th Quality Single Thickness Glass in the Standard Specification F.O.C. Chienmen will be increased to $7.50 per unit as from the 9th November, 1935.

The price of Heavy Grades will be increased by 20% and prices will be quoted on application. Prices for direct shipments by rail to upcountry stations will all be increased by $1.10 per unit of 4th Quality Single Thickness, Standard Specification.

All orders in hand will be executed at the old prices.

Yours faithfully,

E. J. Cowell

TIENTSIN SALES OFFICE.

Copy to:- A.T.

Ag. CWT

TSS(Stat).

译文：
待译成中文

天津　1935年11月7日

18151

致：北平的天源泰玻璃经销商，

敬启者，

请注意，遵照我们在所有市场玻璃价格上涨的决定，从1935年11月9日起，耀华标准规格的四等单厚玻璃的价格将提高到前门离岸价每件7.70美元。

厚玻璃的价格将上涨约20%，价格将在申请时报出。通过铁路直运到内陆各车站的每件四等单厚标准规格玻璃的价格将全部上涨1.10美元。

所有现有订单将按原价格执行。

谨启，

考威尔

天津销售部

抄送：秦皇岛代理商

天津仓储站

To BE TRANSLATERD INTO CHINESE

Tientsin, 30th Dec, 1935

Ref. 18003

Messrs, Tien Yuan Tai.

PEIPING,

Dear Sirs,

 With reference to our recent conversation with your representatives and our Mr. Faulkner in Tientsin, we confirm that our prices for heavy glass will be as hitherto and will not be increased by 20%, as stated in our letter No.18151 of 7th November,1935. In order to compete with Vitrea glass we give you the following attractive prices F.O.C. Chienmen for our 4th Quality, E. Thick glass:-

Sizes	Each Case Containing	Price Per Case
18"*18"	300 sq. ft.	$75.40
80"*14"	-do-	$73.90
80"*15"	-do-	$94.10
84"*16"	-do-	$95.60
86"*18"	-do-	$94.10

 With the above we consider that you should secure all the heavy glass business in your area in due course.

 Regarding the up-country glass prices ,we have reduced our prices for 4th quality, Single Thickness,Standard specification as hereunder:-

Ta Tung	$8.10
Feng Chen	8.20
Suiyuan	8.50
Potou	8.70

Yours faithfully,

TIENTSIN SALES OFFICE.

Copy to: - Agent, C.W.Tao.

 Mr. Chiu

 A.T., T.S.

译文：

待译成中文

天津　　1935 年 12 月 30 日

编号：18003

致：北平的天源泰玻璃店，

尊敬的先生们，

　　根据最近我们与你方代表的谈话及我们与我公司在天津的福克纳先生的谈话，我们确认，我公司 1935 年 11 月 7 日第 18151 号信中所述的厚玻璃的价格将保持不变，不涨价 20%。为了与维特利亚玻璃竞争，我们为四等加厚玻璃提供以下有吸引力的前门离岸价格：

尺寸	每箱容量	每箱价格
18"*18"	300 sq. ft.	$75.40
80"*14"	同上	$73.90
80"*15"	同上	$94.10
84"*16"	同上	$95.60
86"*28"	同上	$94.10

　　综上所述，我们认为贵方应在适当的时候获得贵方区域所有的厚玻璃业务。

　　关于内陆的玻璃价格，我们已经降低了四等单厚标准规格玻璃的价格，列于下表：

大同	$8.10
丰镇	8.20
绥远	8.50
包头	8.70

谨上
齐尔顿
天津经销处

抄送：秦皇岛代理商

　　　邱先生

　　　总局，天津经销处

部门间备忘录三十一
INTER-DEPARTMENTAL MEMORANDUM

To: H.H.Faulkner, Esq.,   Reference（编号）__4601__
CHINWANGTAO.   Serial Number （序号）_____

<u>Tientsin</u>   Agency   <u>14th Feb, 1936</u>

SUBJECT _____

Dear Faulkner,

    I shall be obliged if, at your convenience, you will arrange to let me have a copy of all Sales Contracts negotiated, whether at Chinwangtao or Agencies in order that I may be in a position to check the Terms of Credit, Rebates and Commission Etc.

Yours Sincerely

译文：

参考编号 __4601__
序号 _____
<u>天津</u>   代理处   1936年2月14日

致：秦皇岛的福克纳先生
亲爱的福克纳：

    如贵公司方便，可否将所有经秦皇岛或代理公司谈判的销售合同副本寄给我一份，以便我核对信用证、回扣和佣金等条款。

谨启

M-18003

F.Clark.Esq.
TIENTAIN

Chinwangtao   19th Feb,36

GLASS SALES AGREEMENTS

Dear Clark,

With reference to your letter 4601 at 14th instant regarding the Glass Sales Contracts, I enclose herewith for your retention, copies of the 1936 Agreements for Tientsin, Peiping and Shantung Agencies. Any further agreements negotiated will be sent to you as soon as they are received.

Yours faithfully,

H.H.Faulkner.

ENCLOS.

译文：

M-18003

秦皇岛　　1936年2月19日

18151

致：天津的克拉克先生，

玻璃销售协议

亲爱的克拉克，

关于你方14日第4601号关于玻璃销售合同的来信，现随函附上1936年天津、北平和山东代理公司的协议副本，请保留。任何进一步协商的协议一经收到，我们将立即发送给您。

谨启

福克纳

附件

INTER-DEPARTMENTAL MEMORANDUM

To: H.H.Faulkner, Esq.,   Reference ..... 18068 .....

CHINWANGTAO   Serial Number ....

Tientsin   Agency   28th Feb, 1936

Subject .... STRIP GLASS. ....

CONFIDENTIAL.

Dear Faulkner,

With reference to the last paragraph of your D/O letter M-18119 of 20th inst., I have gone into this question with Mr. Chiu and report as follows:

There is, rather contrary to my expectations, practically no demand for these narrow widths, in any thickness, for shelving, etc: the bulk of the demand being for cutting up for silvering and the production of mirrors.

<u>4th Quality Single Thickness (Yao Hua)</u>

The estimated cost of producing 100 sq.ft. of mirrors is as under:

Cost of glass(36"*8" or 40"*7")	$6.00 per c/s (100 sq.ft)
" " bevelling	6.00 " " "
" " silvering	7.00 " " "
" " framing & boxing	17.00 " " "
" " labour	6.00 " " "
	$42.00 " " "

From 100 sq.ft. 36"*8" can be produced 25 doz. mirrors, cost $42.00:

cost of 1 dozen	$1.68
market selling price per dozen	$1.85-$1.90

Mirrors from coast ports (Japan and Dairen) cost $1.30-$1.40 per dozen, and sell in the market at $1.60-$1.70 per dozen.

Thus the return to Yao Hua is only $0.22 per dozen, compared with $0.30 for the competitors.

Under existing conditions we can sell about 100 cases (of 300 sq.ft.each) per month: but, if you can increase the width of the strips from 6"/8" to 6"/11" in lengths of 40"/50" and authorise adherence to the same price, it is anticipated that sales could be increased by from 50 to 100 cases per month.

With regard to 4th Quality Extra Thick Glass, it is suggested that the dealers be quoted a special price for size 24"*18" (only) of $26.00 per case of 100 sq.ft.,i.e. $0.80 per sheet, in order to compete with Vitrea Glass, which costs $0.90-$0.95 per sheet and is sold at a bout $1.00 (size 24"*18" is common on the market for table pads).

Other Qualities

With the exception of 3rd Quality Double Thickness, none of the other grades and thicknesses appear suitable in the market, even at lowest and most attractive prices.

The following figures regarding 3rd Quality Double Thickness are given for comparison, as to the cost and returns from mirrors, with the figures given above for 4th quality Single Thickness:

Cost of Glass (12"*8" or 10" *7")	$16.50 per case(100 sq.ft).
Cost of bevelling	$7.50 " " "
Cost of silvering	$9.00 " " "
Cost of framing & boxing	$18.50 " " "
Cost of labour	$6.50 " " "
	$58.00 " " "

25 doz. mirrors(8"* 6")cost	$58.00
1 doz. mirrors(8"*6")cost	$2.32
1doz. Mirrors market selling price	$2.40
Return	$0.08

compared with mirror s from Japan/Dairen

1 doz.cost	$1.70-$1.80
1 doz. market selling price	$2.10
Return	$0.30/$0.40

Our sales of 12"*8" 3rd Quality Double Thickness have amounted to only 10 cases in the last two months. In order to promote sales, the following reductions in price are recommended for: sizes 12"*8" and 10"*7":

4th Quality Double Thickness	from $15.00 to $12.00
S/Double "	" $12.00 to $10.00
3rd Qual. Double "	" $16.50 to $13.00
S/Double "	" $13.20 to $10.50

Each for cases of 100 sq.ft. With these reduced prices it is believed that our sales could be increased up to 700/800 cases Double Thickness and 500 cases Semi-Double Thickness per annum.

Yours sincerely,
G.H. Fawcett.

P.S. I shall reply separately in a few days re up-country prices.

译文：

参考编号 __18068__
序号 _____
天津　代理处　__1935年2月28日__

致：秦皇岛的福克纳先生

主题 _____条形玻璃_____

亲爱的福克纳：

  关于您本月20日的M-18119号提货单的最后一段，我已经和邱先生讨论了这个问题，汇报如下：

  与我预计的相反，这些宽度的窄条玻璃，无论任何厚度，几乎都没有市场需求，也没有对做框架的需求等：大部分的需求来自切割镀银以及生产镜子。

  四等单厚玻璃（耀华）玻璃成本（36英寸×8英寸或40英寸×7英寸）生产100平方英尺的镜子的估计成本如下：

玻璃成本（36"*8"或40"*7"）	6.00美元每箱（100平方英尺）
倒角成本	6.00美元每箱（100平方英尺）
镀银成本	7.00美元每箱（100平方英尺）
装框和装箱成本	17.00美元每箱（100平方英尺）
劳务成本	6.00美元每箱（100平方英尺）
	42.00美元每箱（100平方英尺）

100平方英尺36"*8"尺寸的玻璃可以生产25打镜子，成本为42美元。

1打成本	1.68美元
每打市场销售价格	1.85美元～1.90美元

  来自沿海港口（日本和大连）的镜子每打成本为1.30～1.40美元，市场售价为每打1.60～1.70美元。

因此，耀华的收益只有每打 0.22 美元，而竞争对手的收益是 0.30 美元。

在现有条件下，我们每月可以销售约 100 箱（每箱 300 平方英尺）；但是，如果您能将条形玻璃的宽度从 6"/8"增大至 6"/11"，长 40"/50"，并批准维持相同的价格，预计每月销售额可以增加 50 至 100 箱。

为了与"威达利"玻璃竞争，建议对尺寸为 24"*18"（仅此尺寸）的四等加厚玻璃给经销商报一个特价，即：每 100 平方英尺为一箱，售价 26.00 美元，即每片 0.80 美元，维特利亚玻璃每片 0.90~0.95 美元，售价约为 1.00 美元（24"*18"是市场上常见的台垫尺寸）。

其他等级

除了三等双厚度玻璃外，其他等级和厚度的玻璃，即使是以最低和最有吸引力的价格在市场上似乎也不适销。

三等双厚产品的数据如下，供您与上述四等单厚玻璃的数据对比，以了解镜子制作成本和回报。

玻璃成本（12"*8"或 10"*7"）	每箱 16.50 美元（100 平方英尺）
倒角成本	每箱 7.50 美元（100 平方英尺）
镀银成本	每箱 9.00 美元（100 平方英尺）
装框及装箱费用	每箱 18.50 美元（100 平方英尺）
劳务费	每箱 6.50 美元（100 平方英尺）
	每箱 58.00 美元（100 平方英尺）

25 打镜子（8"*6"）成本	58.00 美元
1 打镜子（8"*6"）成本	2.32 美元
1 打镜子（8"*6"）市场售价	2.40 美元
收益	0.08 美元

与日本/大连的镜子相比

1 打，成本	1.70~1.80 美元
1 打，市场售价	2.10 美元
收益	0.30 美元/0.40 美元

在过去的两个月里，我们的 12"*8"三等双厚玻璃的销售量只有 10 箱。为了促进销售，建议对 12"*8"和 10"*7"尺寸的产品进行如下降价。

四等双厚玻璃由 15.00 美元降至 12.00 美元

四等半双厚玻璃由 12.00 美元降至 10.00 美元

三等双厚玻璃由 16.50 美元降至 13.00 美元

三等半双厚玻璃由 13.20 美元降至 10.50 美元

以上均以 100 平方英尺箱计。有了这些降价措施，相信我们的双倍厚度产品销售量每年可以增加至 700/800 箱，半倍厚度产品销售量每年可以增加至 500 箱。

谨上
福西特

又及：关于内陆价格，我将在几天后另行回复。

部门间备忘录三十三
INTER-DEPARTMENTAL MEMORANDUM

To: H.H.Faulkner,Esq.,   Reference   18176

CHINWANGTAO   Serial Number

                                        Tientsin   Agency   2nd March, 1936

Subject

Dear Faulkner,

   At the request of Mr. Yu, I am sending you herewith copy of a letter dated the 28th February, from Mr. Wang Chan Ne, introducing Mr. Liu Ying Kwei, as an applicant as sole agent for the sale of Yao Hua Glass at Sian.

   Mr. Wang Chan Ne is Assistant Chief of the Stores (Purchase Dept.) of the P.N. Railway and the Fu Hsing Glass Store-of which Mr. Liu Ying Kwei is the Assistant Manager-is owned by a Mr. Ma, is also a member of the Stores Dept. of the Railway.

   Mr. Yu feels that it would be impolitic to turn down Mr. Wang's request, and suggests that you write a formal letter direct to Mr. Liu Ying Kwei, advising him that you will call upon him during your next visit to Peiping.

   Will you please let us have a copy of your letter in due course.

                                           Yours sincerely,
                                           G. H. Fawcett.

译文：

参考编号　18176
序号
天津　　代理处　1935年3月2日

致：秦皇岛福克纳先生

主题

亲爱的福克纳，

　　应余先生的要求，我谨寄上2月28日王占和先生的来信一封，并介绍刘英贵先生成为耀华玻璃西安地区销售的独家代理申请人。

　　王占和先生是北平—西安铁路沿线货仓（采购处）的副处长，而福兴玻璃店是此段铁路货仓部的一员，它是马先生的店，刘英贵先生是副经理。

　　余先生认为拒绝王先生的请求不明智，并建议您直接向刘英贵先生书写一封正式信函，通知他您下次到访北平时将会拜访他。

　　敬请于合适时候将您的信件的副本寄给我们。

谨启
福西特

COPY

TRANSIATION

Tientsin, 28th February, 1936

M. T. Yu, Esq.,
K.M.A.,
TIENESIN

Dear Mr. Yu,

I am pleased to have had a conversation with you over the phone just a moment ago.

This serves to introduce to you Mr.Liu Ying Kwei, Assistant Manager of the Fu Hsing Glass Store, Peiping, who intends to undertake the sole Sales of the production at the Yao Hua Glass Works at Sian.

I shall be obliged if you will kindly give Mr. Liu an interview and any assistance you may extend to him will be much appreciated.

Your sincerely,

WANG CHAN HE.

译文：

复本

天津，1936 年 2 月 28 日

致：天津开滦矿物总局的余先生

尊敬的余先生，

我很高兴刚才同你通电话。

现向贵公司介绍福兴北平玻璃店副经理刘永贵先生，他想负责耀华玻璃在西安生产的独家销售。

如果您能给刘先生一次面试的机会，并给予他一些帮助，我将不胜感激。

谨启

王占和

M-18119.

G. H. Fawcett. Esq.,
TIENTSIN.

Chinwangtao　　　3rd March, 36

GLASS SALES.
CONFIDENTIAL.

Dear Fawcett,

　　With reference to your letter 18176 of the 2nd March, as you are aware at present Sian comes under your Agency and Tung Hsiang Yung might object to our slicing into his territory. However, I will be in Tientsin this week-end and will talk to Mr. Yu and yourself about this business. In the meantime I will not write to Mr. Liu Yung Kwei until after our talk.

　　I will be in your office on Saturday morning and would like to meet Mr. Sun if possible sometime on Saturday forenoon.

Yours sincerely,
H. H. Faulkner.

译文：

M-18119.

秦皇岛　　1936年3月3日

致：天津的福西特先生

玻璃销售

亲爱的福西特，

　　根据您3月2日18176号函，如您所知，目前西安归贵方代理处管辖，并且同祥湧可能会反对我们的生意侵入他的领地。但是，我这周末将抵达天津，和余先生以及您本人谈论该事务。同时，在结束我们的谈话之前，我不会向刘永贵去信。

　　我将于周六上午抵达您的办公室。如果有可能的话，我想在周六午前某个时间与宋先生会面。

谨启
福克纳

M-18119.

Tientsin Sales Office,
YIENTSIN

       Chinwangtao 9th March, 36

     <u>GLASS SALES.</u>
     CONFIDENTIAL.

  With reference to Mr. Wang Chan He's application on behalf of Mr. Liu Yung Kwei for a selling agency and Sian, I must point out that this town comes under our contract with Messrs. Tung Hsing Yung and I regret therefore being unable to take advantage of Mr's offer to represent us there.

            H. H. Faulkner
             for AGENT.

译文：

            M-18119.

      秦皇岛 1936年3月9日

致：天津销售处

      玻璃销售

  关于王占和先生代表刘永贵先生申请在西安担任销售代理一事，我必需指出，该地区属于我公司与同祥湧玻璃庄签订的合同范围，因此我很遗憾不能接受他的邀请到那里担任我公司的代理。

              福克纳

部门间备忘录三十四
INTER-DEPARTMENTAL MEMORANDUM

To: H.H.Faulkner, Esq.,　　Reference　18068
　　CHINWANGTAO　　　　Serial Number
　　　　　　　　　　　　　Tientsin　Agency　30th Mar, 1936

Subject

Dear Faulkner,

　　With reference to my letter 18068 of 28th February, I now enclose for your information an original bill, with translation, for four mirrors-one each of Yao Hua and Shoko Glass in double and single thickness-from which you will note that the Shoko mirrors are being marketed at a considerably lower price than mirrors made from Yao Hua Glass.

　　　　　　　　　　　　　　　　　　Yours sincerely,
　　　　　　　　　　　　　　　　　　G. H. Fawcett

Enclos:-(2).

译文：

参考编号　18068
序号
天津　代理处　1935年3月30日

致：秦皇岛福克纳先生

主题

亲爱的福纳克

　　关于我2月28日的18068号信，现随函附上4面镜子的账单正本及翻译件，分别为双厚和单厚的耀华玻璃和曙光玻璃的价格。从中你会注意到，曙光玻璃的售价比耀华玻璃的要低得多。

　　　　　　　　　　　　　　　　　　谨启
　　　　　　　　　　　　　　　　　　福西特

附件：（2）

COPY

Translation:

To Mr. Chiu:

　　1 pce Yao Hua Mirror 8"*6" 3rd quality Double Thickness (28 oz.) at 20 cents = $2.40 per doz.

　　1 pce Shoko Mirror 8"*6" Double Thickness (26 oz.) at 17.5 cents = 2.10 per doz.

　　1 pce Yao Hua Mirror 8"*6" Single Thickness (16-18 oz.) at 15.8 cents = $1.90 per doz.

　　1 pce Shoko Mirror 8"*6" Single Thickness(16 oz.) at 14.1 cents = $1.70 per doz.

　　Total 67.4 cents

(Chop) Yi Hsing Yung Yuan Chi.

27/3/36.

译文：

致邱先生：

　　1 件耀华 8"*6"三等双厚（28 盎司）玻璃镜子，价格为 20 美分，每打 2.40 美元。

　　1 件曙光 8"*6"三等双厚（26 盎司）玻璃镜子，价格为 17.5 美分，每打 2.10 美元。

　　1 件耀华 8"*6"单厚（16~18 盎司）玻璃镜子，价格为 15.8 美分，每打 1.90 美元。

　　1 件曙光 8"*6"单厚（16 盎司）玻璃镜子，价格为 14.1 美分，每打 1.70 美元。

　　总共：67.4 美分

（商号）义祥湧源记

1937 年 3 月 27 日

18119

Tientsin Sales Office,
YIENTSIN

       Chinwangtao 31st March, 36.

<u>GLASS SALES.</u>
CONFIDENTIAL.

With reference to Mr. Fawcett's letter 18068 of 30/3/36 we agree to the price revisions requested in his letter 18068 of the 28/2/36 and which we enumerate hereunder:-

(1) 4th Quality Extra Thick Size 24"*18"only

   $26.00per case of 100 sq.ft.

(2) Sizes 12"*8" and 10"*7"only

4th	Double	$12.00 per case of 100 sq.ft.
4th	S/Double	$10.00 per case of 100 sq.ft.
3rd	Double	$13.00 per case of 100 sq.ft.
3rd	S/Double	$10.50 per case of 100 sq.ft.

          G. H. Fawcett

          for AGENT.

译文：

M-18119.

秦皇岛 1936 年 3 月 31 日

致：天津销售处

<u>玻璃销售</u>

关于福西特先生 1936 年 3 月 30 日的编号为 18068 的来信，我们同意他在 1936 年 2 月 28 日 18068 号信件中所要求的价格修改，现列举如下：

（1）四等加厚玻璃，尺寸为 24"*18"，100 平方英尺每箱仅售 26 洋元；

（2）尺寸为 12"*8" 和 10"*7"，

四等双厚玻璃，100 平方英尺每箱售 12 洋元

四等单双厚玻璃，100 平方英尺每箱售 10 洋元

三等双厚玻璃，100 平方英尺每箱售 13 洋元

三等单双厚玻璃，100 平方英尺每箱售 10.50 洋元

福克纳

部门间备忘录三十五
INTER-DEPARTMENTAL MEMORANDUM

To: Agent　　　　　　　Reference　M-18003
　CHINWANGTAO　　　Serial Number ....

　　　　　　　Tientsin　Agency　30th Mar, 1936

Subject ....

　　We enclose for your information translation copy of a letter dated 28/3/36 from Messrs. Tien Yuen Wai.

　　According to your instructions of 19th March, prices to the upcountry stations in their district are, however, being increased as from 1st April, as per our letter M-18003 of 25th March, and we are advising Messrs. Tien Yuan Tai that no reduction can be considered at present.

G. H. Fawcett
TIENTSIN SALES OFFICE.

Enclos:-(1).

译文：

　　　　　　　参考编号　M-18003
　　　　　　　序号　............
　　　　　　　天津　代理处　1936 年 3 月 30 日

致：秦皇岛代理商

主题 ....

  随函附上天源泰玻璃店1936年3月23日来信的翻译本，以供参考。

  根据贵公司3月19日的指示，按照我公司3月25日的M-18003信的内容，他们地区的内陆车站的价格将从4月1日起上调，特此通知天源泰玻璃店，目前不考虑降价。

福西特
天津销售部

附件：（1）

COPY

TRANSLATION

Peiping, 23/3/36

Tientsin Sales Office
K. M. A.,
TINENTSIN

Dear Sirs,

  With reference to your previous reduction in prices by 50 cents for glass to be sold at Tatung, Feng Chen, Suiyuan and Potou, we beg to advise you that we have sent our representatives to the above named districts to secure glass business. We understand that the Tax charged by the Tax Office at Shahukwan is $0.99 per case. While for Shoko glass only transit dues will be paid and Tax can be exempt.

  Therefore the price of Yao Hua glass is still over $0.50 higher than that of Shoko glass. We shall be obliged if you will kindly take into consideration our difficulties in stimulating sales at the beginning and also the painstaking in travelling and allow us a further reduction of $0.30. By giving the rebate to the buyers our sales can be pushed.

  We shall be glad if you will give this matter your favourable consideration and let us have your reply.

Yours faithfully,
TIEN YUAN TAI.

译文：

北平，1936年3月23日

致：开滦矿物总局天津销售处

敬启者，

  关于贵方先前对在大同、丰镇、绥远和包头销售的玻璃降价50美分一事，为争取玻璃业务，我们已派代表到上述地区，特此奉告。我方了解到沙湖关税务局征收的税是每箱0.99美元。而对曙光玻璃只需征收过境费且豁免税费。

  因此耀华玻璃的价格仍比曙光玻璃的价格高出0.50美元以上。若贵方能考虑到我方在初始阶段促进销售的难处以及差旅的艰苦，并能再给予我方0.30美元的降价，我方将不胜感激。给买主折扣可以促进我方的销售。

  若贵方能考虑此事并给予回复，我方将非常感激。

谨启

天源泰玻璃店

部门间备忘录三十六
INTER-DEPARTMENTAL MEMORANDUM

To: H. H. Faulker	Reference M-18003
CHINWANGTAO	Serial Number
	Tientsin Agency 7th April, 1935

CONFIDENTIAL.

Subject: GLASS PRICES

Dear Faulkner,

  Replying to your letter M-18119 of 27th March, I confirm that the "Shoko Cost Price" is the importer's selling price plus duty and all charges to ex-godown Tientsin with no allowance for dealers' rebates or profit. This cost price, for future suppliers, is calculated to be as under:-

C.I.F. Tientsin	per case	$5.70
Import Duty and Charges G.U. 1.1 479 $227		2.61
		$8.31
Refund of old duty		.86
		$7.45
Unloading charges, etc., say		.05
Nett cost ex godown		$7.50

With regard to the question of increasing the price of our Single Thickness in standard specifications, I think that this could be and should be done, but suggest that no change be made until about 15th of June (notifying our dealers about 1st June), as I am given to understand that the period from May 1st to about the middle of June is a busy buying season, and an increase at this time would be likely to prove prejudicial to our sales.

During the latter part of March all waterways became open and the Tientsi and Peiping and up-country markets became active. From Peiping orders have been received for about 4,500 cases, and for Tientsin and up-country about 11,000 cases. Of the above about 6,000 cases had not been shipped up to the end of March.

At that time-end of March-Shoko dealers had, it is heard, ordered about 2,000 cases 4th Single glass for the replenishment of their April stocks, because the Shoko furnace at Dairen will undertake cold repairs during this month and do not expect to resume output until about the middle of May. Owing, however, to the present high exchange of the Gold Unit, Shoko glass will cost $7.50 per case (as per calculation above) nett ex-godown, Tientsin. Thus, if we maintain our present prices until the middle of June, it is believed that Shoko sales will be reduced to a minimum.

The total imports of Shoko Glass during March was about 1,000 cases

4th quality single thickness. These were ordered last November. Their sales amounted to 3,700 cases, leaving closing stocks, at the end of March, of 3,500 cases. Their next shipment of 2,500 cases is due to arrive in Tientsin on or before 15th April, of which 500 cases represent the balance of last November's orders.

With reference to these imports, I understand that these are not transfers from Dairen to Tientsin for Mitsubishi's godown stocks, but are, in effect, sales to dealers who however have a sort of "free storage on credit" arrangements for 55 days with Mitsubishi, during which period the glass remains in the latter's godown and on which they have a lien covered by the dealers' guarantees for payment.

To summarise: I think that we should increase our prices for 4th single standard specification on or about 15th June and reduce them again about 1st September whereby we should be able to secure business practically up to the date of the Dragon Boat Festival (23rd June) and hold the Tientsin and up-country markets through the summer, at the same time tying up intermediate Shoko stocks, which they will be importing for the early autumn sales, in Tientsin godown, and exposing them to the risk of loss from mildew etc., and a further loss of interest thereon for practically three months.

As to strip glass, this has undoubtedly given a big knock to Shoko and Japanese mirrors, for which reason I suggest that it would be best to follow, in regard to it, the same policy as for 4th single standard specification, as outlined above.

Yours sincerely,

G. H. Fawcett.

译文：

参考编号　M-18003

序号　　　

天津　　代理处　1936年4月7日

致：秦皇岛的福克纳先生

机密件

主题　　玻璃价格

尊敬的福克纳：

　　关于您3月27日编号为M-18119的来信，兹确认"曙光玻璃成本价"是进口商的销售价格加上关税和到天津仓库交货的所有费用，不包括经销商的回扣或利润。本成本价对未来供应商的计算方法如下：

天津到岸价	每箱 5.70 美元
进口关税及费用- G.U. 1.1 479 $227	2.61
	（共）8.31 美元
退还旧税	.86
	（剩）7.45 美元
如：卸货费用等	.05
仓库交货净价	7.50 美元

　　关于提高我们的单厚标准规格玻璃价格的问题，我认为这是可以而且应该做的，但建议在6月15日左右之前不要做任何更改（可通知我们的经销商时间为6月1日左右），因为我了解到从5月1日到6月中旬是繁忙的采购季节，此时增长可能会对我们的销售造成不利影响。

　　三月下旬，所有水路都开放了，天津、北平和内地市场变得活跃起来。从北平收到的订单约4 500箱货品，天津和内地约11 000箱货品。截至3月底，上述订单中有约6 000箱货品尚未发货。

　　有消息称，在3月底的时候，曙光玻璃的经销商已经订购了大约2 000箱四等单厚玻璃，以补充其4月份的库存，因为位于大连的曙光公司熔炉将在本月进行冷维修，预计到 5 月中旬左右才能恢复生产。然而，由于黄金单位目前的高汇率，根据上述天津仓库净货价计算，曙光玻璃每箱售价为 7.50 美元。因此，如果我们将目前的价格维持到 6 月中旬，相信曙光玻璃的销售额将降至最低。

三月份，曙光玻璃的总进口量约为 1 000 箱四等单厚玻璃。这些是去年 11 月订购的。它们的销量达到了 3 700 箱，截至 3 月底，库存剩余 3 500 箱。他们的下一批 2 500 箱玻璃将于 4 月 15 日或之前抵达天津，其中 500 箱是去年 11 月订单的余额。

关于这些进口商品，我了解到，这些不是从大连运往天津的三菱库存，实际上是已经销售给经销商的商品，但经销商与三菱有一种"信用证免费储存"的协议安排，期限为 55 天，在此期间，玻璃仍在三菱的仓库中，他们拥有经销商付款担保所涵盖的留置权。

总结：我认为，我们应该在 6 月 15 日左右提高四等单厚标准规格玻璃的价格，并在 9 月 1 日左右再次降价，这样我们就可以在端午节（6 月 23 日）之前确保业务水平，并在整个夏季保持住天津和内地市场，同时阻碍曙光玻璃在天津仓库的中间库存，这些库存是他们用于早秋销售而进口的商品。这将使他们面临霉变等损失的风险，以及进一步的几乎三个月的利息损失。

至于条形玻璃，这无疑给曙光玻璃和日本镜子带来了巨大的冲击，因此，我建议最好遵循与上述四等单厚标准规格玻璃相同的政策。

谨上

福西特

M-18119

Tientsin Sales Office,
YIENTSIN

        Chinwangtao   8th April, 36

     GLASS PRICES.
     CONFIDENTIAL.

Dear Fawcett,

 Thank you for your letter M-18003 of the 7th April.

 I agree with all your suggestions, but would like to know what the "refund of the old duty" is.

          Yours sincerely,

          H. H. Faulkner.

译文：

M-18119.

秦皇岛 1936 年 4 月 8 日

致：天津销售处

    玻璃价格

亲爱的福西特，

 感谢您 4 月 7 日的 M-18003 的来信。

 我同意你所有的建议，但是我想知道什么是"退旧税"。

        谨启

        福克纳

部门间备忘录三十七

INTER-DEPARTMENTAL MEMORANDUM

To: H. H. Faulker   Reference M-18003

　　　CHINWANGTAO   Serial Number

　　　　　　　　　　　　　Tientsin   Agency   9th April, 1935

Subject

Dear Faulkner,

<u>GIASS PRICES.</u>

　　I have received your Memo. M-18119 of 8th April and am glad that you approve the suggestions contained in my letter of 7th instant.

　　The explanation of "Refund of old duty" is as follows:-

　　Originally, when Shoko Glass was imported for the dealers, the liability for payment of the duty thereon was accepted by Mitsubishi. When, however, the new scale of duties came into force, Mitsubishi would only agree to pay at the old rate; hence the dealers themselves now pay the full duty (at the new rate) and receive from Mitsubishi a "Refund of old duty"- i.e. the amount which would have been payable at the old rate.

　　I hope I have succeeded in making this clear.

　　　　　　　　　　　　　　　　　　　　　　Yours sincerely,

　　　　　　　　　　　　　　　　　　　　　　G. H. Fawcett.

译文：

参考编号　M-18003

序号

天津　　代理处　　1936年4月9日

致：秦皇岛的福克纳先生

主题

亲爱的福克纳，

玻璃价格

我已收到您4月8日的M-18119号备忘录，很高兴您同意我在7日的信中提出的建议。

关于"旧税退款"的解释如下：

最初，经销商进口曙光玻璃时，三菱公司接受了支付相关关税的责任。然而，当新的关税表生效时，三菱只同意按旧的税率支付；因此，现在经销商自己支付全部的关税（按新的税率），然后从三菱那里获得"旧税退款"——即按旧税率应支付的金额。

希望这一点我已经解释清楚了。

谨上
福西特

部门间备忘录三十八
INTER-DEPARTMENTAL MEMORANDUM

To: Agent
    CHINWANGTAO

Reference M-18003
Serial Number
Tientsin Agency 16th May, 1936

Subject

    With reference to your letter No. M-18119 of 5th instant, we enclose herewith copies of letters to Tung Hsiang Yung, Tientsin, and Tien Yuan Tai, Peiping, together with our revised Glass Price List for Tientsin and Peiping, in duplicate, for your approval.

                        G. H. Fawcett
                  TIENTSIN SALES OFFICE.

Enclos:-
  Copy of letters (2)
  Glass Price List (2) in duplicate.

译文：

参考编号 M-18003
序号
天津 代理处 1936年5月16日

致：秦皇岛代理商

主题

    关于你方本月5日M-18119号信，兹随函附上致天津同祥湧玻璃庄和北平天源泰玻璃店的信件副本，以及经修订的天津和北平玻璃价目表一式两份，请批准。

                        福西特
                        天津销售部

附件：
  信件复印件（2）

玻璃价目表（2）

M-18119.

Tientsin Sales Office,
TIENTSIN.

Chinwangtao 5th May, 36

GLASS PRICES.

With reference to our recent conversation in Tientsin I confirm the following arrangements agreed upon:-

(1) As from the 1st June, 1936, the rates for 4th quality, single thickness will be increased by $0.55 per case. This will mean that your Basic Rate for the 60" bracket will be $8.25.

(2) The rate for "Strip" glass will be increased to $19.50 per case of 300 square feet.

(3) The rate for all other thickness will remain unchanged.

(4) Identical increases will be enforced at Peiping.

(5) Rates for Tientsin and Peiping up-country stations will remain unchanged.

Will you kindly arrange to give all concerned the customary notice, and provide us with a copy of your new price schedules for Peiping and Tientsin in duplicate in due course.

for AGENT.

译文：

M-18119

秦皇岛　　1936年5月5日

致：天津销售部

玻璃价格

根据我们最近在天津的谈话，我确认双方已达成下列安排：

（1）从1936年6月1日起，四等单厚玻璃的价格将每箱提高0.55美元。这意味着贵方60英寸级别玻璃的基本价格将为8.25美元。

（2）按每箱300平方英尺计，"条形"玻璃的价格将提高至每箱19.50美元。

（3）所有其他厚度玻璃的价格将保持不变。

（4）北平也将执行相同的涨价。

（5）天津和北平内陆站点的玻璃价格将保持不变。

烦请贵方按照惯例通知所有相关人员，并适时向我们提供您在北平和天津的新价格表，一式两份。

代理商

TO BE TRANSLATED INTO CHINESE

Tientsin, 16th May, 1936

Ref. M-18003.

Messrs. Tung Hsiang Yung,
TIENTSIN.

Dear Sirs,

We shall be glad if you will note that, as from 1st June, 1956, our price for 4th Quality Single Thickness Glass will be increased by $0.55 i.e. from $7.70 to $8.25 per case Standard Specification. Our 4th Quality Single large sizes are automatically increased while the prices for heavy glass and the up-country shipments will remain unchanged.

With regard to the 4th single narrow strip glass 40"*6" to 40"*8" the price will also be increased from $18.00 to $19.50 per case of 300 sq. rt. as from the same date.

Yours faithfully,

G. H. Fawcett

TIENTSIN SALES OFFICE.

Copy to:-

 Agent, Chinwangtao Mr. Fawcett
 SG.   " Mr. Chiu
 A.T., Tientsin.

译文：

　　　　　　　待译成中文
　　　　　　天津，1936年5月16日
　　　　　　　　　编号：M-18003

致：天津的同祥湧玻璃庄
敬启者：
　　请注意，从1936年6月1日起，我方四等单厚玻璃的价格将提高0.55美元，即从每箱标准规格 7.70 美元增加至 8.25 美元。我方四等单厚大尺寸玻璃的价格将随之提高，而厚玻璃和国内运输的价格将保持不变。
　　至于规格为 40"*6" 至 40"*8" 的四等单厚窄条玻璃，按每箱300平方英尺计，自同日起，价格也将从每箱 18.00 美元提高至 19.50 美元。

　　　　　　　　　　　　谨上
　　　　　　　　　　　福西特
　　　　　　　　　　天津营业部

抄送：
秦皇岛代理处，福西特先生
秦皇岛代理商　邱先生
总局，天津

TO BE TRANSLATED INTO CHINESE

Tientsin, 16th May, 1936

M-18003.

Messrs. Tien Yuan Tai,

PEIPING

Dear Sirs,

We shall be glad if you will note that, as from 1st June, 1936, our price for 4th Quality Single Thickness glass will be increased by $0.55, i.e., from $7.50 to $8.05 per case Standard Specification. Our 4th Quality Single large sizes are automatically increased; while the prices for heavy glass and the up-country shipments will remain unchanged.

With regard to the 4th Single narrow strip glass 40"*6" to 40"*8" the price will also be increased from $18.00 to $19.50 per case of 300 sq.ft. as from the the same date.

Yours faithfully,

G. H. Fawcett

TIENTSIN SALES OFFICE.

Copy to:-

Agent, C.W.Tao. Mr. Fawcett.

SG.　　　"　　Mr. Chiu.

A. T., T.S.

译文：

待译为中文

天津，1936年5月16日

M-18003

致：北平的天源泰玻璃店

敬启者：

请注意，自1936年6月1日起，我们的四等单玻璃的价格将提高0.55美元，即每箱标准规格的玻璃从7.5美元提高至8.05美元。我们的四等单厚大尺寸玻璃的价格将随之上涨；而厚玻璃和内陆运输的价格将保持不变。

至于规格为40"*6"至40"*8"的四等单厚窄条玻璃，按每箱300平方英尺计，自同日起，价格也将从每箱18.00美元提高至19.50美元。

谨上

福西特

天津营业部

抄送：

秦皇岛代理处，福西特先生

秦皇岛代理商　邱先生

总局，天津

18119.

Tientsin Sales Office,

TIENTSIN.

Chinwangtao   17th May, 36

TIENTSIN & PEIPING GLASS PRICES

With reference to your letter M-18003 of the 16th, we approve the new Price Lists as submitted.

for AGENT.

译文：

M-18119

秦皇岛   1936年5月17日

致：天津销售部

天津和北平玻璃价格

关于你方16日M-18003号信，我们同意所提交的新价目表。

代理商

INTER-DEPARTMENTAL MEMORANDUM

To: H.H.Faulkner, Esq.,   Reference 18003
     CHINWANGTAO   Serial Number _____

                                   Tientsin Agency 3rd June, 1936

Subject _____

Dear Faulkner,

    I enclose translation copy of a letter from Tung Hsiang Yung dated 1st instant.

    There is, so far as I can trace, no record, nor have I any recollection, of any such arrangement being agreed to by you; but, before replying to Tung Hsiang Yung, shall be glad to have your confirmation or denial thereof.

    It occurs to me that the wish may be father to the thought and that they may be seeking to establish as a precedent, the privilege granted to them last year when they were permitted to pay for their orders at the old rate although delivery thereof was completed only after a price increase had become effective (Ref. our letter to you No.18151 of 8th November 1935).

                                              Yours sincerely,
                                                G. H. Fawcett.

Enclo. (1)

译文：

参考编号　18003

序号

天津　　代理处　1936年6月3日

致：秦皇岛福克纳先生

主题

尊敬的福克纳：

随函附上同祥湧本月1日来信的翻译本。

据我所知，没有任何记录，我也不记得您同意过这样的安排；但是，在答复同祥湧之前，我很乐意您对此作出确认或否认。

我突然想到他的这种愿望可能是这种想法的根源，他们可能是试图借由去年给予他们的特权开一个先例，尽管当时是在涨价已生效后才完成交货，我们还是允许他们按旧价格支付订单（参考我们1935年11月8日给您的第18151号信）。

谨上
福西特

附件（1）

TRANSLATLON

Tientsin Sales Office,   Tientsin. 1/6/36.

K.M.A.,

TIANTSIN.

Dear Sirs,

We have not anticipated that the recent sales of your Yao Hua Glass have been very brisk. This must be due to your Administration's endeavours. We are as well fortunate.

We are in receipt of a letter from our Manager, who is now in Peiping, advising us of the increase in price for your glass. It is remembered that when you were contemplating to increase prices on the 8th November last year, your Mr. Faulkner came to Tientsin on official business. During an interview with Mr. Faulkner, our Manager was told that if the price should be increased next time your Administration would supply us with 1,000 cases of glass at the previous rate as a special arrangement to Contractors.

Your Administration is hereby requested to supply us, in accordance with Mr. Faulkner's intentions, with 1,000 cases of glass, for which we shall be obliged.

                                        Yours faithfully,

            (Chop)   Tung Tsiang Yung.

译文：
翻译

1936 年 6 月 1 日

开滦矿物总局天津销售营业部

敬启者：

出乎我方意料，最近贵方耀华玻璃的销售非常火爆。这一定是总局的努力，我们也有幸沾光。

我方收到了目前在北平的我方经理来函，告知我方贵公司玻璃的价格上涨。记得去年 11 月 8 日，当贵方考虑涨价时，贵方的福克纳先生因公来到天津。在与福克纳先生的会谈中，我方经理得知，如果下次涨价，你们总局将按先前的价格向我们提供 1 000 箱玻璃，作为给承包商的特别安排。

特此请求你们总局按照福克纳先生的意思，按先前的价格向我们提供 1 000 箱玻璃，我们将对此表示感谢。

谨上

（商号） 同祥湧

部门间备忘录四十
INTER-DEPARTMENTAL MEMORANDUM

To: H.H.Faulkner, Esq.,　　　Reference   M-18003
　　　CHINWANGTAO　　　　　　Serial Number

　　　　　　　　　　　　　　　Tientsin   Agency   6th June, 1936

Subject

Dear Faulkner,

　　With reference to Your letter No.18119 of the 4th of June, I had an interview yesterday with Mr.Sung of Tung Hsiang Yung as a result of which I am convinced that the impressions conveyed to you in my letter of the 3rd of June are substantially correct, and as a result politely declined to agree to Tung Hsiang Yung's request that we should supply them with the 1,000 cases of glass at the old prices, asked for in their letter of the 1st of June, that is to say, one day after the increased prices became effective and do not think that this attitude will prove prejudicial to our relations with this dealer.

　　In my opinion the request appears to have been made partly as the result of a misunderstanding of our attitude last November and partly as a "try on" to secure similarly favourable treatment on this occasion, since I am convinced that for these 1,000 cases Tung Hsiang Yung have not themselves bona fide orders and hope merely to secure this glass for stock and subsequent speculative sales at the old prices.

　　　　　　　　　　　　　　　　　　　　　　Yours sincerely,
　　　　　　　　　　　　　　　　　　　　　　G. H. Fawcett.

译文：

参考编号　M-18003

序号　　　

天津　　代理处　　1936年6月6日

致：秦皇岛福克纳先生

主题

亲爱的福克纳：

　　关于您6月4日的第18119号信件，我与同祥湧玻璃庄的宋先生进行了会谈，因为我确信我在6月3日的信中给您传达的印象基本上是正确的。也因此，我婉拒了同祥湧玻璃庄的要求，即我们应按他们在6月1日，即有关涨价生效后一天，信中要求的按照旧价格向他们提供1000箱玻璃，我认为这种态度不会损害我们与该经销商的关系。

　　在我看来，他们之所以提出这一要求，部分是由于去年11月对我方态度的误解，部分是为了"试探"一下，好在今年这种情况下获得类似的优惠待遇，因为我相信，同祥湧玻璃庄本身并没有这1000箱玻璃的真正的订单，他们只是希望把这批玻璃作为存货，随后按旧价格进行投机性销售。

谨上

福西特

18119.

G. H. Fawcett, Esq.,
TIENTSIN.

Chinwangtao   4th June, 36

CONFIDENTIAL.

Dear Fawcett,

With reference to your letter 18003 of the 3rd June, 1936, I certainly have no remembrance of ever having agreed to the arrangement put forward by Tung Hsiang Yung. If I had, it would have been set down in writing, as I trust the memory of nobody in matters of this nature.

However I do know that Tung Hsiang Yung received very generous treatment at our hands when the increase was made in November last, and I imagine this is a try-on to extort further favours and perhaps, as you suggest, to establish a precedent. In this connection please read my letter X-18119 of the 8th November, 1935, in reply to Cowell's letter X-18119 of the 7th November, 1935.

Nevertheless we do not wish to weaken our present strong position, and you should go into the whys and wherefores of his request before definitely turning it down, and if he can put forward a reasonable case we will concur with a fair settlement. It must be understood, however, that this particular instance would in no way establish a precedent.

Yours sincerely,
H.H.Faulkner.

译文：

18119.

秦皇岛，1936年6月4日

致：天津的福西特先生

机密文件

亲爱的福西特：

关于您1936年6月3日的第18003号信，我当然不记得我曾同意过同祥涌提出的安排。如果我有，也会以书面形式记录下来，因为在这种性质的问题上我不相信任何人的记忆。

然而，我确实知道，去年11月涨价时，同祥涌在我们手中得到了非常慷慨的待遇，我想他这是在尝试索要更多的好处，也许正如您所说，开一个先例。关于这一点，请看我1935年11月8日的X-18119号信，该信是对考威尔1935年11月7日的X-18119号信的答复。

然而，我们不希望削弱我们目前的强硬立场，在明确拒绝他的请求之前，您应该深入了解他提出要求的原因和动机，如果他能提出合理的理由，我们将同意公平解决。然而，必须理解的是，这个特例绝不会成为先例。

谨上

福克纳

部门间备忘录四十一

INTER-DEPARTMENTAL MEMORANDUM

To: H.H.Faulkner, Esq.,   Reference 18119

      CHINWANGTAO   Serial Number

                                       Tientsin Agency 10th July, 1936

Subject   GLASS FOR SUIYUAN

Dear Faulkner,

     During the past few days we have had an exchange correspondence with Tung Tsiang Yung and Tien Yuan Tai with regard to the supply of glass by direct shipment to Suiyuan to meet the requirements of a customer of Tung Hsiang Yung's.

     This merchant, who trades under the name of Yuan Sheng Tai Glass Store in Suiyuan has apparently, for some reason, an objection to dealing through Tien Yuan Tai, and there would appear to be price competition between this firm and Tung Hsiang Yung in respect of the prospective Suiyuan business。

     For your better understanding of this matter I enclose copies of letters received from Tung Hsiang Yung and Tien Yuan Tai on the subject, and in order not to lose the chance of securing this business, suggest for your consideration that Tung Tsiang Yung be permitted to negotiate for it at our standard price of $9.00 per case F.O.C. Suiyuan (less whatever rebate he himself may be prepared to give to his customer) and that we grant to Tien Yuan Tai (say) $1\frac{1}{2}$% (instead of the customary 3%) as a "consolation" for invading Peiping dealers territory.

     I think you will agree that any reduction in price is, at the moment, out of the question.

     Will you please let me know your views regarding the above as soon as possible?

                                                 Yours sincerely,

                                                G. H. Fawcett.

Enclos:-(2)

译文：

参考编号　__18119__

序号　　　_____

天津　　代理处　__1936年7月10日__

致：秦皇岛福克纳先生

主题　　　　　　　……………绥远玻璃……………………………………

亲爱的福克纳：

在过去的几天里，我们与同祥湧和天源泰进行了通信交流，讨论直接向绥远供应玻璃以满足同祥湧的一名客户的要求一事。

该商人在绥远以元盛泰玻璃店的名义进行玻璃交易，显然由于某种原因，他反对通过天源泰进行交易，而且该商行与同祥湧之间在绥远的潜在业务方面似乎存在价格竞争。

为了让您更好地了解此事，我附上了从同祥湧和天源泰那里收到的关于这一问题的信件的副本，为了不失去获得这笔生意的机会，建议您考虑允许同祥湧以我们的标准价格，即每箱绥远离岸价9美元（减去他自己可能准备给客户的回扣）进行谈判，并且我们给予天源泰（比如）1.5%（而非按例3%）作为其涉足北平经销商地盘的"安抚金"。

目前没有任何降价空间，我想您会认同这一点。

您能尽快告诉我您对上述问题的看法吗？

谨上

福西特

附件：（2）

Copy

Peiping, 7th July, 1936

Chiu Shao Tang, Esq.,
K. M. A.

Dear Mr. Chiu,

  When sometime ago Mr., Huang Wei San was in Tientsin, you said that no carload glass had as yet been shipped to Suiyuan for sale. Your Administration quoted us $9,00 per case and we quote our Suiyuan customers, Ching Hsiang Cheng, Yuan Sheng Tai and Kuei Chu Hsing, $8.80 per case of No.46 glass, f.o.c., Suiyuan Station. They all declared that on Yao Hua glass a tax at $0,99 must be paid at Sha Hu Kuan while that on Shoko glass was exempted. Therefore Yao Hua glass cannot be sold there. If you quote us $8,30, the price for Yao Hua glass will equal that of Shoko glass. Please try to consult with your Chief Managers in the matter for their approval of a reduction of $0.50, in order to effect brisky sales of your glass. As to whether or not this is in order, kindly make us a reply. Sometime ago we urged you by letter to despatch us 30-40 tons of large sized glass but we have not received same up to now.

  Please press your factory for their immediate despatch to Peiping of the glass mentioned above.

Your faithfully,

Tein Yuan Tai Glass Store.

译文：

1936年7月7日，北平

致：邱绍棠先生

尊敬的邱先生，

　　前段时间黄伟三先生在天津的时候，您说过还没有玻璃运到绥远出售过。贵方总局报价为每箱9美元，我方为绥远客户庆祥盛、源盛泰和贵珠兴报价为46号玻璃每箱8.80美元，绥远站离岸价。他们都宣称，耀华玻璃必须在沙湖关缴纳0.99美元的税。而曙光玻璃则是免税的。因此耀华玻璃无法在那里销售，如果你报8.30美元的价格，耀华玻璃的价格将与曙光玻璃等价。为了促进你们玻璃的销售，请试着就此事与你们的总经理协商，让他们同意降价0.50美元。前段时间，我们曾写信催你方向我方运送30~40吨大尺寸玻璃，但至今未收到。

　　请催促贵厂立即将上述玻璃运往北平。

谨启，

天源泰玻璃店

The Tientsin Sales Office,

K.M.A.

Dear Sirs,

　　A glass merchant (Our customer for many years) has come from Suiyuan to Tientsin contemplating to purchase from us carload glass destined for Suiyuan f.o.c. Suiyuan Station. Asked quotation per case and period of delivery, we made a reply that Yao Hua glass supplies for the said city were under the management of Tien Yuan Tai, Peiping Agents for Yao Hua glass along the P.S.R. line. and advised him to take up the matter with your Peiping Sales Agents. Strongly refusing to do so, and declaring that in our transactions with him for these many years we had shown honesty and trustworthiness, he requested us to bring the matter to you for action.

We are now writing you this letter to enquire of you into your attitude toward this matter, stating, in detail, the advantages and disadvantages, and the detailed conditions the merchant has set forth. We venture to request your early consideration and reply, for negotiation and action.

The said merchant has established in Suiyuan the Yuan Sheng Tai Glass Store for many years and transports about 1,000 cases of glass from us in Tientsin every year. Since the adoption of the through consignment system by your Administration, Tien Yuan Tai, Peiping, has also supplied him at $9.00 per case, f.o.c. at Suiyuan Station, cartage and local taxes (octroi) being borne by the purchaser, without any rebate. On account of the heavy local taxes, he later dealt in Shoko glass, instead. (No local taxes levied on Shoko glass after payment of import duty.) During the period from last autumn to the present, he has had about 1,000 cases of Shoko glass transported to the said city. If this lasts long, Yao Hua glass would suffer a great loss. Since we are informed of the situation in detail, we have to report to you by letter. We wonder whether the quotation for glass f.o.c. at said station is $9.00. If this is the case, we are simply willing to sacrifice our 2% rebate and give it to the said merchant in order to wage a competition with Shoko glass and to avoid damage to your business. Kindly make us a reply as to whether or not this is in order.

Yours faithfully,
TUNG HSIANG YUNG, TIENTSIN.

译文：

致：开滦矿物总局天津经销处，

敬启者，

　　一位玻璃商人（我们多年的客户）从绥远来到天津，打算从我们这里购买一车厢玻璃，运往绥远。询问每箱报价和交货期限时，我方答复说，上述城市供应的耀华玻璃由北平天元泰公司管理，该公司负责供应北平—绥远铁路沿线的耀华玻璃，并建议他与你们北平的销售代理人交涉此事。他坚决拒绝这样做，并宣称在与他多年的生意交往中我方是诚实可靠的，他要求我们将此事提交给你方来处理。

　　我们现在写这封信是为了询问你对此事的态度，并详细说明其利弊，以及商家提出的详细条件。我们冒昧地请求你方尽早考虑并答复，以便协商和采取措施。

　　该商家在绥远经营源盛泰玻璃店多年，每年从天津我公司运输玻璃约1 000箱。自从总局采用直运制度以来，北平天源泰已开始给他报价每箱9美元，绥远站到岸价，运费和地方税由买方负担，不退还。由于当地赋税过重，他后来转而经营"曙光"玻璃。（曙光玻璃在缴纳进口关税后不征收地方税。）从去年秋天到现在，他已经将大约1 000箱曙光玻璃运到了这座城市。如果这种情况持续太久，耀华玻璃将蒙受巨大损失。既然我们已经详细了解了情况，我们不得不写信向你汇报。我们不知道该地点玻璃离岸价是否为9美元。如果是这样的话，我们愿意牺牲我们2%的回扣，把它给上述商家，以便与曙光玻璃进行竞争，避免对您的业务造成损害。请答复我们这样做是否妥当。

　　　　　　　　　　　　　　　　　　　　谨启，
　　　　　　　　　　　　　　　　　　　　同祥湧玻璃庄，天津

INTER-DEPARTMENTAL MEMORANDUM

To: H.H.Faulkner,Esq.,　　　Reference　18119
　　　CHINWANGTAO　　　　Serial Number
　　　　　　　　　　　　　　Tientsin Agency 25th July, 1936

Subject　　　　　　GLASS FOR SUIYUAN

Dear Faulkner,

　　Upon receipt of your letter Ref.18119 of the 11th instant, I arranged for representatives of the Peiping Glass Dealers to come and see me to discuss the question of shipments to Suiyuan. The net result of our conversation is that they (that is the Peiping dealers) intend to work this Suiyuan business themselves by taking advantage of the 200 sq. ft. per case packing, in the hope that they will be able to pass these larger pieces through the Shahhukwan Tax Office at the same rate of 99 cents per case (as the small cases of 100 sq. ft). If they succeed, they are confident that, with the assistance of the rebate offered them on the 200 sq. ft. cases they will be able to do business, and expect shortly to send in their first orders.

　　It was made quite clear to them that we could not permit competition in each other's areas by our Tientsin and Peiping dealers, and they fully appreciated our attitude, and I do not think that we need fear loss of business from this source.

　　A careful watch will be maintained for this upcountry business and the dealers are fully aware that we expect them to extend their sales to these points more vigorously than in the past.

　　　　　　　　　　　　　　　　　　Yours sincerely,
　　　　　　　　　　　　　　　　　　G. H. Fawcett.

译文：

参考编号 18119
序号
天津　代理处　1936年7月25日

致：秦皇岛福克纳先生

主题　　　　　　　绥远玻璃

亲爱的福克纳：

收到您本月11日的第18119号信后，我安排了北平玻璃经销商的代表与我见面，讨论向绥远运货的问题。我们谈话的最终结果是，他们（即北平的经销商）打算利用每箱容量200平方英尺的箱子来装货，自己来做绥远的生意，希望他们能够以每箱99美分的价格（与100平方英尺的小箱一样）让这些大件货通过沙湖关税务局。如果他们成功了，他们有信心，有了200平方英尺箱装货的回扣，他们的生意能做成，预计不久就能发出他们的第一批订单。

我们已经很清楚地告诉他们，我们不允许天津和北平的经销商在对方的地区进行竞争，他们完全理解我们的态度，我认为我们不需要担心失去这个来源的业务。

我们将对这一内陆业务保持谨慎的关注，经销商们也充分意识到我们希望他们能比过去更积极地将销售扩展到这些地点。

谨上
福西特

18119.

G. H. Fawcett, Esq.,
TIENTSIN.

Chinwangtao   11th July, 36

CONFIDENTIAL.

GLASS FOR SUIYUAN

Dear Fawcett,

With reference to your letter 18119 of the 10th Instant, I wired you this morning agreeing to your proposal to meet this special case in order not to lose immediate business, but we cannot agree to treat further cases or this kind in the same manner. An agreement must be reached between our Tientsin and Peiping dealers to meet instances where they become competitors, and I suggest you call them in to arrive at an understanding before the autumn buying season commences.

If you would like me to negotiate with them personally I am at your service to run up for a day any time you say.

I agree with you that it is out of the question to consider reducing prices for any interior business at the moment.

Yours sincerely,
H. H. Faulkner.

译文：

18119.

秦皇岛　　1936 年 7 月 11 日

致：天津的福西特先生

机密件

绥远地区玻璃业务事宜

亲爱的福西特：

　　关于您本月 10 日的 18119 号来信，我今天上午给您发了电报，同意贵方为了不失当前商机而处理这一特殊情况的建议，但我们不能同意再以同样的方式处理其他此类情况。我们的天津经销商和北平经销商之间必须达成协议，以应对他们之间相互竞争的情况，我建议您在秋季采购季节开始之前召集他们达成谅解。

　　如果您想让我亲自与他们谈判，您随时吩咐我，我愿意为您效劳。

　　我同意您的观点，目前不可能考虑针对内陆业务的任何降价举措。

谨上
福克纳

部门间备忘录四十三
INTER-DEPARTMENTAL MEMORANDUM

To: H.H.Faulkner, Esq., Reference ...... 1000 ......
      CHINWANGTAO Serial Number ....
                                Tientsin Agency 27th July, 1936

Subject ....

Dear Faulkner,

    It has been arranged that I proceed tomorrow to Tongku to relieve Carter for three weeks while he takes the Summer Holiday at Chinwangtao.

    There are, so far as I am aware, no outstanding matters of importance and I have arranged for the routine work in connection with [Brick and] Glass business to be carried on by Messrs. S. C. Chiu, C. C. Chang in conjunction with Henry Yueh and P. Y. Wang.

    I expect to be back at my desk in Tientsin about the 18th of August.

                                                    Yours sincerely,
                                                    G. H. Fawcett.

译文：

                          参考编号 ...... 1000 ......
                          序号 ....
                          天津   代理处   1936 年 7 月 27 日

致：秦皇岛福克纳先生

主题 ....

亲爱的福克纳，

    根据安排，卡特去秦皇岛度暑假，我明天前往塘沽接替他三周的工作。

    据我所知，没有什么重要的未处理事项，我已经安排了邱先生、张先生、Henry Yueh 和王先生共同完成（砖瓦和）玻璃业务有关的日常工作。

    我预计在 8 月 18 日左右回到天津的岗位上。

                                                                  谨上
                                                                  福西特

部门间备忘录四十四
INTER-DEPARTMENTAL MEMORANDUM

To: Agent, Reference 18068
CHINWANGTAO Serial Number
Tientsin Agency 5th Aug, 1936

Subject

CONFIDENTIAL.

We regret the delay in replying to your letter Ref. 18119 of the 17th July, as we have only just received Messrs. Tung Hsiang Yung's offer today. It is apparent that our dealers in Peiping and Tientsin have exchanged views on the subject, because they both offer $6.00 per case.

In view of the instructions contained in the last paragraph of your letter under reply, we shall endeavour to send for Messrs. Tung Hsiang Yung and see if we can obtain a better offer from them. In the meantime, however, we shall be pleased to know of what price you will eventually consider to dispose of the unsold stock.

TIENTSIN SALES OFFICE.

译文：

参考编号 18068
序号
天津　代理处　1936年8月5日

致：秦皇岛代理商

主题

机密文件

关于您7月17日的编号为18119号的信件，迟复为歉，因为我们今天才收到同祥湧玻璃庄的报价。显然，我们在北平和天津的经销商已经就此问题交换了意见，因为他们的报价都是每箱 6 美元。

鉴于您回信中最后一段的指示，我们将尽力请来同祥湧，看看我们是否能从他们那里得到更好的报价。但与此同时，贵公司最终会考虑以什么价格来处理未售出的存货，敬请告知。

天津营业部

M-18119.

Tientsin Sales Office,
TIENTSIN.

Chinwangtao   17th July, 36

CONFIDENTIAL.

UNSOLD STOCK

We have in the factory the following unsold stock which we are anxious to dispose of and would like you to offer to either your Tientsin or Peiping dealers:

(1) 135 cases of 100 sq.ft. 4th Single, paper packed, 11"*29". Price $7.25 per case ex-godown Tientsin or f.o.c. Peiping.

(2) 5 cases of 200 sq. ft. 4th Single, straw packed, 5"*35" and 1 case of 200 sq.ft. 4th Single, straw packed, 7"*35". Price $12.00 per case ex-godown Tientsin or f.o.c. Peiping.

These are the minimum rates we will consider and you should endeavour to obtain better if possible. It must be clearly understood, however, that these prices are special to dispose of unsold stock, and any further orders for these sizes will be in accordance with the standard price list prevailing at the time.

For AGENT.

译文：

M-18119.

秦皇岛　　1936 年 7 月 17 日

致：天津销售部

机密件
<u>未售存货</u>

我们在工厂里有以下未售出的库存，急于处理，希望您能供应给天津或北平的经销商。

（1）100 平方英尺箱装纸包装 11"*29"规格四等单厚玻璃 155 箱。每箱天津出厂价或北平出厂价 7.25 美元。

（2）200 平方英尺箱装稻草包装 5"*55"规格四等单厚玻璃 5 箱、200 平方英尺箱装稻草包装 7"*35"规格四等单厚玻璃 1 箱。每箱天津出厂价或北平出厂价 12.00 美元。

这些是我们考虑的最低价格，如果可能的话，贵方应该争取获得更好的价格。不过，我们必须清楚了解，这些是针对未售存货而定的特价，今后对于任何以上尺寸货物的订单都将按照当时的标准价格表交易。

代理人

18119.

Tientsin Sales Office,
TIENTSIN.

　　　　　　　　　　　　　　　Chinwangtao　　4th Aug, 36

We shall be much obliged if you will reply to our letter 18119 of the 17th ultimo at your early convenience.

H. H. Faulkner
for AGENT.

译文：

M-18119.

秦皇岛　1936 年 8 月 4 日

致：天津销售部

如能尽早回复我方上个月 17 日的 18119 号信，将不胜感激。

福克纳

部门间备忘录四十五
INTER-DEPARTMENTAL MEMORANDUM

To: Agent,　　　　　　　Reference ____18068____
　　CHINWANGTAO　　　Serial Number _____
　　　　　　　　　　　　Tientsin Agency 10th Aug, 1936

Subject _____UNSOLD STOCK_____

　　With further reference to our letter No.18068 of the 5th instant, Messrs. Tung Hsiang Yung have increased their offer to $6.50 per case. They claim that the sizes are unsuitable and it will be difficult to effect sales.

　　In view of the instructions contained in your letter No.M-18119 of the 17th July, we shall consider the matter closed unless we receive further advice from you.

　　　　　　　　　　　　　TIENTSIN SALES OFFICE.

译文：

  参考编号 18068
  序号
  <u>天津</u> 代理处 1936 年 8 月 10 日

致：秦皇岛代理商

主题   <u>未售的存货</u>

  进一步参考我方本月 5 日 18068 号函，同祥湧先生已将他的报价提高至每箱 6.50 美元。他们声称因尺寸不合适，难以出售。

  鉴于贵方 7 月 17 日 M-18119 号信函中的指示，若未收到贵方进一步通知，我方将认为此事已结案。

天津销售处

18119

Tientsin Sales Office,
TIENTSIN.

            Chinwangtao 7th Aug, 36

    UNSOLD GLASS STOCKS

  With reference to your letter 18068 of the 5th instant, the minimum prices we will consider were given in our letter M-18119 of the 17th July.

              H. H. Faulkner
                 for AGENT.

译文：

                 M-18119.
        秦皇岛 1936 年 8 月 7 日

致：天津销售部

     <u>未售出的玻璃库存</u>

  关于你方 5 日 18068 号来信，我方将考虑的最低价格已在 7 月 17 日信 M-18119 中给出。

福克纳

INTER-DEPARTMENTAL MEMORANDUM

To: Agent,　　　　　　　Reference .....18068.....
　　　CHINWANGTAO　　　Serial Number ....
　　　　　　　　　　　　Tientsin　Agency　14th Aug, 1936

Subject ....UNSOLD STOCK........................

With reference to your letter No.18119 of 12th instant, we enclose herewith copy of Sales Note No.TS.257 covering 135 Units of 4th Single Glass (odd sizes) and shall be obliged if you will arrange to despatch the above to Tientsin at your convenience.

　　　　　　　　　　　　TIENTSIN SALES OFFICE.

译文：

　　　　　　　　参考编号 .....18068.....
　　　　　　　　序号　　 ....
　　　　　　　　天津　代理处　1936 年 8 月 14 日

致：秦皇岛代理商

主题 ....未售的存货........................

　　根据贵方本月 12 日 18119 号函，我方现随函附上编号为 TS.257 的销售单据，涉及号 135 件 4 等单厚玻璃（非标准尺寸），若贵方方便时安排将上述货物运至天津，我方将不胜感激。

　　　　　　　　　　　　　　　　　　天津销售处

18119

Tientsin Sales Office
TIENTSIN

Chinwangtao   12th Aug, 36

UNSOLD STOCK

With reference to your letter 18068 of the 10th instant, we accept Messrs. Tung Hsiang Yung's offer of $6.50 per case for the 135 cases of 100 sq,ft., 4th Single, paper packed 11"*29", offered in our letter M-18119 of the 17th July.

Will you kindly let us have your Sales Note covering the business, which should be marked, "To be supplied from Unsold Stook".

H. H. Faulkner

for AGENT.

译文：

18119

秦皇岛　1936年8月12日

致：天津销售处

未售的存货

根据贵方本月10日的18068号函，我方接受同祥湧在7月17日M-18119号函中的报价，即100平方英尺装的四等单厚玻璃，尺寸为11"*29"，纸箱包装，每箱6.50美元，135箱。

烦请您寄给我方该笔生意的销售单据，并注明"代售库存货物供应"。

福克纳

第四章

开滦矿务总局耀华公司玻璃经销函电（共16份）

函电一[①]

E. J. Cowell, Esq.,
TIENTSIN

Chinwangtao 4th Jan., 35

Dear Cowell,

With reference to your letter 18119 of the 3rd instant, I am leaving for Shanghai on Sunday or Monday and will not have time to make the trip to Tientsin as I have several things to clear up before I can leave.

However, carry on with your conversations with Mr. Sung on the lines you suggest, but I would be careful about the point of the "Overhead" account.

I agree with you about longer credit and stocks and the question of commission for Tientsin sales, but I am not sure of whether making two contracts would be the wisest plan. However, I will study the matter further during my journey and we can get together when I pass through Tientsin about the middle of the month.

Yours sincerely,
(Sgd) H. H. F.

[①] 关于同一事务的前后多份档案归类于同一序号函电下面，本章共有16份档案。

译文：

11819.

秦皇岛　　　　　　　　　　（19）35 年 1 月 4 日

致：天津的考威尔先生

亲爱的考威尔先生：

回应您本月 3 日编号 18119 的信函，我将于星期天或星期一动身前往上海，没有时间去天津了，因为在我离开之前，还有几件事要处理。

不过，请按照您建议的内容继续与宋先生谈话，但我会谨慎对待"间接费用"账目的问题。

我同意您关于延长信贷和库存以及天津销售佣金的提议，但我不确定签订两份合同是否是最明智的计划。不过，我会在旅途中进一步研究这件事，大约在本月中旬我经过天津时，我们可以聚一聚商讨此事。

谨上

（签字）福克纳

函电二

18119

Tientsin Sales Office
TIENTSIN　　　　　　　Chinwangtao　　　　11th Feb., 35

We enclose herewith, for your information and necessary action, an original letter dated the 9th instant from Mr. H.T. Kuo, Manager of the Hua Sheng Tung Glass company, Tientsin.

H. H. Faulker
for AGENT.

译文：

18119

秦皇岛　1935年2月11日

致：天津销售处

兹随函附上天津华盛堂玻璃公司经理郭先生本月9日来函原文，以供贵方参考并采取必要措施。

福克纳

函电三

G.H.A. Snow, Esq.,
TIENTSIN

Chinwangtao 12th Feb., 35
M-18119

Dear Snow,

Many thanks for your letter 2563 of 11th instant. Your suggestion to make 18119 an "M" File will meet our requirements nicely so will kindly cancel file 18504.

Yours sincerely,
(Sgd) H. H. F.

译文：

致：天津斯诺先生

秦皇岛　1935 年 2 月 12 日
M-18119

非常感谢您本月 11 日发来 2563 编号的来信。您建议将 18119 号文件作为"M"文件很符合我们的要求，所以请取消 18504 号文件。

谨上
福克纳

函电四

```
                                                          18119
Tientsin Sales Office
TIENTSIN              Chinwangtao           23rd Feb., 35

                    CONFIDENTIAL.

Further to our letter No. 18119 of the 11th instant, we attach hereto a
further letter from Mr. H.T.Kuo of Tientsin for your necessary action.
                                          H. H. Faulker
                                             for AGENT.
```

译文：

18119

秦皇岛　1935年2月23日

致：天津销售处

继我方本月11日第18119号函之后，兹附上天津郭先生的来信，要求你方采取必要行动。

福克纳

18119

2nd March, 1935

Mr. H. T. Kuo

Hua Sheng Tung Glass Co.,

Hope i, Tientsin.

Dear Sir,

GLASS SALES AGENCY

You letter of February the 9th and February the 20th, addressed to Chinwangtao, have been passed to us, and we regret the delay in replying to your letters which has been due to the illness of the undersigned.

With reference to your request for a sole glass sales agency, we regret that our 1935 sales agreements do not permit us to appoint you in this capacity, neither do they permit us to grant you special prices or credit terms.

We shall, of course, be pleased to supply you at any time with your requirements at market price rates and for cash.

With regard to your Bank Guarantee, we have asked our Accounts Department to return this to you as it will no longer be required by us during 1935.

Yours faithfully,

TIENTSIN SALES OFFICE.

Copy to:- Ag.,CWT.

译文：

18119
1935年3月2日

致：天津希望路华盛堂玻璃公司郭先生
尊敬的先生：

玻璃销售代理

您于2月9日和2月20日写给秦皇岛的信已转交给我们，由于签名人生病，我们未能及时回信，对此深表歉意。

关于贵方要求做独家玻璃销售代理一事，我们很遗憾不能答应您，因为我们1935年的销售协议不允许我们任命贵方做独家销售代理，也不允许我们给予贵方特殊价格或信用条款。

当然，我们很乐意随时以市场价格和现金交易形式，按照您的需求向您供货。

关于贵方的银行保函，我方已要求会计部门将其退还给贵方，因为我方在1935年不再需要该保函。

谨上
考威尔
天津销售部

抄送：秦皇岛代理

函电五

CONFIDENTIAL.

18119.

E. J. Cowell. Esq.
TIENTSIN.

CWT. 13th May, 35

Dear Cowell,

<u>Upcountry Glass Sales</u>

With reference to your letter 18119 of the 9th instant. I take it that the comparison of our quotations for direct shipment and the cost price of the via Tientsin route is as follows:

	Direct	Via Tientsin
Shihchiachuang	$7.60	$7.62
Chengchow	8.00	8.09
Kaifeng	7.90	8.01
Tsinanfu	7.20	7.08

I quite agree that there is very little difference. And perhaps the direct shipment method will not appear in a very attractive light to Tung Hsiang Yung, but it must be remembered that (a) the risk of breakage will be less by the elimination of the several handling necessitated by the via Tientsin route, (b) the inland dealers will not have the expense of going to Tientsin on their buying trips, and (c) Tung Hsiang Yung will be able to keep in closer contact with the interior markets and expand his business with good profits, as the present interior selling prices will show.

He must understand, however, that our plans in that direction are not being formulated to increase his profits, but he should be able to visualise that any extensions of sales should mean increased returns to him in the long run, especially when he establishes a direct contact with the interior trade.

    Our quotations for direct shipment are present ex-factory returns from the via Tientsin route plus actual charges to the various stations, and we consider it unnecessary to consider a reduction. I suggest therefore you place these rates before Tung Hsiang Yung and impress upon him that our desire to expand our interior sales is earnest, and if he is unwilling to co-operate with us, we must explore other means.

Yours sincerely,
H. H. Faulker.

译文：

机密文件

18119
秦皇岛　1935 年 5 月 13 日

致：天津的考威尔先生

亲爱的考威尔：

内陆玻璃销售

贵方本月 9 日 18119 号函已收悉。我认为我方直运报价与经由天津的成本价比较如下：

	直运	经天津
石家庄	$7.60	$7.62
郑州	8.00	8.09
开封	7.90	8.01
济南府	7.20	7.08

我完全同意两者差别甚微。也许直运方式对同祥湧并不是很有吸引力。但必须记住的是（a）由于取消了经天津路线所必需的几次转运，破损风险将会降低，（b）内陆经销商将不必破费前往天津采购，（c）如目前的内陆销售价格所示，同祥湧将能够与内陆市场保持更密切的联系，获得丰厚的利润，扩大他的业务。

然而，他必须明白，我们朝这个方向制定计划之意不在增加他的利润，但他应该可以想见，任何销售的扩张应该都意味着他的长期回报会提高，当他建立起与内陆贸易的直接联系时尤为如此。

我们的直运报价是目前经由天津路线的出厂价加上到各车站的实际费用，我们认为没有必要考虑降价。因此，我建议您把这些价格告知同祥湧，让他明白我们衷心希望扩大内陆销售，如果他不愿意合作，我们就必须另谋他法。

谨上

福克纳

函电六

Tientsin Sales Office,
TIENTSIN.

Chinwangtao, 16th July,35

UP — COUNTRY SALES

With reference to your letter 18119-X of the 12th inst., we have the following remarks to make:

(1) Yi Sheng Chang-Kaifeng.

According to our figures the charges from Shanghai to Kaifeng amount to $1.70 per case and we consider it very unlikely that our glass from Shanghai is offered at less than $7.70 per case f.o.c. Kaifeng.

We have authorised you to quote as low as $7.90 f.o.c. Kaifeng for direct rail shipments.

(2) Teh Yuan Tai-Tsinanfu.

We have authorised you to quote $7.20 per case for standard specifications, f.o.c Tsinanfu, therefore the dealers offer of $7.45 should be accepted on an f.o.c. delivery basis.

(3) Kwang Tai Hsiang-Chengchow.

Our information is that the charges from Shanghai to Chengchow amount to $1.80 and we consider that our glass from Shanghai is not offering at less than $7.80 per case, whereas you have been authorised to quote $8.00 per case f.o.c. Chengchow.

(4) Teh Sheng Heng-Tayuanfu.

This is first information we have had of Shoko being able to load 350 cases to the 20-ton carload, and we would like you to investigate in Tientsin as according to the railway regulations here we are allowed 16 cases to the ton only.

(5) You ask us to give you quotations for Shihohiachwang and Taiyuanfu. Please refer to Mr. Faulkner's letter to Mr. Cowell No.18119 of the 3rd April, 1935, in which you will find these prices together with the minimum rates for the other places mentioned above.

(6) We shall be pleased if you will let me have Messrs. Tung Hsiang Yung's answer to the first paragraph of our letter 18119 of 10/7/35 as soon as possible.

for AGENT.

译文：

秦皇岛，1935 年 7 月 16 日

致：天津经销处

国内销售

关于贵方本月 12 日 18119-X 号函，我们有以下意见：

（1）义盛昌—开封。

根据数据显示，从上海到开封的费用为每箱 1.70 美元，但我们认为上海的玻璃报价不可能低于开封到岸价每箱 7.7 美元。

我方已授权你方铁路直运到开封，报价最低要每箱 7.90 美元。

（2）德源泰—济南府。

我们已批准你方每箱标准规格的玻璃 7.20 美元的济南府到岸价，因此经售人提出的 7.45 美元的济南府到岸价可以接受。

（3）康泰祥—郑州。

我们得到的信息是，从上海运至郑州的费用报价达到每箱 1.80 美元。我们认为上海的玻璃报价不能低于每箱 7.8 美元，而且贵方已被授权每箱玻璃郑州到岸价报价为 8 美元。

（4）德盛恒—太原府。

我们得到的第一条消息是 Shoko 公司用火车装载 350 箱玻璃，总运载量达到了 20 吨，我们希望您能在天津进行深入调查，因为根据这里的铁路规定，每吨只允许装 16 箱玻璃。

（5）贵方要求我们对石家庄和太原府的玻璃进行报价。请参阅福克纳先生 1935 年 4 月 3 日致考威尔先生的第 18119 号信，在信中您可以看到上述价格以及上述其他地方的最低玻璃价格。

（6）如果您能把同祥涌玻璃庄对于 35 年 7 月 10 日 18119 号信第一段的答复尽快给我，则甚为感激。

函电七

M-18119

Tientsin Sales Office,
TIENTSIN.

Chinwangtao, 23rd Oct., 35

GLASS

CONFIDENTIAL.

In view of fall in exchange I shall be obliged if you will endeavour to restrict further booking at the present prices and inform Messrs. Tung HsingYung, in accordance with Clause 4 of their agreement dated March 28th, 1935, that an increase in price of glass is anticipated to be effective immediately.

Amended price list will be forwarded as early as possible.

Chilton

For agent.

译文：

M-18119

致：天津销售处

秦皇岛，1935 年 10 月 23 日

玻璃

机密文件

鉴于汇率的下降，我将不得不尽力限制今后的现价订购，并根据 1935 年 3 月 28 日签订的协议第 4 条，通知同祥湧玻璃庄，玻璃的价格将立即上调。

修改后的价目表将尽快寄上。

谨上

齐尔顿

函电八

M-18119

E.J.Cowell, Esq.,
TIENTSIN.

Chinwangtao, 24th Oct., 35

DROP IN EXCHANGE

Dear Cowell,

With reference to my letter No. 18119 of yesterday's date and your telegram No.180 of even date, will you please keep me informed regarding any increase in Shoko's quotations as a result of the fall in silver.

I presume that it would be necessary for them to consider an immediate increase if they are to obtain a satisfactory return in the early advice of any move they make will be much appreciated.

Yours sincerely,

Chilton

for Agent.

译文：

M-18119

致：天津的考威尔先生

秦皇岛，1935年10月24日

汇率下跌

亲爱的考威尔，

关于我昨天第18119号信和您同日第180号电报，如果曙光玻璃公司因银价下跌而报价增加，请随时通知我。

我认为，如果他们想要获得令人满意的回报，他们就有必要考虑立即涨价，他们所做的任何变动，如果您能及早告知我方，我们将不胜感激。

谨上

齐尔顿

函电九

Copy

18119

Accountant,
TIENTSIN.

Tientsin　　17th Jan., 36

TIENTSIN GLASS DEALER'S AGREEMENT 1935
REFUND OF INITIAL REBATE

With reference to our Glass Sales Agreement with Messrs. Tung Hsiang Yung of Tientsin, dated 28th March 1935, it is stated in Clause (7):-

"That the Administration agrees to advance the initial rebate by crediting it in the monthly settlements of accounts and that the additional rebates if earned will be paid on the final settlement of the Contractor's account at the termination of this Agreement. The Contractor agrees, however, that should he fail to purchase the guaranteed minimum quantity of 60,000 standards he will refund to the Administration the full amount of the initial rebate advanced to him by the Administration."

We beg to advise you, however, that although, during the calendar year 1935, the Contractor did not purchase the minimum quantity of 60,000 standards as laid down in the agreement, it has been agreed to waive the refund of the initial rebate advanced to him, since his default was attributable in some measure to the Factory being short of stock and unable to supply his full requirements during the earlier part of the year and to other causes beyond his control; and we are satisfied that he used his best endeavours to promote sales throughout the year.

Please, therefore, cancel any debits which may have been made to Tung Hsiang Yung's account for refund of advances of initial rebate during 1935.

(signed)　G. H. Fawcett
TIENTSIN SALES OFFICE.

Copy to:-Ag. CWT.

译文：

致：天津财务处　　　　　　　　　　　　编号：18119

天津，1936年1月17日

1935年天津玻璃经销商退还最初返利协议

关于1935年3月28日我们与天津同祥湧玻璃庄签订的玻璃销售协议，第（7）条规定：

"总局同意预支最初的返利，将其记入每月结算的账户中，如果获得额外返利的话，则将在本协定终止时在分销商账户的最后结算中支付。但是，分销商同意，如果他未能购买保证的最低数量6万标准件，他将把最初预支的全额退还给总局。"

但是我们也建议您，尽管在1935年度分销商没有按协议规定，购买最低数量60 000标准件，分销商已同意放弃最初的退款折扣。他的违约在一定程度上归因于今年年初工厂缺乏库存，无法供应他的全部需求，和超出他控制的其他原因。但我们很满意，他全年都在尽最大努力推销产品。

因此，取消任何可能记入同祥湧账户的借记，以退还1935年首次退款的预付款。

（签名）福西特

天津经销处

M-18119

G.A. Fawcett, Esq.
　　TIENTSIN.

Chinwangtao　20th Feb., 36

UP-COUNTRY SALES

Dear Fawcett,

　　I attach hereto a statement I have prepared showing the present returns on Tientsin, Peiping and the up-country sales: From it you will see that most of the latter do not compare very favourably with the former and it appears to me that at Kaifeng, Chengchow, Yutse and Taiyuanfu under the Tientsin area and Ta Tung, Feng Chen, Suiyuan and Potou under the Peiping area we are selling our glass too cheaply.

　　I understand that at certain points Yao Hua glass is subjected to certain provincial taxes that are not levied on the Shoko, but it seems to me that our prices could go up and still meet Shoko competition from Tientsin. This particularly applies to the stations under the Peiping area.

　　Last year your dealers put up the plea that at certain southern points along the Peiping Hankow Line they would meet competition from Shanghai if our rates were too high, but under present conditions there is no fear of such a contingency arising, as our Shanghai selling prices are now far too high to allow them to market so far afield to the North.

　　I realise the sales at the places mentioned above are very small and any increases made will do but little to augment the average returns from your Agency, but the point is that we want to obtain the very best rates possible everywhere, and it seems that this is not being done at the abovementioned stations.

I would also like to remind you of the question of finding a market for the long narrow strips of the heavy grades, which I brought up when last in Tientsin. I can offer you very attractive prices for strips 6 to 8 inches wide up to 50 inches long in all the heavy grades if taken in 200 or 300 sq. ft. cases, if your Peiping and Tientsin dealers are interested.

Yours sincerely,

H. H. Faulker.

ENCLOS.1.

译文：

M-18119

致：天津的福西特先生

秦皇岛　　　　1936年2月20日

内陆销售

亲爱的福西特：

随函附上我准备的一份报告，说明天津、北平和内地销售的目前收益情况：从报告中您可以看出，后者的收益大都不如前者。而且，我认为，在属于天津片区的开封、郑州、榆次和太原府，以及北平片区的大同、丰镇、绥远和包头，我们玻璃的销售价格太低了。

我理解"耀华玻璃"受某些省份税收的影响，而这些税是不向"曙光"玻璃征收的。但在我看来，我们的价格可以上涨，而且依然面临着来自天津方面的"曙光"玻璃的竞争。北平片区的销售站点尤其如此。

去年，贵方的经销商曾提出请求，称如果我方价格太高，在北平汉口线沿线的某些南方销售站点，他们就要面对来自上海方面的竞争，但在目前情况下，不必担心发生这种意外情况，因为目前我们在上海的销售价格太高了，所以他们无法将产品远销北方。

我知道上述地方的销售额很小，无论销量提高多少，对于提高贵方代理的平均收益都是杯水车薪。但关键是，我们希望在任何地方都能获得最好的价格，而上述销售站点似乎并没有做到这一点。

我还想提醒您，上次在天津时，我曾提出过为重型狭长条形玻璃产品找销路的问题。如贵方北平和天津的经销商感兴趣，我可以给您为全部50英寸长，6至8英寸宽，按200或300平方英尺规格装箱的条形重玻璃提供非常有吸引力的价格。

谨上

福克纳

附件：1

函电十一

TO BE TRANSLATED INTO CHINESE.

Tientsin, 17th March, 1936

Ref. M-18003

Messrs. Tung Hsiang Yung,

TIENTSIN

Dear sirs,

    With reference to present upcountry glass sales, we find that from our existing f.o.c. prices at the undermentioned six stations, our return is unsatisfactorily low, and confirm, therefore, that our prices for 4th Quality Single Thickness in standard specification will be increased. The new prices, effective as from 1st of April, 1936, will be as unders:

F.O.C. Kaifeng Station,	Honan	$9.00 per unit
F.O.C. Chengchow Station,	Honan	$9.10 per unit
F.O.C. Loyang Station,	Honan	$9.30 per unit
F.O.C. Sian Station,	Shensi	$9.60 per unit
F.O.C. Yutse Station,	Shensi	$9.20 per unit
F.O.C. Taiyuanfu Station,	Shensi	$9.40 per unit

Yours faithfully,

G. H. Fawcett

TIENTSIN SALES OFFICE.

Copy to:- A.T.

       Ag. CWT.

译文：

　　　　　　　　　　待译成中文
　　　　　　　　　天津，1936年3月17日
　　　　　　　　　　编号：M-18003

致：天津的同祥涌玻璃庄

敬启者：
　　关于目前内陆玻璃的销售情况，从我们目前在以下六个站点的离岸价格来看，我们发现，我们的利润低得令人不满意。因此，我们确认，我们将提高标准规格的四等单厚玻璃的价格。从1936年4月1日起生效的新价格如下：

　　河南开封离岸价　　　　　每箱$9.00
　　河南郑州离岸价　　　　　每箱$9.10
　　河南洛阳离岸价　　　　　每箱$9.30
　　陕西西安离岸价　　　　　每箱$9.60
　　山西榆次离岸价　　　　　每箱$9.20
　　山西太原府离岸价　　　　每箱$9.40

　　　　　　　　　　　　　　　　谨启，
　　　　　　　　　　　　　　　　福西特
　　　　　　　　　　　　　　　天津销售部

抄送：总局
　　　秦皇岛销售处

M-18119

Tientsin Sales Office.

TIENTSIN.   Chinwangtao   19th March, 36

<u>GLASS SALES</u>

We are pleased to note from your letter M-18003 of 17/3/36 addressed to Messrs. Tung Hsiang Yung the increases you have effected to six up-country stations in his territory, and trust you are arranging to do likewise for Ta Tung, Feng Chen, Sui Yuan and Potou in the Peiping Agency area.

H. H. Faulkner

for AGENT.

译文：

M-18119

致：天津销售处

秦皇岛　　1936 年 3 月 19 日

玻璃价格

从 1936 年 3 月 17 日贵公司致同祥湧玻璃庄的编号为 M-18003 号信中获悉，贵公司已对其管辖内 6 个内地车站实施了涨价，相信贵公司也会对北平地区的大同、丰镇、绥远、包头采取同样的措施。

福克纳

PRIVATE AND CONFIDENTIAL

Chinwangtao.

27th March, 1936

M-18119.

G.H. Fawcett, Esq.

TIENTSIN.

Dear Fawcett,

GLASS PRICES

In your Monthly Report for January 1936, last paragraph narrative section, you state that "if we maintain our present Tientsin and up-country prices, sales of Shoko Glass will be eliminated when their present stocks are cleared, as $7.50 (Shoko cost price) cannot compete with $7.70 (Yao Hua gross price) under the present conditions."

I presume you mean by "Shoko cost price" the Shoko importer's selling price plus duty and all charges to ex-godown Tientsin with no allowance for dealer's rebates or profit? If such is the case, do you not think that our single thickness rate for standard specifications could stand increasing, say about the 1st May, when most of the Spring buying has been placed and there is no danger of losing forward booking to Shoko?

From your February Report I note that there were no imports of Shoko Glass during February, (but we have to thank the ice conditions for that) and that Shoko stocks at the end of the month were 6,200 cases. It would be interesting to know whether there have been any imports since the river opened, and if so were they transfers from Dairen to Mitsubishi's Tientsin godown stocks, or were they sales to dealers.

I am sure we will never be able to eliminate Shoko entirely out of the Tientsin proper markets as there will be always some demand from Japanese buyers: But if we can monopolise the interior trade we will be more than satisfied, and I think our present method of direct shipment is carrying us toward that goal.

Will you therefore kindly let me have your views regarding this matter of prices? I would also like to increase the 300 sq. ft. cases of strip glass to $19.50 per case. Will you please let me know if this can be done without killing the demand?

Yours sincerely,
H.H.Faulkner.

译文：

私人机密件

秦皇岛
1936年3月27日
M-18119

致：天津的福西特先生

亲爱的福西特：

玻璃价格

在您1936年1月月报的最后一段叙述部分中，您说："如果我们维持目前天津和内陆的价格，在'曙光'玻璃库存清仓后，我们就会停止销售该产品，因为在目前条件下，7.50美元（曙光玻璃成本价）无法与7.70美元（耀华毛价）相竞争。"

我想您说的"曙光玻璃成本价"是指曙光玻璃进口商的销售价加上关税和到天津仓库交货的所有费用，不包括经销商的回扣或利润吧？如果是这样的话，您认为我们标准规格的单厚玻璃率不会继续增加吧？比如在5月1日左右，那时春季采购的大部分货物都已订购完毕，订单无落入曙光玻璃之手之虞。

从您 2 月份的报告中，我注意到 2 月份无曙光玻璃进口（但我们得将此归功于结冰期的天气条件），而曙光玻璃该月底库存量为 6 200 箱。我很想知道开河后是否有曙光玻璃进口呢？如果有，它们是从大连转运到三菱的天津仓库交货，还是出售给经销商呢？

我相信我们永远不可能把曙光玻璃从天津的市场上根除，因为总会有一些日本买家对此有需求；但如果我们能继续垄断内陆贸易，我们就会非常满意。我认为我们目前的直接运输方式正带领我们朝着这个目标前进。

因此，请您谈谈您对这个价钱问题的看法好吗？我还想将 300 平方英尺的箱装条形玻璃每箱价格提至 19.50 美元。请告知我是否可以在不扼杀需求的情况下实现这一点。

谨上

福克纳

函电十三

TO BE TRANSLATED INTO CHINESE.

Tientsin, 28th March, 1936

Ref. M-18003

Messrs. Tung Hsiang Yung,

TIENTSIN

Dear sirs,

With reference to present upcountry glass sales, we find that from our existing f.o.c. prices at the undermentioned four stations, our return is unsatisfactorily low, and confirm, therefore, that our prices for 4th Quality Single Thickness in standard specification will be increased. The new prices, effective as from 1st of April, 1936, will be as unders:-

F.O.C. Tatung Station,	$8.60 per unit
F.O.C. FengChen Station,	$8.70 per unit
F.O.C. Suiyuan Station,	$9.00 per unit
F.O.C. Potou Station,	$9.20 per unit

Yours faithfully,

G. H. Fawcett

TIENTSIN SALES OFFICE.

Copy to:- Ag. CWT.
        A.T. TS.
        Mr. Chiu

译文：

待译成中文

天津，1936年3月28日
编号：M-18003

致：北平的天源泰玻璃庄

敬启者：

  关于目前内陆玻璃的销售情况，从我们目前在以下四个站点的离岸价格来看，我们发现，我们的利润低得令人不满意。因此，我们确认，我们将提高标准规格的四等单厚玻璃的价格。从1936年4月1日起生效的新价格如下：

大同离岸价	每箱$8.00
丰镇离岸价	每箱$8.70
绥远离岸价	每箱$9.00
包头离岸价	每箱$9.20

谨启，
福西特
天津销售部

抄送：秦皇岛代理处
   总局，天津销售处
   邱先生

函电十四

<u>TO BE TRANSLATED INTO CHINESE</u>

Tientsin, 1st April, 1936

Ref. No. 18068.

Messrs Tien Yuan Tai, PEIPING.

Dear Sirs,

In order to meet the competition of Vitrea Glass and Japanese mirrors, we wish to inform you that our prices of the undermentioned qualities and sizes of Yao Hua Glass will be revised with effect from to-day's date as follows:-

1. 4th Quality Extra Thick Glass Size 24"*18" only 26.00 per case of 100 sq.ft . F.O.C. Chienmen Station, Peiping.

2. 4th S'double Sizes 12"*8" and 10"*7" only 10.00 per case of 100 sq.ft. F.O.C. Chienmen Station, Peiping.

4th Double Sizes 12"*8" and 10"*7" only 12.00 per case of 100 sq. ft. F.O.C Chienmen Station, Peiping.

3rd S'double Sizes 12"*8" and 10"*7" only 10.50 per case of 100 sq.ft. F.O.C. Chienmen Station, Peiping.

3rd Double Sizes 12"*8" and 10"*7" only 13.00 per case of 100 sq.ft. F.O.C. Chienmen Station, Peiping.

Yours faithfully,

G. H. Fawcett

TIENTSIN SALES OFFICE.

Copy to：-

Agent, Chinwangtao.

AT.,T.S.

Mr. chiu（T.s.s.）

译文：

待译成中文

天津，1936年4月1日
编号：18068

平地区的天源泰

敬启者：
  为适应与维特利亚玻璃和日本镜子的竞争，我方望在此通知贵方，即日起我方将对以下质量和尺寸的耀华玻璃的价格作出以下调整：
  1. 四等加厚玻璃，尺寸为12"*8"，100平方英尺每箱仅售26洋元，北平前门交货价。
  2. 四等单双厚玻璃，尺寸为12"*8"和10"*7"，100平方英尺每箱仅售10洋元，北平前门交货价。
  四等双厚玻璃，尺寸为12"*8"和10"*7"，100平方英尺每箱仅售12洋元，北平前门交货价。
  三等单双厚玻璃，尺寸为12"*8"和10"*7"，100平方英尺每箱仅售10.50洋元，北平前门交货价。
  三等双厚玻璃，尺寸为12"*8"和10"*7"，100平方英尺每箱仅售13洋元，北平前门交货价。

天津经销部
福西特

抄给：
秦皇岛代理商
总局天津销售部
邱先生（天津销售商）

第五章
秦皇岛港藏"滦外档"耀华玻璃经销翻译及研究

第一节 秦港藏"滦外档"民国时期耀华英文档案中地名、人名、商号名的翻译规律

"滦外档"中涉及大量的地名、人名和玻璃商号名,这些名称的翻译和现在的拼音不甚相同,用的是威妥玛式拼音法(Wade-Giles romanization),该方法由英国人、剑桥大学教授、英国驻华公使威妥玛(Thomas F. Wade)首创,又称威妥玛—翟理斯式拼音,简称威氏拼音法。1867年,在英国使馆任中文秘书的威妥玛出版《语言自迩集》,其中以罗马字母为汉字注音,创立威氏拼音法。后来翟理斯(H. A. Giles)在其1912年出版的《华英字典》中,对威妥玛的标音系统又略加改良,形成了威妥玛—翟理斯式拼音。威氏拼音法是根据北京话读音,用拉丁字母给汉字注音的拼音方案。如:北京为 Peking,苏州为 Suchow,青岛为 Tsingtao,汉口 Hankow,贵州是 Kweichow,茅台是 Moutai,功夫是 Kungfu,太极是 Taichi,易经是 Ching,清明节是 Chingming Festival,毛泽东是 Mao Tsetung,蒋介石是 Chiang Kaishek,宋庆龄是 Soong Chingling,宋美龄是 Soong Mayling。

清末至1958年汉语拼音方案公布前,威氏拼音法是中国和国际上流行的中文拼音方案,被广泛地运用于邮政电信、海外图书馆中文藏书编目、外交护照之中文人名及地名的译音等。1958年《现代汉语拼音方案》公布以后,威氏拼音在中国大陆基本不再使用了,但一些在西方流传度很广的名字还保留着当时的叫法。为保证历史的延续性,少量享誉海内外的商标

至今仍旧使用威妥玛拼音法，如茅台（Moutai）、中华（Chunghwa）、张裕葡萄酒（Changyu）；像功夫（Kungfu）这样使用威妥玛拼音的专有名词已被吸纳为英文的外来语；某些历史名人的名字在西方学术界仍采用威妥玛拼音。

为了能准确地还原这些地名、人名和玻璃商号名，笔者总结了秦皇岛港藏"滦外档"中民国时期耀华英文档案中地名、人名、商号名的汉语拼音和威妥玛式拼音的转换规律。为了准确记录历史，笔者对其中的每一个玻璃商号的名字都做了详尽的历史考证。

（1）汉语拼音声母 q，一般英文写成 Ch，如：Chinwangtao（秦皇岛）、Chienmen（前门）、Ching Shun Ho（庆顺和）、Ching Yuan Teh（庆源德）、Chien Hsing Hou（乾兴厚）、Mr. Chiu（天源泰玻璃店的邱经理）；或英文写成 ts，如：Tsingtao（青岛）。

（2）汉语拼音声母 d，一般英文写成 t，如：Chinwangtao（秦皇岛）、Tsingtao（青岛）、TaTung（大同）、Teh Yuan Tai（德源泰）、Teh Sheng Heng（德盛恒）、Shantung（山东）、Ching Yuan Teh（庆源德）、Peitaiho（北戴河）。

（3）汉语拼音声母 j，一般英文写成 ts，如：Tientsin（天津）、Tsinanfu（济南府）；或英文写成 ch，如：Shihchiachuang（石家庄）、Li Shu Chih（李书吉）、Yi Hsing Yung Yuan Chi（义祥湧源记）。

（4）汉语拼音声母 b，一般英文写成 p，如：Peiping（北平）、Potou（包头）、Paodingfu（保定府）、Peitaiho（北戴河）。

（5）汉语拼音声母 x，一般英文写成 Hs，如：Tung Hsiang Yung（同祥湧玻璃庄）、Kuang Tai Hsiang（康泰祥）、HengYuan Hsiang（恒元祥）、Wen Hsiang Yung（文祥湧）；有时英文也写成 s，如：Sian（西安）、shansi（山西）。

（6）汉语拼音声母 zh，一般英文写成 ch，如：Chengchow（郑州）、Fengchen（丰镇）、Kuang Chu Cheng（康珠正）、Shihchiachuang（石家庄）、Wang Chanho（王占和）。

（7）汉语拼音韵母 an，一般英文写成 en，如：Tientsin（天津）、Tien Yuan Tai（天源泰）、Chienmen（前门）、Chien Hsing Hou（乾兴厚）。

（8）汉语拼音韵母 ou，英文有时写成 ow，如：Chengchow（郑州）；英文有时写成 ou，如：Heng Yee Hou（恒义厚）、Chien Hsing Hou（乾兴厚）、Potou（包头）。

（9）汉语拼音声母 c，一般英文写成 tz，如：Yutze（榆次）。

（10）汉语拼音韵母 ong，一般英文写成 ung，如：TaTung（大同）、Tung Hsiang Yung（同祥湧玻璃庄）、Mr. Sung（同祥湧玻璃庄的宋经理）、Shantung（山东）。

（11）汉语拼音声母 g，一般英文写成 k，如：Chao Sheng Kuan（朝胜关）、Shahhukwan（沙湖关）、Tongku（塘沽）、Mr. Kuo（华盛堂玻璃店的郭经理）、liu Ying Kwei（刘英贵）。

（12）汉语拼音韵母 i，一般英文写成 ee，如：Shun Tai Yee（顺泰义）、Heng Yee Hou（恒义厚）。

（13）汉语拼音韵母 e，一般英文写成 eh，如：Ching Yuan Teh（庆源德）、Teh Yuan Tai（德源泰）；有时也写成 o，如：Honan（河南）、Peitaiho（北戴河）、Wang Chanho（王占和）、Ching Shun Ho（庆顺和）。

（14）汉语拼音韵母 ao，英文可能写成 o，如：Potou（包头）；或可能写成 ao，如：Paodingfu（保定府）。

（15）汉语拼音韵母 uo，英文可能写成 o，如：Loyang（洛阳）；或英文写成 uo，如：Mr. Kuo（华盛同玻璃店的郭经理）。

（16）汉语拼音声母 l，一般英文写成 r，如：Dairen（大连）。

（17）汉语拼音韵母 ang，一般英文写成 ong，如：Tongku（塘沽）。

第二节　秦港藏"滦外档"民国时期耀华英文档案合同翻译中的时代特色

历史档案翻译不同于文学翻译，亦不同于科技翻译，往往需要综合上述二者的经验。不仅在内容上要做到客观、忠实原文，为了维持档案材料的原貌，还要尽量还原源语言所具有的时代特色，以使译文和原文发挥相同或相似的语言交际功能。历史档案翻译给译者留下的创作空间不大，反而对译者的知识面、责任心要求极高，要做到让译文既保留原意，又维持文体语气不变，同时还留有时代特色。五四前后，革新思潮澎湃，先进知识分子提出了"文学革命"的口号，提倡新文学，反对旧文学。新文学不是指新时期的文学，而是指新性质的文学，它的特点是文体是白话的，内容是新颖的，思想是革命的。语言是一种交流工具，白话文体现了语言与社会发展之间的相关性和互动性，充分体现了其作为交流工具的特质。因为是新的书面表达形式，人们在使用它时会时而和文言文混用，即文言文和白话文没有实现完全抽离，所以有一种"半文半白"的风格。这类文体既有文言的简洁、精练，又有白话的通俗、晓畅，特别适用于公私函电。下面以秦皇岛港藏"滦外档"之耀华玻璃经销合同中开滦矿务总局耀华机器制造玻璃有限公司与同祥湧玻璃庄1934年和1936年签订之合同以及开滦矿务总局耀华机器制造玻璃有限公司与北平地区经销商签订之合同为例，说明历史档案翻译如何保留时代特色。

一、"时间"翻译的时代特色

1934年1月18日开滦矿务总局耀华机器制造玻璃有限公司与同祥湧玻璃庄签订之合同：

前言英文：

> MEMORANDUM OF AGREEMENT made and entered into this 18th day of January 1934, at Tientsin, North China, between the Kailan Mining Administration, as General Managers of the Yao Hua Mechanical Glass Co.,Ltd., (hereinafter referred to as the Administration) of the one part and the Tung Hsiang Yung (hereinafter referred to as the Contractor) of the other part, WHEREBY it is mutually agreed:

前言中文：

> 本合同于中华民国二十三年一月十八日在华北天津订立。此造为经理耀华机器制造玻璃有限公司营业事宜之开滦矿物总局（此后称总局）彼造为同祥涌玻璃庄（此后称分销人），兹将两造之认可之条件列左。

合同前言中英文"18th day of January 1934"不能直译为一九三四年一月十八日，译为"中华民国二十三年一月十八日"更符合民国时期的语言特色。1911年，武昌起义推翻了清朝帝制，1912年，中华民国成立，开始使用中华民国纪年，故此处1934年译为中华民国二十三年更恰当。

二、词汇翻译的时代特色

（1）在以上合同前言中 the one part 译为"此造"，the other part 译为"彼造"，mutually 译为"两造"；合同第13条中"in the event of any dispute arising as to its interpretation, the English version shall be binding on both parties"译为"如有争执，两造应以英文为准"，此处的"both party"也译为"两造"，这样的翻译更符合民国时期语言的"半文半白"特点。在现代汉语词典中"造"的第3条含义为"指相对两方面的人，法院专用于诉讼的双方，如：两造，甲造"，故"此造"意为"此方"，"彼造"意为"彼方"，"两造"意为"双方"。笔者查阅了清朝祝庆祺著、2004年北京古籍出版社出版的半文半白著作《刑案汇览三编（全四卷）》，该书作为中国古代篇幅最大、涉及范围最广、分类最为详细的案例编纂类图书，由任职刑部两代老吏历时数十年精心编纂而成，其所具备的史料价值是弥足珍贵的。在这部著作的刑案汇览卷六十中，有如下表述"若两造情罪两不相侔如此造系干犯尊长不能宽减则彼造虽系寻常斗杀亦不准减死者与此造凶手并无服制则彼造死者虽系彼造凶手有服亲属亦不准减所以昭限制也如谓此造应抵彼造可减则设有此造殴死彼造二命而彼造殴死此造一命及此造故杀彼造一命而彼造斗杀此造一命之案亦将一抵一命有是理乎"。在现代汉语中合同的双方被称作甲方、乙方。但考虑到民国时期的语言时代特色，故将合同当事人译为"此造""彼造"和"两造"。

（2）在合同前言中"WHEREBY it is mutually agreed"译为"兹将两造之认可之条件列左"，这里的"whereby" 译为"左"，而不译为"下"。合同第 6 条中 "Should the amount of glass purchased by the Contractor during the period of this Contract exceed 50,000 standards, additional rebates will be given as detailed hereunder"，译为：分销人在本合同期限以内购买玻璃过单位数五万以上者期当照左开情形加给回用。此处的"hereunder"也译为"左"，不译为"下"。第 9 条中 "The definition or a 'Standard Specification' is as follows"，译为：兹将通常尺寸之意义解释列左。此处的"as follows"也译为"左"，不译为"下"。第 10 条中 "That for the purposes of the rebates set forth in Clause 6, the better qualities and heavier grades will be computed as follows"，译为：凡较佳及较重之玻璃当按左开办法计算第六条规定之回用。此处的"as follows"也译为"左"，不译为"下"。

中国传统的书写方式是竖向，且由右至左。清朝末年，一些知识分子学习西方文化，提倡汉字改革和拼音文字，力主改变传统书写方式，改用从左到右的"横行"排列方式。1909 年中国已有了"横行"排版的书，它就是提倡拼音文字改革的刘世恩写的《音韵记号》，但绝大部分人的书写和书籍的排版都是由右至左竖向排列的。中华人民共和国成立初期，时任教育部部长的郭沫若先生便向毛主席提议：改过去竖向的书写方式为横向书写方式，把从右往左改为从左往右。因为人的眼睛，左右转动所看到的角度和区域，要比上下转动所看到的角度和区域广阔得多，横着书写和看书会减轻眼睛的疲劳程度。1954 年的学生课本正式变为由左至右，由上到下。1955 年 10 月，教育部和文改会联合召开了全国文字改革会议，建议全国印刷品采用横写印刷。1955 年 1 月 1 日《光明日报》首先实现横排。1956 年 1 月 1 日,《人民日报》和地方报纸一律改为横排。因此民国二十三年的书写方式是竖向，且由右至左。故此处译为"兹将两造之认可之条件列左"。另如：民国时期保定一合资经营卷烟厂业务的合同中类似内容表述为"议定条件于左"，还有民国时期一份证券经纪人合同文书类似内容表述为"兹公共议定办法条列于左"。

（3）合同第 1 条中 "the Administration reserve the right to cancel forthwith this Contract, and withhold payment of any rebate outstanding"，译为"总局可立即取消本合同及停付未结清之回用"，此句中的"rebate"一词，根据民国时期语言的"半文半白"的时代特色，译为"回用"。回用，现代汉语中表述为佣金，即买卖货物时，中间人所得的酬劳。晚清文学家吴趼人创作的一部带有自传性质的长篇小说《二十年目睹之怪现状》，有一段这样描述："此时他更乐得拿腔了，说已经说煞了，挽回不明，必要三成回用。"而"佣金"和"回扣"则为现代汉语表达。

（4）在 1934 年 1 月 18 日开滦矿务总局耀华机器制造玻璃有限公司与同祥湧玻璃庄签订之合同，1936 年 1 月 1 日开滦矿务总局耀华机器制造玻璃有限公司与同祥湧玻璃庄签订之合同，以及 1936 年 1 月 1 日开滦矿务总局耀华机器制造玻璃有限公司与北平地区经销商签订之合同这三份合同落款处均有 "Witness to the signature of" 这样的表达，根据民国时期的语言特色，译为"在见人"，即合同中的"中人"。

在古代传统社会，契约不仅仅需要双方当事人的意思表示一致，还需要有第三人参与进来，中人在习惯法的维系与发展中扮演着重要的角色。订立契约后保障契约的履行，在很大程度上也依靠第三方"中人"的力量。契约中的中人，其称谓多种多样，有"凭中""凭证""中证""证人""凭中人""凭众""在见""见证""见议"等，他们在契约中所起的作用是基本相同的，都是以第三方证人的身份参加契约的签订，在契约成立过程中起直接见证者的作用。在传统中国民法不完善的情况下，需要借助人际关系来"评理"，主持公道。中人应当具有一定的社会地位、声望和影响力，并能够为双方所信服，在合同订立的过程中以及一方违约时能够从中调处。

（5）1936 年 1 月 1 日开滦矿务总局耀华机器制造玻璃有限公司与北平地区经销商签订之合同，第三条英文 "Each of the Dealers agrees to lodge with the Administration a first glass shop guarantee to the value of \$3,000"，译文为"经售人承认各兑价值三千元之一等铺保交与总局"。根据民国时期北京地区的特色，此处"shop guarantee"译为"铺保"。对于风险的承担,在开滦矿务总局耀华机器制造玻璃有限公司与北平地区经销商签订之合同中是以"铺保"的形式约定的。而在开滦矿务总局耀华机器制造玻璃有限公司与同祥涌在天津签订的两份合同中,并没有出现"铺保"一词,而是向总局交付三万元国币,作为对于各欠款之保证金。民国时期北京地区的工商业管理中铺保较为常见。它曾经广泛存在于老北京的借贷、租赁、买卖、学徒或店员入号等担保情事中,对老北京人或进京寻生计之人顺利地找到工作或生活起着十分重要的作用。但"铺保"一词现在北京的年轻人知之甚少,就连一些老年人也已淡忘或并不熟悉,甚至在今天的多数汉语词典、辞海、辞源等工具书中,我们也找不到"铺保"的踪影。旧时担保分人保与铺保。铺保在担保中的地位与作用优于人保,为交易的安全性提供了较为可靠的保障。所谓商业铺保,通常是指旧时以商号名义出具证明所做的担保,它广泛存在于诉讼、商业管理、宗教管理和市民经济交往等地方社会生活的实践中。一般要店铺出具保证书,并在保单上盖店铺的印章方为有效。从法律的角度看,商业铺保制度是一种人身担保和物质担保相结合的契约,它通过第三方的商业信誉和商业资本,保证当事方履行义务,否则商号按照约定履行债务或者承担相应的责任。铺保制度由来已久,至少在汉代,我国就已经出现最早的商业铺保形式,当时称之为"任者",唐代称为"保见",宋元时期将商业铺保和牙人合称为"牙保",明清时期则称为"中保"。从北京的史料看,早在明朝年间的行业碑刻中,就有"保"的字样出现,在明清地方史志文献和档案资料中,也有多种商业铺保的说法,如:"铺保""庙保""中保""具保人""铺伙""铺户"和"伙友"等。民国北京商业铺保制度的形式有:工商业管理铺保、诉讼责任担保、宗教管理铺保、信贷风险铺保、学徒铺保。铺保所承担的责任可以分为监督责任、偿付责任和中介责任。当然,这种划分并不是绝对的和孤立的,一些铺保常常肩负两种甚至三种担保的责任。民国时期的北京城正处在现代化的转型过程中,商业铺保深深地融入了北京地方社会,在经济、社会和法律生活中发挥着独特的作用。

三、同素异序词翻译的时代特色

合同第 1 条英文：

> In the event of the Contractor being no interested directly or indirectly in the sale and/or purchase of any articles or commodities competing with the products of the Yao Hua Mechanical Glass Co.,Ltd., the Administration reserve the right to cancel forthwith this Contract, and withhold payment of any rebate outstanding.

合同第 1 条中文：

> 分销人有直接或间接买卖与耀华玻璃公司产品对竞之货物情事，总局可立即取消本合同及停付未结清之回用。

合同第 2 条英文：

> Should he for any reason be unwilling to transact business with an individual or individuals, he will report the circumstances to the Administration with full explanation, and the Administration reserve the right to undertake the business subject to Clause 7 of this Agreement.

合同第 2 条中文：

> 如对某某有不愿与之交易情事，应将事实详细向总局述明，总局依据各本合同第七条之规定有办理此项业务之权。

此处第 1 条中的"in the event of"和第 2 条中的"business"按照民国时期的语言时代特色，译为"情事"，而不是现代汉语中的"事情"，二者意思相同，这样的词汇叫作同素异序词。更多的同素异序词，如：演讲—讲演、寻找—找寻、力气—气力、悲伤—伤悲、叫喊—喊叫、牵挂—挂牵、感情—情感、觉察—察觉、声名—名声、代替—替代、粮食—食粮、积累—累积、救援—援救、到来—来到、康健—健康、询问—问询、整齐—

齐整、奋发—发奋、寂静—静寂、夜半—半夜、羊羔—羔羊、开放—放开、焰火—火焰等。在词语发展过程中，由于词汇处于不稳定状态之中，所以出现了许多同素异序词，尤其是民国时期。比如老舍先生用过的同素异序词有：限制—制限，玩赏—赏玩，灵魂—魂灵，地道—道地，尝试—试尝等。有时老舍先生颠倒字序来满足用韵需求，如：运输—输运，心腹—腹心，光荣—荣光，声响—响声，凄惨—惨凄，合适—适合等。当五四白话文运动轰轰烈烈展开之时，一大批同样出色的文人也和老舍一样在尝试着语言的创新，并推动着现代汉语词汇的完善。异序词的使用，可以看作是此时期一个典型的语言现象，许多作家也都不同程度地使用异序词。比如鲁迅先生曾使用过语言—言语，痛苦—苦痛等。这些同素异序词，有的仅仅在此时期使用，使用频率低，在现代汉语口语中几乎已经不再使用了，有的在现代汉语中依然使用。

四、货币翻译的时代特色

合同第 4 条英文：

> That the Contractor shall provide security against sums due to the Administration in the form of a cash deposit of Thirty Thousand Chinese Standard Dollars (c.s.$30,000) whereon the Administration will credit the Contractor's account with interest calculated at 6% per annum.

合同第 4 条中文：

> 分销人尤备中国国币三万元交付总局，作为对于各欠款之保证金。总局尤按年息六厘付息计入分销人账内。

此处的"Thirty Thousand Chinese Standard Dollars (c.s.$30,000)"根据民国时期的货币流通情况，译为"国币三万元"。另外。1936 年 1 月 1 日开滦矿务总局耀华机器制造玻璃有限公司与同祥湧玻璃庄签订之合同的第 6 条"That the administration agrees to grant the Contractor an initial rebate or 35 cents per standard on all glass purchased by him up to the guaranteed minimum of 60,000 standards."译为"总局承认对于分销人购买各种玻璃，遇其担保之至少数量六万箱时，每箱给予最初回用洋三角五分"，此处的"35 cents"译为"洋三角五分"。

民国时期各地政府更迭频繁，银行等金融单位缺乏统一的管理，发行的货币也多种多样。庚子后，银元在全国范围内取代了清朝使用的铜钱和元宝，但各地银行发行的钱币制式不尽相同，这些不同的银元同时流通。20世纪20年代邮政系统英文文件中常出现的就有 Peking Dollar、Shanghai Dollar、Canton Dollar，这些货币不能按照今天的语言习惯直译为北京元、上海元等，应按照当时中文的官称统一将 Dollar 译为"银元"，即北京银元、上海银元、广东银元。在香港流通的货币更为复杂，包括 Hongkong Dollar（香港银元）、Rupee（印度卢比）、Gold Dollars（联邦金币）、Straits Dollar（叻币）、Sterling（英镑）等。其中叻币为马来西亚、新加坡与文莱等地在被英国殖民的时期，由当时的叻屿呷政府发行的货币。联邦金币也是美国在1849—1889年暂时发行的一种美元金币。这两种货币都已退出历史舞台，译者只有不厌其烦地多方查证才能保证译文准确，符合时代语境。

五、合同文本体例、行文和用语的时代特色

综合三份合同：1934年1月18日开滦矿务总局耀华机器制造玻璃有限公司与同祥涌玻璃庄签订之合同，1936年1月1日开滦矿务总局耀华机器制造玻璃有限公司与同祥涌玻璃庄签订之合同，以及1936年1月1日开滦矿务总局耀华机器制造玻璃有限公司与北平地区经销商签订之合同的文书，能看出民国时期的合同文书与清代相比，在体例、行文和用语上均发生了变化，表现了社会变革、人际交往和商务合同中人与人的关系发生的深刻变化。在分析之前，须先厘清"合同"和"契约"的概念。契约又称契，广义是指立约各方一定的权利义务，狭义是指当事人之间关于民事关系的协议。契约在我国商周的青铜器铭文中已普遍存在。

《周礼·秋官·朝士》中有"判书"一词，贾公彦疏："之判，半分而会者，即质剂传别分支合同，两家各得其一者也。"将各方商定的权利义务各书一份，待有需要时双方将之前所书权利义务取出，合而同之，以资判别。至清代，无论是从形制（一式一份或一式多份）还是从当事人具体关系的性质上区分，"契约"与"合同"在外延上都是包含关系，"合同"是"契约"的一种。契（约）包含单契和合同，单契以田房买卖、典、租佃、借贷为主要内容。合同以分家析产、祖产管理、换产、合伙为主要内容。

这三份合同的文书特点如下。

（1）去掉了合同文本对人际互信的表述。在清代契约中，开头多有"知契同心""管鲍信胜"之类的表述，强调立约人之间的意见一致和互相信任。本书所举民国时期的三份合同与之相比，此类表述几乎没有，没有强调彼此间的信任关系。

（2）对立约人的要求更加具体、规范。清代合同在正文中常有对立约人尽职尽责的要求，对盈亏的分担要求，但表述比较抽象笼统，没有具体的行为规范和处理办法，指向道德层面，缺乏可操作性。例如"务宜尽心竭力，不得各存私心，如有此情，神灵鉴察，亏折盈余各安天命。岁首盈结公品公支"；"全始而全终，经营惘懈。愿协心而协力，正直无私"；"倘年景不济，或有亏本，亦财运使然，毋得别生异言"。本文所举三份合同中没有涉及道德精神层面的要求，但作出了具体的操作规范。对于利润分享、损失承担、风险处置均有较为详细的条款。如利润分享分别列于1934年1月18日和1936年1月1日开滦矿务总局耀华机器制造玻璃有限公司与同祥湧玻璃庄签订之合同的第6条，以及1936年1月1日开滦矿务总局耀华机器制造玻璃有限公司与北平地区经销商签订之合同的第9条中；损失承担分别列于1934年1月18日和1936年1月1日开滦矿务总局耀华机器制造玻璃有限公司与同祥湧玻璃庄签订之合同的第4条、第8条，以及1936年1月1日开滦矿务总局耀华机器制造玻璃有限公司与北平地区经销商签订之合同的第3条中；风险处置分别列于1934年1月18日和1936年1月1日开滦矿务总局耀华机器制造玻璃有限公司与同祥湧玻璃庄签订之合同的第 14 条，以及 1933 年 1 月 1 日开滦矿务总局耀华机器制造玻璃有限公司与北平地区经销商签订之合同的第 11 条中。

（3）与传统的契约相比，去掉了合同结尾处的"恐后无凭""永远存照"之类的程式化表述。在清代的各类契约中，在正文末尾一般要写明"恐后无凭，立此存照"之类的话。这种表述虽为套话，但在当时并非没有意义，具有"结信"和"止讼"的作用。这些套话强调了文件的重要性和效力。然而随着现代化进程的推进，商事法规陆续颁布，法治意识渐入人心。北洋政府于 1914 年颁布了《公司条例》。法律对于商事合同的设立、违约等已作出了较为明确的规定。合同文本只需写明要件，它的效力不需要自我强调，而是来自法律。另外，这也表明随着商品经济发展，商务活动日益增多，自愿订立契约、自觉履行契约的意识越来越深入人心，无须在契约中赘述合同效力。

第三节 秦港藏"滦外档"民国时期耀华英文档案中地名的考证

秦皇岛港藏"滦外档"中民国时期耀华英文档案中出现了大量的地名，地名的拼写虽然采用的是威妥玛式拼音法，但大多数地名能猜测出来。但有些地名的威妥玛式拼音与现在的汉语拼音相去甚远，如：Kalgan（张家口）、Cherfoo（烟台）。有的地名或行政区划已被撤销，现代人们已不甚熟悉，但在档案中多次提到，历史上也有着重要的商贸地位，如：Feng Chen（丰镇）、Sui Yuan（绥远）等。因此，笔者对这些重要的地名做了历史考证。

一、张家口（Kalgan）

Kalgan 是蒙古语，即汉语中地名"张家口"，意为"关卡""边境"或"货物买卖的口子"。张家口的英文今名是汉语拼音 Zhangjiakou，《大英百科全书》（Encyclopaedia Britannica）是英文百科全书的传统权威，其所收录的张家口，目前用的还是旧称 Kalgan。若以今名 Zhangjiakou 搜索，《大英》返回的也是 Kalgan，可见这个旧称在西方学术界的地位。俄语和其他斯拉夫语也用 Kalgan 来指称张家口。《大英百科全书》对张家口的定义如下：Kalgan, the name by which the city is most commonly known, is from a Mongolian word meaning "gate in a barrier" or "frontier"。1908 年上海商务印书馆出版的《英华大辞典》和 1911 年出版的《英汉辞典》中，张家口一词的对照词条也都是"KALGAN"。

有学者认为，Kalgan 这个名称，是蒙古语指称的大境门，如图 5-1 所示，后经语义扩展，成了整个张家口的代名词。大境门是古代屏障汉蒙边境的城门，是长城内外交通要道上的关卡，也是清政府所设的陆上通商口岸，是汉蒙贸易的商品集散地。大境门是中国万里长城众多关隘中一个十分特殊的关口。在国内外学术界已被列入与山海关、居庸关、嘉峪关同样重要的关口。我国万里长城的关口都以"关""口"称谓，而只有张家口的这个关口被称作"境门"，其中即包含着"商文化"和"武文化"的魅力，也流淌着民族融合的历史渊源。"关"和"口"意味着战争和防御，而"门"恰恰是开放的、积极拓展的，这也正是大境门自身具备的独特魅力。"境门"是指边境之门。从公元 1571 年起，张家口大境门外元宝山一带，逐渐形成了在历史上被称为"贡市"和"茶马互市"的边贸市场。来自蒙古草原和欧洲腹地的牲畜、皮毛、药材、毛织品、银器等在这里被换成了丝绸、茶叶、瓷器和白糖，大境门外成为我国北方国际易货贸易的内陆口岸。封建王朝以长城和门为界，做生意的外族人只能在城外交易。当时，在长城脚下，在大境门内外，店铺林立，牛马驼成群，各类货物堆积如山。此地也被称为"路陆商埠""皮都"，著名的张库商道的集散点就是大境门。甚至到 19 世纪末，张家口依然十分繁华，贸易额曾达到 1.5 亿两白银。由于张库大道的繁荣，1909 年清朝政府把中国第一条实用铁路"京张铁路"从北京修至张家口。

大境门街景市场、大境门外滩市场中进行羊只交易的商人如图 5-2、图 5-3 所示。

图 5-1 大境门

图 5-2 大境门街景市场

图 5-3 在大境门外滩市场中进行羊只交易的商人

但是大境门建于公元 1644 年，如前文所说大批蒙古人来张家口其实并不始于清初，而始于明朝隆庆、万历年间。1571 年明蒙议和，张家口成为长城一线最大的马市，马市举办期间，成千上万的蒙古人来到张家口。那时的蒙古人怎样称呼张家口呢？如果也称张家口为 kalgan，那就说明 Kalgan 实际所指并非大境门，而是小境门。

台湾中国文化大学金荣华先生所撰写的《张家口和北方丝茶之路》一文中，有如下记载：1618 年 5 月，俄国派出裴特林出使中国，历时四个月，经张家口到达北京。在裴特林的出使报告里写道："穿过（长城）城墙的边界后，就进入中国城市锡喇喀勒噶（译注：即张家口市，此从蒙古语译）。"艾梅霞女士在《茶叶之路》一书中也写道："张家口这个城市的蒙古名字是 kalgan，最早则叫 chuulalthaalga，意思是聚集之门，至今内蒙古的蒙古族人仍然这么称呼。"因此，虽然锡喇喀勒噶这个译名与后来的 kalgan 虽稍有不同，但其实为同一个名字。张家口地方文史学者一般都认为，小境门最晚与来远堡同时建筑，即最晚建于 1613 年，也很有可能建于 1571 年明朝与鞑靼部实现和议之时。由此说明 kalgan 最初所指为小境门。

因此准确说来 kalgan 之名的发端应该是西境门（小境门）和后来的大境门，西境门和大境门的文化内涵，就是 kalgan 的文化定位。

汉语"张家口"之名始于明代，明朱棣迁都北京后，为充实京畿人口，巩固边防，增加兵源，有计划地从山西人员稠密的县区移民到直隶一带。在北部边疆地区，由官方修建长城，在宣化、张家口一带，筑起驻军城堡。这些军堡中，就有始建于 1429 年的张家堡，是张家口城市的发祥地。张家堡由驻军指挥官张文所建，故名张家堡。后来公元 1529 年，当地守备张珍在北城墙开一小门，因门小如口，是方方正正的"口"字型，加上又是由张珍开筑，两人都是张姓，所以就把"张家堡"改成了"张家口"。后来"张家口"名称内涵和外延不断扩大，变成了现在的区域名称。

二、烟台（Chefoo）

前文提到威妥玛式拼音法和现在的汉语拼音虽然拼写有所不同，但是在发音上，这些英文名字听起来和原名差不太多。但是有一座城市。他的英文发音和汉语差距很大，那就是烟台（Chefoo），这与它的汉语名称的演变有关系。

"Chefoo"之名，旧时是烟台的英文名称，因烟台旧称芝罘，至今一些国家的海图上标注烟台依旧是"Chefoo"。

烟台之名见之于史籍最早叫"转附"（见《孟子·正义》），从秦朝到清朝则称为"之罘"，后改"芝罘"。从行政组织上讲，明清两朝的地方组织结构为县、保、社、村四级，现烟台市芝罘区当时为福山县东北保芝罘社和奇山社。可见，"芝罘"这个名字从古到今中国人使用了 2 000多年，到了近代，当外国人到了芝罘之后，根据中文的音译拼为英语的"Chefoo"。

"烟台"之名，相对于"芝罘"而言则年轻得多了。公元 1398 年，明政府在现芝罘区内设"奇山守御千户所"屯兵设防，守军在海边一个叫"北熨斗山"的小山上设墩台狼烟，以为传讯之用，当地民众称为"烟台"，将小山称为"烟台山"，其后相当长一段时间"烟台"一词只是一个地理标志物，并不是一个行政机构名。

到 1908 年福山县废保社，全县划为 20 个区，现芝罘区范围内设置了三个区：芝罘区、奇山区和烟台商埠区，直到这时"烟台"作为一级行政组织才名列册籍。1913 年又被称为"福山县烟台特别警察区"，1934 年成为山东省直辖的"烟台特别行政区"，1938 年日军侵占烟台后改为烟台市，1945 年烟台解放后一直设市，1983 年地改市，原烟台市域再叫"芝罘区"。

需要特别指出的是：尽管有了"烟台特别行政区""烟台市"的名号，"Chefoo"这个名字还是沿用了很长时间。如：1968 年中国人民解放军总参谋部批准烟台港实行单航次对外开放时，当时的"烟台外轮理货公司"所用的对外文件仍将"烟台"译为"Chefoo"。1973 年烟台港、中央军委批准为对外开放港口后的几年间对外文件仍将"烟台"译为"Chefoo"，直到 20 世纪 70 年代末才统一译为"Yantai"。

第四节　秦港藏"滦外档"民国时期耀华玻璃经销英文档案中"退旧税"的考证

在前面第四章开滦矿务总局耀华公司玻璃经销部门间备忘录三十六和部门间备忘录三十七中，天津销售处的福西特与秦皇岛经理处的福克纳三次讨论了"退旧税"的问题。其中 1936 年 4 月 7 日福西特致福克纳的备忘录中如此记录：

Replying to your letter M-18119 of 27th March, I confirm that the "Shoko Cost Price" is the importer's selling price plus duty and all charges to ex-godown Tientsin with no allowance for dealers' rebates or profit. This cost price, for future suppliers, is calculated to be as under:-	
C.I.F. Tientsin	per case $5.70
Import Duty and Charges　G.U. 1.1479 $227	2.61
	$8.31
Refund of old duty	.86
	$7.45
Unloading charges, etc., say	.05
Nett cost ex godown	$7.50

译为：

关于您 3 月 27 日编号为 M-18119 的来信，兹确认"曙光玻璃成本价"是进口商的销售价格加上关税和到天津仓库交货的所有费用，不包括经销商的回扣或利润。本成本价对未来供应商的计算方法如下：

天津到岸价	每箱 5.70 美元
进口关税及费用- G.U. 1.1 479 $227	2.61
	（共）8.31 美元
退还旧税	.86
	（剩）7.45 美元
如：卸货费用等	.05
仓库交货净价	7.50 美元

这里第一次提到了"Refund of old duty"（退旧税），每箱曙光玻璃退还旧税 0.86 洋元。紧接着在 4 月 8 日福克纳追问福西特："I agree with all your suggestions, but would like to know what the 'refund of the old duty' is."（我同意你所有的建议，但是我想知道什么是"退旧税"。）在 4 月 9 日福西特回复福克纳：

> The explanation of "Refund of old duty" is as follows:-
> Originally, when Shoko Glass was imported for the dealers, the liability for payment of the duty thereon was accepted by Mitsubishi. When, however, the new scale of duties came into force, Mitsubishi would only agree to pay at the old rate; hence the dealers themselves now pay the full duty (at the new rate) and receive from Mitsubishi a "Refund of old duty"- i.e. the amount which would have been payable at the old rate.

译为：

关于"旧税退款"的解释如下：

最初，经销商进口曙光玻璃时，三菱公司接受了支付相关关税的责任。然而，当新的关税表生效时，三菱只同意按旧的税率支付；因此，现在经销商自己支付全部的关税（按新的税率），然后从三菱那里获得"旧税退款"——即按旧税率应支付的金额。

考证：这里"退旧税"是在关税提高的前提下发生的。市场发展的基本条件是物畅其流，而流通领域的各种苛捐杂税则是商品营销的障碍，因而也是制约市场发展的重要因素。据考证，民国以后，在征税方面大多数的企业都不再享有以前政府给予的"待遇"，有时候不仅政府的保护支持没有了，还受到军阀和政府的税负加征，各类企业不得不疲于应付，或忍气吞声。一旦时局不稳、政局不宁、战事四起，各路军阀和政府部门为了军费开销和办公经费就会不顾中央政府的政令，私自设立各种名目，巧取豪夺，企业不得不多方寻求帮助，想方设法消除各种不必要的税务负担。这些税额的征收，从征收主体看，均属于地方行为；从征收的税种看，既有附加税、营业税，又有出品税、牌照税，内容丰富，比例不等。

不过在国家层面，当时的政府还是积极为企业发展创造了不少税收优惠条件，如提高关税比率。国民政府决定从1930年1月1日起，"进口货颁行新税一种，计外国敌货进口税十八年颁定应纳海关银五钱二分，每箱者现已改按金单位征收，计每箱应纳关税金元九角一分，外国玻璃每箱新税征收海关金元九角七分，若按银价流通，玻璃进口税以现时与上年此时相较，每箱计增加天津大洋七角三分"。增加税负的地区不仅限于天津一处，1930年9月奉天地方收税所开始加征货物进口税，征税基数上调，遭殃者不仅耀华一家，昌光玻璃估价每箱由原来的大洋四元增加至大洋六元，耀华玻璃则由原来的五元增至七元，之后则按此项基数缴纳地方营业税。1935年6月间，国民政府原本拟修改税则，以期保护本国工商业，但是汪精卫害怕国际指责，影响外交，主张普遍增加，大约按照附加税办法加征10%。

第五节　秦港藏"滦外档"民国时期耀华英文档案中"Shoko""昌光"和"Vitrea"的考证

在秦皇岛港藏"滦外档"民国时期耀华英文档案中提及Shoko玻璃的有20份文件72次，列举如下：

第一份文件是1934年12月29日：

It was because of our ability to compete with the Shoko glass and control the market price.

译文：这是因为我们有能力与曙光玻璃竞争，并控制市场价格。

On account of sharp competition with the Shoko glass, our profits are entirely sacrificed in these recent two years.

译文：由于与曙光玻璃的激烈竞争，近两年我们的利润亏损殆尽。

第二份是1935年1月3日：

Tientsin local sales.

We think an increase in commission for Tientsin sales should be dependent upon Tung Hsiang Yung being able to arrange for the Shoko dealers to cooperate with them and the amount of commission necessary to secure this cooperation. We presume 1.5 % to 2% would be sufficient for this.

译文：

天津本地销售

我们认为，天津销售佣金的增加应取决于同祥湧玻璃庄能否安排曙光玻璃经销商与他们合作，以及足够确保这种合作所需的佣金。我们推测1.5%到2%足矣。

第三份文件是1935年1月28日：

> According to him, the Mitsubishi people are making strong efforts to interest some of the Peiping dealers in selling Shoko glass, offering to quote the same price for Shoko as Yaohua glass and in addition to give a rebate of 5% to the dealers. An independent investigation carried out by us confirms that attempts are being made to put Shoko glass on the Peiping market, but we are unable to confirm whether the rebates offered for this business are as stated by the Peiping dealer. The attitude of Tien Yuan Tai was that he was not asking for a price reduction or for a rebate, but he considered that unless we did something we must face the possibility of some of our dealers going over to Shoko. We therefore consider that we should take immediate steps to prevent this happening.
>
> His idea is that we should keep our price unchanged, but should give Peiping dealers a commission of 5% on their sales. He maintained that this would suffice to keep the combine together, and that as soon as the Shoko overtures have been definitely rejected, we could recoup ourselves by increasing the Peiping price.
>
> Without committing ourselves we suggested that if any rebate was granted, it should be on a sliding scale basis and in accordance with quantity sold in a similar manner as that of Tientsin, but Tien Yuan Tai considered that

> would not be satisfactory.
>
> We believe that, on the whole, the position as outlined by Tien Yuan Tai is correct and that it would probably pay us to keep the combine in being and Shoko glass off the market even if we have to give some kind of rebate. Once Shoko Glass is sold in quantity on the market, it will be difficult to revert to the former conditions and undoubtedly by price cutting, etc.. We should lose considerably. We therefore recommend a) that we offer a flat 3% commission to Peiping dealers or b) that we offer them a rebate increasing up to 5% in accordance with quantities sold.

译文：

据他说，三菱公司的人正在大力吸引北平的一些经销商销售曙光玻璃，条件是曙光玻璃的报价与耀华玻璃持平，此外还可以给经销商5%的佣金。我们进行的独立调查证实，有人正试图将曙光玻璃投放到北平市场。但我们无法确认为这项业务提供的返利是否如北平经销商所言。天源泰的态度是他并不要求我们降价或给佣金，但他认为，除非我们采取行动，否则我们必须面对一些经销商转向曙光玻璃的可能性。因此，我们认为应该立即采取措施，防止这种情况发生。

他的想法是，我们应该保持我们的价格不变，但应该给北平的经销商们提供5%的销售佣金。他坚持认为，这些将足以使经销商联合组织团结一心，而且，一旦曙光玻璃的提议被明确拒绝，我们就可以通过提高北平的价格来收回成本。

我们建议，在不作出承诺的条件下，如果给予任何返利，应该以递增佣金为基础，以类似天津的做法，根据销售数量返利，但天源泰认为这不会令人满意。

我们认为，总体而言，天源泰的观点是正确的，即使我们不得不给予某种形式的返利，只要能够保住经销商联合组织，让曙光玻璃退出市场，这就很有可能会给我们带来好处。一旦曙光玻璃在市场上大量销售，就很难恢复到以前的局面，而且无疑要通过降价等方式来收拾局面。我们应该会有很大的损失。因此，我们建议：a）我们向北平的经销商提供统一的

3%的佣金，或者 b）我们根据销售数量将给他们的返利增加至 5%。

第四份文件是 1935 年 3 月 6 日：

If we can give a contract to them, they mill cease to sell Shoko glass and sell ours instead.

译文：如果我们能与他们签订合同，他们就会停止销售曙光玻璃，转而销售我们的玻璃。

In the past three years, glass sales made by Messrs. Tung Hsiang Yung have gradually diminished. On the other hand, those dealing in Shoko glass have increased their sales by leaps and bounds. The reason is that the said Tung Hsiang Yung refuse to associate with the local dealers with the result that they have been completely isolated. There is no wonder that Yao Hua glass has been seriously affected by the Shoko glass competition.

译文：

在过去三年中，同祥湧玻璃庄的玻璃销售额逐渐减少。另一方面，他们对曙光玻璃的销售额大幅增长。原因是同祥湧拒绝与当地经销商联合，结果他们被完全孤立。难怪耀华玻璃受到了曙光玻璃销售竞争的严重影响。

第五份文件是 1935 年 3 月 15 日：

It is stated that sales of Shoko Glass have increased by "leaps and bounds". Sales of Shoko increased by 1,200 standards during 1934, but the information at our disposal shows that this was primarily due to the attractive prices quoted and the better condition of the glass market, rather than to any lack of energy on the part of our dealer.

With regard to Hua Sheng Tung, it is true this concern was a considerable business in Shoko Glass, but it is hardly correct to state that they control Sales of this Glass. They are some of a combine of 8 dealers selling this glass and they were actually out of the market for some months last year owing to a lawsuit between themselves and the other Shoko dealers who claimed they had infringed their agreement by importing Soviet Glass without the cognisance of the rest of the combine. Hua Sheng Tung lost the case and had to pay the costs and compensation before being readmitted into the combine.

We have no idea what quantity of Yao Hua Glass Hua Sheng Tung could sell if appointed our contractor, but we consider it highly unlikely that this action would result in a cessation of Shoko sales, since this obviously cannot be arranged without the agreement of the Japanese themselves. The defection of a Shoko dealer or dealers would only result in others being appointed.

译文：

据称，曙光玻璃的销量"突飞猛进"。1934 年，曙光玻璃的销售额增加了 1 200 标准件，但我们掌握的信息表明，这主要是由于报价吸引人，以及玻璃市场状况较好，而不是因为我们的经销商没有尽力。

关于华盛堂，确实我们担心它与曙光玻璃有大量销售业务，但说他们控制了整个曙光玻璃的销售是不正确的。他们只是和其他 7 家销售商联合起来组成一个商会销售曙光玻璃，去年他们实际上已经退出了市场几个月，由于他们和其他曙光玻璃经销商之间的诉讼，其他经销商声称华盛堂违反了他们的协议，在没有其他经销商的许可的情况下进口了苏联玻璃。华盛堂败诉，在交了赔偿金之后才被重新纳入商会。

如果指定华盛堂为我们的销售承包商，我们不知道耀华玻璃能卖出去多少，但我们认为这一行为不太可能导致曙光玻璃销售的停止，因为没有日本人自己的同意，这显然是无法安排的。一个或几个曙光玻璃经销商的退出只会导致其他人被任命。

第六份文件是 1935 年 4 月 3 日：

However before giving these prices to Messrs.Tung Hsing Yung We suggest you obtain some idea of the costs of delivering to these points by the present via Tientsin method for both shoko and our own glass.

译文：

不过，在把这些价格告诉同祥湧玻璃庄之前，我们建议你先了解一下经由天津的曙光玻璃和我们自己的耀华玻璃目前交货到这些地点的成本。

第七份文件是 1935 年 5 月 9 日：

I now enclose a statement showing the F.O.C. to Tung Hsiang Yung and Shoko dealers costs of glass at inland centres as compared with the proposed direct shipment costs given by you and the reported selling prices at inland towns.

译文：

现随函附上一份报表，说明给同祥湧玻璃庄的离岸价和给内陆中心的曙光玻璃公司经销商的成本价，以和贵方提出的直接运输成本及报告记载的内陆城镇售价作比较。

第八份文件是 1935 年 7 月 12 日：

Mr Sung has requested us to obtain for him f.o.c. prices at Shihchiachwang and Taiyuanfu and reports that in the latter town competition from Shoko glass is at the moment very keen.

译文：

宋先生要求我们为他索取石家庄和太原府的离岸价，并报告说，在太原府，目前与曙光玻璃的竞争非常激烈。

第九份文件是 1935 年 7 月 13 日：

Now, we are in receipt of letters from those dealers who have most of your goods, saying that the prices fixed by you are higher than the selling price ruling at the sport. The reason is that the price of Shoko Glass is cheaper and the price of your glass shipped from Shanghai to the districts is also cheaper than that shipped from Tientsin.

We are hereby asking you to devise way and means without delay so as to compete with the Shoko Glass, as it would otherwise not only affect the sales of your goods, but we shall also sustain a heavy loss.

译文：

现在，我们收到了那些拥有贵方大部分货物的经销商的来信，他们说贵方所定的价格高于本地区规定的售价。原因是曙光玻璃的价格比较便宜，贵方从上海到各区的玻璃价格也比从天津到各区的便宜。

我们在此要求你们尽快设计出与曙光玻璃竞争的方法，否则不仅会影响你们的销售，我们也将蒙受重大损失。

第十份文件是 1935 年 7 月 16 日：

This is first information we have had of Shoko being able to load 350 cases to the 20-ton carload, and we would like you to investigate in Tientsin as according to the railway regulations here we are allowed 16 cases to the ton only.

译文：

我们得到的第一条消息是旭硝子公司用火车装载 350 箱玻璃，总运载量达到了 20 吨，我们希望您能在天津进行深入调查，因为根据这里的铁路规定，每吨只允许装 16 箱玻璃。

第十一份文件是 1935 年 8 月 9 日：

We are, however, rather satisfied with our present total annual sales results so far as the present adverse business condition is concerned. But the business of this year has been prosperous. Kalgan has been put under the control of Peiping, most of the Shantung ports under Tsingtao, the interior of Honan has been affected by Shanghai, and the district of Tientsin by Shoko Glass.

译文：

然而，就目前不利的商业情况而言，我们对目前的全年总销售业绩还是相当满意的。但今年的生意很兴隆。张家口的业务归属于北平，山东大部分港口的业务归属于青岛，河南的内陆业务被上海所控制，天津地区业务被曙光玻璃所控制。

第十二份文件是 1935 年 10 月 24 日：

With reference to my letter No.18119 of yesterday's date and your telegram No.180 of even date, will you please keep me informed regarding any increase in Shoko's quotations as a result of the fall in silver.

译文：

关于我昨天第 18119 号信和您同日第 180 号电报，如果曙光玻璃公司因银价下跌而报价增加，请随时通知我。

第十三份文件是 1935 年 11 月 8 日：

I consulted with Mr. Chilton on this point and in our opinion we considered this the best policy to adopt having regard to the future of our sales in Tientsin, and our desire to strengthen his hand against the Shoko.

译文：

在这一点，我和齐尔顿先生商量过，我们认为，考虑到我们在天津市场的未来，以及我们想要加强他的力量来让他对抗曙光玻璃，这是我们能采取的最好的办法了。

第十四份文件是 1936 年 2 月 20 日：

I understand that at certain points Yao Hua glass is subjected to certain provincial taxes that are not levied on the Shoko, but it seems to me that our prices could go up and still meet Shoko competition from Tientsin. This particularly applies to the stations under the Peiping area.

译文：

我理解"耀华玻璃"受某些省份税收的影响，而这些税是不向"曙光"玻璃征收的。但在我看来，我们的价格可以上涨，而且依然面临着来自天津方面的"曙光"玻璃的竞争。北平片区的销售站点尤其如此。

第十五份文件是 1936 年 3 月 23 日：

> With reference to your previous reduction in prices by 50 cents for glass to be sold at Tatung, Feng Chen, Suiyuan and Potou, we beg to advise you that we have sent our representatives to the above named districts to secure glass business. We understand that the Tax charged by the Tax Office at Shahukwan is $0.99 per case. While for Shoko glass only transit dues will be paid and Tax can be exempt.
>
> Therefore the price of Yao Hua glass is still over $0.50 higher than that of Shoko glass. We shall be obliged if you will kindly take into consideration our difficulties in stimulating sales at the beginning and also the painstaking in travelling and allow us a further reduction of $0.30. By giving the rebate to the buyers our sales can be pushed.

译文：

关于贵方先前对在大同、丰镇、绥远和包头销售的玻璃降价 50 美分一事，为争取玻璃业务，我们已派代表到上述地区，特此奉告。我方了解到沙湖关税务局征收的税是每箱 0.99 美元。而对曙光玻璃只需征收过境费且豁免税费。

因此耀华玻璃的价格仍比曙光玻璃的价格高出 0.50 美元以上。若贵方能考虑到我方在初始阶段促进销售的难处以及差旅的艰苦，并能再给予我方 0.30 美元的降价，我方将不胜感激。给买主折扣可以促进我方的销售。

第十六份文件是 1936 年 3 月 27 日：

> In your Monthly Report for January 1936, last paragraph narrative section, you state that "if we maintain our present Tientsin and up-country prices, sales of Shoko Glass will be eliminated when their present stocks are cleared, as $7.50 (Shoko cost price) cannot compete with $7.70 (Yao Hua gross price) under the present conditions."
>
> I presume you mean by "Shoko cost price" the Shoko importer's selling price plus duty and all charges to ex-godown Tientsin with no allowance for dealer's rebates or profit? If such is the case, do you not think that our single thickness rate for standard specifications could stand increasing, say about the 1st May, when most of the Spring buying has been placed and there is no danger of losing forward booking to Shoko?
>
> From your February Report I note that there were no imports of Shoko Glass during February, (but we have to thank the ice conditions for that) and that Shoko stocks at the end of the month were 6,200 cases. It would be interesting to know whether there have been any imports since the river opened, and if so were they transfers from Dairen to Mitsubishi's Tientsin godown stocks, or were they sales to dealers.
>
> I am sure we will never be able to eliminate Shoko entirely out of the Tientsin proper markets as there will be always some demand from Japanese buyers: But if we can monopolise the interior trade we will be more than satisfied, and I think our present method of direct shipment is carrying us toward that goal.

译文：

在您 1936 年 1 月月报的最后一段叙述部分中，您说："如果我们维持目前天津和内陆的价格，在'曙光'玻璃库存清仓后，我们就会停止销售该产品，因为在目前条件下，7.50 美元（曙光玻璃成本价）无法与 7.70 美元（耀华毛价）相竞争。"

我想您说的"曙光玻璃成本价"是指曙光玻璃进口商的销售价加上关税和到天津仓库交货的所有费用，不包括经销商的回扣或利润吧？如果是这样的话，您认为我们标准规格的单厚玻璃率不会继续增加吧？比如在 5 月 1 日左右，那时春季采购的大部分货物都已订购完毕，订单无落入曙光玻璃之手之虞。

从您 2 月份的报告中，我注意到 2 月份无曙光玻璃进口（但我们得将此归功于结冰期的天气条件），而曙光玻璃该月底库存量为 6 200 箱。我很想知道开河后是否有曙光玻璃进口呢？如果有，它们是从大连转运到三菱的天津仓库交货，还是出售给经销商呢？

我相信我们永远不可能把曙光玻璃从天津的市场上根除，因为总会有一些日本买家对此有需求；但如果我们能继续垄断内陆贸易，我们就会非常满意。我认为我们目前的直接运输方式正带领我们朝着这个目标前进。

第十七份文件是 1936 年 3 月 30 日：

With reference to my letter 18068 of 28th February, I now enclose for your information an original bill, with translation, for four mirrors-one each of Yao Hua and Shoko Glass in double and single thickness-from which you will note that the Shoko mirrors are being marketed at a considerably lower price than mirrors made from Yao Hua Glass.

译文：

关于我 2 月 28 日的 18068 号信，现随函附上 4 面镜子的账单正本及翻译件，分别为双厚和单厚的耀华玻璃和曙光玻璃的价格。从中你会注意到，曙光玻璃的售价比耀华玻璃的要低得多。

第十八份文件是 1936 年 4 月 7 日：

Replying to your letter M-18119 of 27th March, I confirm that the "Shoko Cost Price" is the importer's selling price plus duty and all charges to ex-godown Tientsin with no allowance for dealers' rebates or profit. This cost price, for future suppliers, is calculated to be as under:-

C.I.F. Tientsin	per case $5.70
Import Duty and Charges G.U. 1.1 479 $227	2.61
	$8.31
Refund of old duty	.86
	$7.45
Unloading charges, etc., say	.05
Nett cost ex godown	$7.50

With regard to the question of increasing the price of our Single Thickness in standard specifications, I think that this could be and should be done, but suggest that no change be made until about 15th of June (notifying our dealers about 1st June), as I am given to understand that the period from May 1st to about the middle of June is a busy buying season, and an increase at this time would be likely to prove prejudicial to our sales.

During the latter part of March all waterways became open and the Tientsi and Peiping and up-country markets became active. From Peiping orders have seen received for about 4,500 cases, and for Tientsin and up-country about 11,000 cases. Of the above about 6,000 cases had not been shipped up to the end of March.

At that time-end of March-Shoko dealers had, it is heard, ordered about 2,000 cases 4th Single glass for the replenishment of their April stocks, because the Shoko furnace at Dairen will undertake cold repairs during this month and do not expect to resume output until about the middle of May. Owing, however, to the present high exchange of the Gold Unit, Shoko glass will cost $7.50 per case (as per calculation above) nett ex-godown, Tientsin.

Thus, if we maintain our present prices until the middle of June, it is believed that Shoko sales will be reduced to a minimum.

The total imports of Shoko Glass during March was about 1,000 cases 4th quality single thickness. These were ordered last November. Their sales amounted to 3,700 cases, leaving closing stocks, at the end of March, of 3,500 cases. Their next shipment of 2,500 cases is due to arrive in Tientsin on or before 15th April, of which 500 cases represent the balance of last November's orders.

With reference to these imports, I understand that these are not transfers from Dairen to Tientsin for Mitsubishi's godown stocks, but are, in effect, sales to dealers who however have a sort of "free storage on credit" arrangements for 55 days with Mitsubishi, during which period the glass remains in the latter's godown and on which they have a lien covered by the dealers' guarantees for payment.

To summarise: I think that we should increase our prices for 4th single standard specification on or about 15th June and reduce them again about 1st September whereby we should be able to secure business practically up to the date of the Dragon Boat Festival (23rd June) and hold the Tientsin and up-country markets through the summer, at the same time tying up intermediate Shoko stocks, which they will be importing for the early autumn sales, in Tientsin godown, and exposing them to the risk of loss from mildew etc., and a further loss of interest thereon for practically three months.

As to strip glass, this has undoubtedly given a big knock to Shoko and Japanese mirrors, for which reason I suggest that it would be best to follow, in regard to it, the same policy as for 4th single standard specification, as outlined above.

译文：

关于您3月27日编号为M-18119的来信，兹确认"曙光玻璃成本价"是进口商的销售价格加上关税和到天津仓库交货的所有费用，不包括经销商的回扣或利润。本成本价对未来供应商的计算方法如下：

天津到岸价	每箱 5.70 美元
进口关税及费用- G.U. 1.1 479 $227	<u>2.61</u>
	（共）8.31 美元
退还旧税	<u>.86</u>
	（剩）7.45 美元
如：卸货费用等	<u>.05</u>
仓库交货净价	<u>7.50</u> 美元

关于提高我们的单厚标准规格玻璃价格的问题，我认为这是可以而且应该做的，但建议在 6 月 15 日左右之前不要做任何更改（可通知我们的经销商时间为 6 月 1 日左右），因为我了解到从 5 月 1 日到 6 月中旬是繁忙的采购季节，此时增长可能会对我们的销售造成不利影响。

三月下旬，所有水路都开放了，天津、北平和内地市场变得活跃起来。从北平收到的订单约 4 500 箱货品，天津和内地约 11 000 箱货品。截至 3 月底，上述订单中有约 6 000 箱货品尚未发货。

有消息称，在 3 月底的时候，曙光玻璃的经销商已经订购了大约 2 000 箱四等单厚玻璃，以补充其 4 月份的库存，因为位于大连的曙光公司熔炉将在本月进行冷维修，预计到 5 月中旬左右才能恢复生产。然而，由于黄金单位目前的高汇率，根据上述天津仓库净货价计算，曙光玻璃每箱售价为 7.50 美元。因此，如果我们将目前的价格维持到 6 月中旬，相信曙光玻璃的销售额将降至最低。

三月份，曙光玻璃的总进口量约为 1 000 箱四等单厚玻璃。这些是去年 11 月订购的。它们的销量达到了 3 700 箱，截至 3 月底，库存剩余 3 500 箱。他们的下一批 2 500 箱玻璃将于 4 月 15 日或之前抵达天津，其中 500 箱是去年 11 月订单的余额。

关于这些进口商品，我了解到，这些不是从大连运往天津的三菱库存，实际上是已经销售给经销商的商品，但经销商与三菱有一种"信用证免费储存"的协议安排，期限为 55 天，在此期间，玻璃仍在三菱的仓库中，他们拥有经销商付款担保所涵盖的留置权。

总结：我认为，我们应该在 6 月 15 日左右提高四等单厚标准规格玻璃的价格，并在 9 月 1 日左右再次降价，这样我们就可以在端午节（6 月 23 日）之前确保业务水平，并在整个夏季保持住天津和内地市场，同时阻碍曙光玻璃在天津仓库的中间库存，这些库存是他们用于早秋销售而进口的商品。这将使他们面临霉变等损失的风险，以及进一步的几乎三个月的利息损失。

至于条形玻璃，这无疑给曙光玻璃和日本镜子带来了巨大的冲击，因此，我建议最好遵循与上述四等单厚标准规格玻璃相同的政策。

第十九份文件是 1936 年 4 月 9 日：

Originally, when Shoko Glass was imported for the dealers, the liability for payment of the duty thereon was accepted by Mitsubishi. When, however, the new scale of duties came into force, Mitsubishi would only agree to pay at the old rate; hence the dealers themselves now pay the full duty (at the new rate) and receive from Mitsubishi a "Refund of old duty"- i.e. the amount which would have been payable at the old rate.

译文：

最初，经销商进口曙光玻璃时，三菱公司接受了支付相关关税的责任。然而，当新的关税表生效时，三菱只同意按旧的税率支付；因此，现在经销商自己支付全部的关税（按新的税率），然后从三菱那里获得 "旧税退款"——即按旧税率应支付的金额。

第二十份文件是 1936 年 7 月 7 日：

They all declared that on Yao Hua glass a tax at $0.99 must be paid at Sha Hu Kuan while that on Shoko glass was exempted.

译文：

他们都宣称，耀华玻璃必须在沙湖关缴纳 0.99 美元的税。而曙光玻璃则是免税的。

On account of the heavy local taxes, he later dealt in Shoko glass, instead. (No local taxes levied on Shoko glass after payment of import duty.) During the period from last autumn to the present, he has had about 1,000 cases of Shoko glass transported to the said city. If this lasts long, Yao Hua glass would suffer a great loss. Since we are informed of the situation in detail, we have to report to you by letter. We wonder whether the quotation for glass f.o.c. at said station is $9.00. If this is the case, we are simply willing to sacrifice our 2% rebate and give it to the said merchant in order to wage a competition with Shoko glass and to avoid damage to your business. Kindly make us a reply as to whether or not this is in order.

译文：

由于当地赋税过重，他后来转而经营"曙光"玻璃。（曙光玻璃在缴纳进口关税后不征收地方税。）从去年秋天到现在，他已经将大约1 000箱曙光玻璃运到了这座城市。如果这种情况持续太久，耀华玻璃将蒙受巨大损失。既然我们已经详细了解了情况，我们不得不写信向你汇报。我们不知道该地点玻璃离岸价是否为9美元。如果是这样的话，我们愿意牺牲我们2%的回扣，把它给上述商家，以便与曙光玻璃进行竞争，避免对您的业务造成损害。请答复我们这样做是否妥当。

在秦皇岛港藏"滦外档"民国时期耀华英文档案中2份文件提及"昌光"玻璃：

1935年8月15日德源泰致同祥湧：

Besides, we should like to inform you that the prices for "Chang Kuang" glass and Yao Hua glass are the same at present.

译文：此外，我们想告知您，"昌光"玻璃和耀华玻璃目前的价格是一样的。

1935年9月6日同祥湧玻璃庄致天津销售处：

Besides, the Japanese "Chang Kuang" glass has flooded the Tientsin market.

译文：此外，日本"昌光"玻璃大量涌入天津市场。

在秦皇岛港藏"滦外档"民国时期耀华英文档案中6份文件提及"Vitrea"玻璃：

第一和二份文件是1935年8月15日：

We therefore suggest that our price for Extra Thick glass in Tientsin be reduced in the following six sizes:-

EXTRA THICKK	YAO HUA CURRENT PRICE	PROPOSED PRICE	VITREA CURRENT PRICE
24 × 18	$34.00	$24.00	$28.00
30 × 20	34.00	29.00	34.00
36 × 24	34.00	29.00	39.00
44 × 28	39.00	32.00	39.00
52 × 36	45.00	36.00	46.00
60 × 40	52.00	42.00	51.00

译文：

因此，我们建议将天津以下六种尺寸特厚玻璃进行价格下调：

特厚	耀华现价	建议价	维特利亚现价
24 × 18	$34.00	$24.00	$28.00
30 × 20	34.00	29.00	34.00
36 × 24	34.00	29.00	39.00
44 × 28	39.00	32.00	39.00
52 × 36	45.00	36.00	46.00
60 × 40	52.00	42.00	51.00

附件：

PRICES OF YAO HUA AND VITREA GLASS (EXTRA THICK)

YAO HUA CURRENT PRICE PER SHEET	VITREA CURRENT PRICE PER SHEET	PROPOSED PRICE FOR YAO HUA PER SHEET
$1.03	$0.85-$0.90	$0.73
1.44	1.40	1.21
2.00	2.30	1.70
3.25	3.30	2.67
5.62	5.70	4.50
8.66	8.50	7.00

译文：

耀华玻璃与维特利亚玻璃价格对比（加厚）

耀华玻璃目前每片价格	维特利亚玻璃目前每片价格	建议耀华玻璃每片价格
$1.03	$0.85～$0.90	$0.73
1.44	1.40	1.21
2.00	2.30	1.70
3.25	3.30	2.67
5.62	5.70	4.50
8.66	8.50	7.00

第三和四份文件是1935年12月30日：

齐尔顿致同祥湧玻璃庄：

In order to compete with Vitrea and secure all the heavy grades glass business in your area, we wish to inform you that our heavy glass prices will not be in creased by 20% as stated in our letter No.18119 of 7th November but the old prices remain in force from today. We also give you a few attractive prices for our 4th quality, E. Thick Glass as follows.

译文：

为了与维特利亚竞争并确保你方地区的所有重玻璃业务，我们在此通知你方，我们的重玻璃价格不会如我们11月7日第18119号信中所述的那样上涨20%，但从今天起旧价格仍然有效。我们也给你一些四等玻璃有吸引力的价格，我们的四等加厚玻璃信息如下。

齐尔顿致天源泰玻璃店：

In order to compete with Vitrea glass we give you the following attractive prices F.O.C. Chienmen for our 4th Quality, E. Thick glass.

译文：

为了与维特利亚玻璃竞争，我们为四等加厚玻璃提供以下有吸引力的前门离岸价格。

第五份文件是1936年2月28日：

With regard to 4th quality Extra Thick Glass, it is suggested that the dealers be quoted a special price for size 24"*18"(only) of $26.00 per case of 100 sq.ft.,i.e. $0.80 per sheet, in order to compete with Vitrea Glass, which costs $0.90-$0.95 per sheet and is sold at a bout $1.00 (size 24"*18" is common on the market for table pads).

译文：

为了与"维特利亚"玻璃竞争，建议对尺寸为 24"*18"（仅此尺寸）的四等加厚玻璃给经销商报一个特价，即：每 100 平方英尺为一箱，售价 26.00 美元，即每片 0.80 美元，威达利玻璃每片 0.90～0.95 美元，售价约为 1.00 美元（24"*18"是市场上常见的台垫尺寸）。

第六份文件是 1936 年 4 月 1 日：

In order to meet the competition of Vitrea Glass and Japanese mirrors, we wish to inform you that our prices of the undermentioned qualities and sizes of Yao Hua Glass will be revised with effect from to-day's date as follows.

译文：

为适应与维特利亚玻璃和日本镜子的竞争，我方望在此通知贵方，即日起我方将对以下质量和尺寸的耀华玻璃的价格作出以下调整。

考证：秦皇岛港藏"滦外档"民国时期耀华英文档案中提及的 Shoko 玻璃是日本旭硝子株式会社生产的一款玻璃。日本旭硝子株式会社（Asahi Glass Company），有的文献中也根据英文名称翻译成亚沙海玻璃公司，是日本三菱公司的子公司，1907 创立于日本兵库县尼崎市，创建者是三菱公司首任总裁岩崎弥太郎的次子。昌光玻璃是昌光硝子株式会社生产的一款玻璃，昌光硝子株式会社是日本在 1925 年于大连创建的。关于昌光硝子株式会社的建立，有两种说法：第一种说法是 1921 年秋，日本南满洲铁道株式会社所属的南满洲硝子株式会社筹建大连玻璃厂，于 1923 年冬建成。当 1924 年 1 月准备投产时，旭硝子株式会社向日本当局控告南满洲硝子株式会社侵犯专利权。1924 年 4 月，经日本当局判决该厂由旭硝子株式会社经营，厂名改为昌光硝子株式会社。第二种说法是当时旭硝子株式会社找到满铁提出联营，满铁随即同意。工厂设董事 5 人，其中满铁方面1人，旭硝子方面4人。无论哪一种说法都说明Shoko玻璃和昌光玻璃都是由日本旭硝子株式会社生产的玻璃。

硝子也称人造水晶，其实就是玻璃制品。中国是最早发明玻璃的国家之一，中国唐代称玻璃为硝子，此后这一名称流传到日本，至今日本的玻璃名称仍沿用"硝子"这一名词。作为最古老的人工合成材料，其历史可追溯到公元前4 000年以前，世界公认最早的玻璃制造者为古埃及人。

耀华玻璃公司自1925年投放市场以来经过多年的市场竞争，最终在国内市场站稳了脚跟，1934年到1936年耀华玻璃在国内市场所占比例如表5-1所示，历年销售比例都在65%~75%，反映出了耀华在这一时间段的市场占有率。

表5-1 1934—1936年历年销售比例表

年份/年	销售总量/平方米	进口数量/平方米	耀华数量/平方米	耀华比例/%
1934	5 238 510	1 579 700	3 658 810	75
1935	6 172 274	2 184 180	3 988 094	65
1936	5 576 910	1 419 840	4 157 070	75

耀华想要操纵远东市场，攫取高额利润，就必须首先考虑与远东各玻璃厂家，尤其是日本昌光公司达成协议，共同操控市场价格。经过数次协商，首先耀华和昌光两家公司于1926年12月7日签了一份临时合约，大致划分了远东市场上日本和耀华的销售份额和数量。随后又联系比利时方面的厂家，最终三方于1927年年初签订了一份临时协议，主要内容包含中国市场和日本市场以及各家公司的权利义务。这一协议也可以使耀华和昌光两家公司更好地合作，避免无谓的竞争使两家企业两败俱伤。可惜的是，这一协议有效期仅仅一年，之后耀华再也没有和其他玻璃企业进行过联营活动，市场再次恢复到没有秩序的相互竞争中。1933年后，耀华的利润率逐渐下降，这与"九一八事变"之后日本对中国东北、华北各地的疯狂侵略以及日金的跌价有着直接的关系。"九一八事变"后，一向被耀华视为最重要的玻璃销售市场之一的东北被日本占领，尤其伪满洲国成立后，日本更是加紧了对中国东北的控制。在日本的指使下，伪满洲国政府于1932年开始征收耀华玻璃出品税百分之十五，虽经耀华递禀反对缴纳，

但结果无效，只得照缴。只此一项税收已使耀华玻璃的成本上升15%，再加上其他费用的增加，挤压了耀华的利润空间。1931年"九一八事变"后，日本开始侵略中国东北三省，到1932年2月，东北全境被占领。继东北之后，华北顺理成章地成为日本侵略的下一个目标。紧接着日军将魔爪伸向华北，制造了"察哈尔事件""河北事件"和"张北事件"，阴谋策动"华北自治"。1935年6月，国民党军委会华北分会代理委员长何应钦与日本华北驻屯军司令官梅津美治郎谈判，达成了所谓的《何梅协定》，日本帝国主义实际取得了对华北的控制权。《塘沽停战协定》《何梅协定》、策动华北五省自治、成立伪冀东防共自治委员会等一系列的日本侵华行为，都为日本玻璃在华北市场上与耀华开展激烈的争夺提供了便利条件。同时，当局对耀华等民族企业强征赋税，而耀华的劲敌——大连昌光过津运赴内地的各批玻璃却时有免税情况发生。

笔者将华北地区各处销售情况单列出来，同样证明随着日本玻璃在华北销售的扩张，耀华玻璃市场销量受到很大影响，销售量呈减少趋势，如表5-2所示。

表5-2 1932年、1933年华北地区耀华玻璃销售统计表

华北各地	1932年	1933年
天津	62 560 箱	63 871 箱
唐山	5 589 箱	3 519 箱
北平	15 877 箱	12 782 箱
秦皇岛	1 757 箱	938 箱
总数	85 783 箱	81 110 箱

上表显示，华北四地销售市场中只有耀华的大本营天津销售量略有增加，但也仅仅增加1 311箱，唐山、北平、秦皇岛三地销量均呈下降趋势，无序的市场竞争，带来的必定是商品市场价格的下降。

随着日本在中国侵略势力的不断加大，日本玻璃不断涌入中国市场，给耀华带来了巨大的竞争压力。日本企业还利用其军事占领优势，组织船

只私运玻璃到中国各地，更加重了耀华玻璃的竞争压力。随着日本玻璃在华北销售的扩张，耀华玻璃市场销量受到很大影响，销售量呈减少趋势。激烈的市场竞争导致企业间为争夺市场纷纷压价，甚至偶尔出现低于成本价格销售的情况，带给企业的是较低利润率，这也是耀华虽然经营多年，市场占有率也不断升高，但是公司却始终没能很好摆脱资金紧张束缚的原因。以 1933 年全年的市场售价比较为例，耀华、昌光年初的市场售价都远高于年末的售价，如表 5-3 所示，这就说明各家企业都在采用降价竞销的手段抢夺市场占有份额。

表 5-3　1933 年耀华与昌光在华北玻璃售价比较一览表

地区	厂家	时间		降价率
		1933 年 1 月 1 日	1933 年 12 月 31 日	
华北	耀华	10 元	8 元	20.00%
	昌光	9.1 元	7.48 元	17.80%

1925—1935 年每标准箱玻璃成本、售价一览表如表 5-4 所示。

表 5-4　1925—1935 年每标准箱玻璃成本、售价一览表　　（单位：银元）

年份/年	成本	售价	利润率
1925	5.25	5.81～6.08	10.67%～15.81%
1926	5.12	5.6～6.2	9.37%～21.09%
1927	4.77	5.2	9.01%
1928	4.5	6.9	53.33%
1929	4.25	7.25	70.59%
1930	4.65	8.9～11.15	91.40%～139.78%
1931	5.29	10.5	98.49%
1932	5.21	9.8～10.2	88.10%～95.78%
1933	4.84	8～9.5	65.29%～96.28%
1934	4.62	6.6～7.7	42.86%～66.67%
1935	4.42	6～7.7	35.75%～74.21%

上表显示，耀华玻璃投放市场的时间是 1925 年。利润率最低的是 1927 年，仅有 9.01%。从 1928 年，开始有了明显提升，而利润率最高的是 1930 年。从 1933 年至 1935 年，耀华的利润率持续下跌，这与日军侵占华北有着密切联系。

无独有偶，继而又有苏俄、比国玻璃及其他玻璃相继来中国竞销，如：捷克斯洛伐克的玻璃品牌维特利亚（Vitrea）和越南的玻璃品牌"海防"。为求扩大市场，各品牌争相贬价，甚至出现低于成本价格出售的情况。

第六节　秦港藏"滦外档"民国时期耀华英文档案中"耀华"玻璃销售的考证

秦皇岛港藏"滦外档"民国时期耀华英文档案中有三份开滦矿务总局与同祥湧玻璃庄及北平地区玻璃庄签订的经销合同，三份关于简化档案手续的文件，同时多处提及玻璃经销方式的改革，列举如下：

1934 年 12 月 7 日福克纳致考威尔：

> If you are satisfied that our best interests have been served by the 1934 arrangement, we must consider the facts that we desire, (a) to extend our sales in our "Home Markets" of North China to the elimination of all competition, and (b) that according to the recent survey there is a possibility of effecting an increase. However, to realise these increased sales it will be necessary to alter our selling methods to meet the recommendations of direct shipments, sub-agents and the carrying of stocks at the main centres.
>
> I consider, therefore, your first plan should be to explain to Tung Hsiang Yung our ambition in North China and our ideas of expanding sales by direct rail shipments, and the maintenance of a closer contact with the distant markets. I suggest you have a talk with Mr. Sung and obtain his views, particularly on the question of direct shipments and the holding of stocks at the various large centres. If you think I would be of any help in your dealing I can run up.

译文：

如果您认为1934年的协议符合我们的最大利益,我们必须考虑以下情况：(a)我们希望扩大我们在华北"本土市场"的销售,以消除所有竞争；(b)根据最近的调查,有可能实现销售增长。然而,为了实现销售额增长,有必要改变我们的销售方法,以满足直接发货、分代理和在主要中心储备库存的建议。

因此,我认为,您的第一个计划应该是向同祥湧玻璃庄解释我们在华北的雄心壮志,以及我们通过铁路直接运输扩大销售的想法,并与远一些的市场保持更密切的联系。我建议您和宋先生谈谈,征求他的意见,特别是关于直接装运和在各大中心储藏存货的问题。若您觉得我能为您的交易助一臂之力,我愿效犬马之劳。

1934年12月9日同祥湧玻璃庄致天津销售处：

> Our firm may establish branch offices or agencies in Shansi, Kalgan, Chengchow of Honan and Tsinan of Shantung. Goods will be shipped to them by you by direct rail shipments for our accounts. We will settle the accounts monthly together with the payments due on local sales. But the annual overhead charges as fire insurance, godown charges and other expenses for their branch offices shall be for your account. The total amount is about $7,000 yearly (Shansi, $2,000; Chengchow, $2,000; Shantung and Kalgan, $1,500 each).
>
> On account of sharp competition with the Shoko glass, our profits are entirely sacrificed in these recent two years. If no adequate commission is allowed, we cannot carry on the struggle. We, therefore, request you to increase our commission. If the annual sales are below 50,000 cases, 5% commission shall be allowed; If it is above 50,000 to $55,000 cases, 5.5% shall be allowed; If it is above 55,000 to 60,000 cases, 6% shall be allowed; if it is above 60,000 to 65,000 cases, 6.5% shall be allowed. If the sales reach 100,000 cases, 10% shall be allowed. For other bonuses in addition to monthly payments, the commission shall be allowed in accordance with the rates for 50,000 cases as per the actual sales. If the sales exceed 50,000 cases, the total amount of extra commission shall be settled at the end of year.

译文：

我公司可在山西、张家口、河南郑州、山东济南等地设立分公司或代理机构。货物将由贵方通过铁路直接运给他们，费用由我方承担。我们将按月与当地销售的应付款项一起结账。但其销售办事处每年的间接费用，如火灾保险、仓库费和其他费用应由贵方负担。总金额约为每年7 000元（山西，2 000元；郑州，2 000元；山东和张家口各1 500元）。

由于与曙光玻璃的激烈竞争，近两年我们的利润亏损殆尽。如果不能获得足够的佣金，我们很难继续下去。因此，我们请求贵方提高佣金。如果年销售量低于5万箱，佣金应为5%；超过5万至5.5万箱，佣金为5.5%；超过5.5万至6万箱，佣金为6%；超过6万至6.5万箱，佣金为6.5%。如果销量达到10万箱，佣金应为10%。对于除按月支付外的其他奖金，根据实际销售情况，按5万箱费率给予提成。如果销售量超过50 000箱，额外佣金的总额将在年底结清。

1935年2月13日考威尔致福克纳：

we will always sell to him at market rates and for cash, but that our 1935 sales arrangements do not permit us to grant him any sole sales contract, nor to extend credit terms to him.

译文：

我们将始终以市场价格和现金向他出售，但我们1935年的销售安排不允许我们授予他任何独家销售合同，也不允许我们向他提供信贷条款，但须经贵方批准。

1935年4月3日福克纳致考威尔：

with reference to your letter 18119 of yesterday's date regarding the Freight Rates from Chinwangtao to upcountry stations, I confirm that these rates include Railway Risk charges.

译文：

关于你昨天18119信中关于从秦皇岛到内陆站的运费的问题，我确认这些运费已包括铁路风险费用。

考证：耀华公司一向非常重视玻璃销售。1925年8月正式点火生产前，开滦组织专人赴沈阳、大连、青岛、烟台、上海、北平等处实地调查。截至1925年3月25日，各地市场平板玻璃销售的数量、来源、等级、规格、售价、税收、库存、销售淡旺季、玻璃经销商等信息收集完毕，并撰写书面调查报告。

在二号窑炉建成投产后，耀华充分发挥"国货"优势，打入内地市场。1934年8月，公司派人专程沿京汉、京绥、承太等铁路线到大、中、小城市调查玻璃市场情况。先后调查了张家口、阳高、大同、丰镇、绥远、包头、保定、石家庄、顺德、新乡、郑州、榆次、太原等城镇。对各地的自然经济状况、历年玻璃销量、品种、规格、货源、用途、售价、各种费用等情况做了详细调查，还拜会了各地较大的玻璃经销商。通过调查，提出耀华在内地开拓、扩大销售市场的意见。主要是在大的站点建立经销代理人，小的站点可直接销售；在通火车又有铁路货运保险的地方，从秦皇岛直接发货到销售点，以降低商人花费的中间费用，利于耀华玻璃销售量的扩大；在较大城市——保定、石家庄、新乡等地建立仓储点，存放一些玻璃，以及时满足用户需要。

对市场的调查工作，耀华从1924年投产到1950年一直很重视。开滦在各地的销售处实行每月坚持报送市场调查报告制度，内容包括市场情况概述；耀华玻璃每月销售数量、规格、品种、价格；各国进口玻璃销售数量、规格、品种、价格；耀华玻璃与各国玻璃优劣的比较；市场竞争情况；前景展望。开滦销售处把各地报来的月报汇总整理，报送开滦总经理和耀华公司总董、协董。另外，每年有一份年报，总结当年各地玻璃销售情况，分析市场变化和前景，提出下一年经销方针和经营策略。这种月报、年报制度在1950年以前，无论是开滦代理经销处、三菱公司包销，还是耀华自己销售，一直坚持，从未废除。

在产品销售中，耀华充分利用开滦矿务总局已有的市场优势，迅速地打开了销售市场，在华北、东北、上海等国内市场快速地占领了重要份额，尤其是华北，一直是耀华的主要销售市场。本册"滦外档"记录的是1934—1936年间耀华公司在华北市场的销售情况。

1934年开始，耀华与天津的代理商同祥湧玻璃庄以及北平地区的天源泰等八家代理商签订合同，作为经理耀华在天津和北平地区的售品处。从第二章开滦矿务总局与天津的同祥湧玻璃庄以及北平地区的天源泰等八家代理商签订的三份合同看出：合同规定每月开滦供给的玻璃售款必须于次月10日前全数付清，开滦给代理商开出的酬报条件是与商品销售数量挂钩的，销售得越多，回扣的比例越高，销售商获得的收入越高。通常尺寸的单厚玻璃市场价格由总局随时规定，但是价格的增长必须于两星期前通告代理商。这种办法可更好地激励代理商努力想办法多卖公司的产品，每月争取最好的销售量以便获取更高比例的回扣。

从上述合同的规定中可看到，耀华在产品销售方面与代理商合作的模式基本有两种，一种是降价售予，即按耀华规定的价格降价，比例视市场情况和玻璃等级、品种、规格而定，一般为5%~10%，玻璃商再按耀华规定的价格在市场出售，赚取价差；一种是给予回扣，回扣的比例视售出玻璃数量多少而定，1%~5%不等，按每月结算货款的实际数核发。为了保住市场，合同中还规定了："and in turn the Contractor undertakes not to be interested directly or indirectly in the sale and /or purchase of any articles or commodities competing with these products.In the event of the Contractor being no interested directly or indirectly in the sale and/or purchase of any articles or commodities competing with the products of the Yao Hua Mechanical Glass Co.,Ltd., the Administration reserve the right to cancel forthwith this Contract, and withhold payment of any rebate outstanding."即：经销耀华玻璃的商人不得再经销其他厂家的玻璃，如发现经销其他厂家玻璃，降价和回扣全部取消。

耀华销售商品的管理模式中第一种给予经销商的利润空间是有限的，这种方式可旱涝保丰收，适合于一些销售能力有限的小型代理商人；第二种方式与现代企业的销售方式类似，通过不同比例的销售回扣来激励商家努力多销货物，在规定的时限内完成额定的销售数量。如：1934年开滦矿务总局与天津的同祥涌玻璃庄签订的合同中规定，分销人在合同期限以内购买玻璃单位最低数是五万箱，1936年开滦矿务总局与天津的同祥涌玻璃庄签订的合同中规定最低数是六万箱，1936年开滦矿务总局与北平的天源泰等八家代理商签订的合同中规定最低数是两万箱。拿到更高一级的销售回扣点数，挣得更多的利润收入，这种方式更适合于一些有较好销售途径，可以保证时限内销出一定数量的商品，较有实力的大代理商。

开滦矿务总局代管耀华的销售工作后，随即通过它在全国各地的销售处建立了销售耀华玻璃的经销点，有的地方由开滦销售处直接销售，有的地方由开滦委托经销商代销。耀华玻璃以现货、期货两种方式供应客户，为方便推销，自出产后即在各地经销处储存相当数量的玻璃，以保障能够及时供应。

对于大宗供货，开滦对耀华采取便捷的管理方法。由各地经销商每月向该地的开滦销售处提出需货数量、品种、规格、等级，开滦销售处汇总后直接交秦皇岛经理处发货；开滦秦皇岛经理处负责从工厂把玻璃运出，运往沿海各城市的玻璃主要是由开滦矿务局运煤船代运，船运不到的地方由火车运输，耀华付给开滦由工厂运到码头的搬运费和火车、轮船运输费；玻璃运到各地后，按协议规定的条件，在码头交货的，由经销商自行提走，在货栈交货的先运至开滦在各地的仓库存储，由经销商在限期内提走，代为储存的时间一般不许超过半个月，过期不提走的，按日计收仓储费。这种方法使耀华产品既可以充分利用开滦设在各地经销处的便利条件，又可以满足客商的提货要求，更好地为客户提供服务，赢得客户的信赖，方便商品的销售。

凡是采用经销商代理经销方式的，都由开滦矿务局与各地经销商签订合同，合同内容主要涉及保证金、每月销售数量、价格管理、商品供应地点、每月与公司结账规定以及商家报酬办法等方面。首先，经销商人必须有可靠的殷实保证人，或缴纳一定数量的保证金；其次，每月销售玻璃的最低数量有明确的规定；再次，商品售价必须按耀华公司规定的价格，不许任意提价；最后，限定每月供给玻璃价款的交纳时间，一般不许超过一个月。发展到1936年，耀华各处代理商多已比较固定，玻璃也已深受市场欢迎。

开滦矿务局为了减少总局与秦皇岛之间的信函往来麻烦，方便经销商与公司的销售买卖，于1930年年底对耀华玻璃销售管理模式进行了改革。改革前，开滦总局"各经理处销售玻璃各项事宜向系在天津总局办理，多年以来因工厂设于秦皇岛，时有各经理处来函询及总局，总局又须询问工厂，往返函询每感不便"。此时开滦局办理售卖玻璃事宜的人员恰巧提出辞职，正好可以借此机会"将售卖玻璃方面日常应办各事移至秦皇岛办理，俾可与工厂接近"。"至于营业方针及其他重要事项仍应由总局主持，其各经理处与秦皇岛售玻璃处往来各项函件，凡不属日常应办之事者，亦须送总局裁夺。"这样就减少了很多经理处、总局、秦皇岛工厂之间的信函往来烦琐的弊端，节省了办事时间，提高了办事效率，进一步完善了管理体制。同时，耀华与各代理处所订售卖玻璃的办法也进行了相应的调整。在天津、奉天、北京、秦皇岛、上海以及开滦矿区各处所有卖玻璃事宜，一概由各该地的开滦矿务分局经理，各处的经售手续均照耀华与开滦历次所订代管营业办法办理，没有多少变化。开滦各地分局代售耀华玻璃均无佣金。

各地售卖玻璃的事项则由开滦委托的代理开滦局业务的各商行兼办，各地开滦代理处商行均登记在册，开滦将其印制成广告性质的小册子供客户查阅参考。开滦局用自己的运货轮船将耀华玻璃与开滦局的各种出品一同运往各代理处。各代理处等到玻璃运到后，即对卸货及其他一切手续均负照料的义务，开滦不付分文报酬，因此，开滦给每家以代理人的名义作为回报。各代理处售卖耀华玻璃的报酬办法各异，由开滦视情形而定，售卖货物的多寡、推销产品的难易以及公司对于该处销售市场的销售目的都是开滦核定报酬多少的考虑因素。总的情况是，耀华的出品供不应求，本着能够获取最大利润的市场尽量供应，其他获利较微的市场较少供货的原则，对各销售处提供不同数量的货源。耀华经过多年的市场竞争，最终在国内市场站稳了脚跟。

参考文献

[1] 艾梅霞. 茶叶之路[M]. 北京：中信出版社，2007.

[2] 陈凯. 近代中国第一家中外合资企业——耀华玻璃公司[J]. 文史天地，2015（12）.

[3] 陈厉辞，王莲英，李艾. 耀华玻璃厂比利时股权被日强购始末[J]. 遗产与保护研究，2018（8）.

[4] 陈支平，卢增荣. 从契约文书看清代工商业合股委托经营方式的转变[J]. 中国社会经济史研究，2000（2）.

[5] 丁抒明. 烟台港史（古近代部分）[M]. 北京：人民交通出版社，1988.

[6] 董劭伟，袁媛，岳晓蕊.《耀华机器玻璃股份有限公司筹备情形报告书》整理[J]. 中华历史与传统文化研究论丛，2020（6）.

[7] 董晓萍. 流动代理人：北京旧城的寺庙与铺保（1917—1956)[J]. 北京师范大学学报（社会科学版），2006（6）.

[8] 方强. 中比合办时期秦皇岛耀华玻璃公司研究（1921—1936)[D]. 保定：河北大学，2015.

[9] 葛庆成. 秦皇岛港百年记事[M]. 秦皇岛港务集团有限公司，2009.

[10] 郝莹玉. 作为一个张家口人你知道城市名字的由来吗？[N]. 张家口新闻网，2019-06-27.

[11] 黄化."诸者平衡"原则——以民国英文档案汉译实践为例[J]. 上海翻译，2005（5）.

[12] 菅荣军. 保定民国时期一份合资经营卷烟厂业务的合同[J]. 档案天地，2015（10）.

[13] 李保平. 开滦煤矿档案史料集[M]. 石家庄：河北教育出版社，2012.

[14] 李娜. 民国时期白话文中的同素异序词研究[J]. 华夏文化论坛, 2013（2）.

[15] 李向. 民国档案翻译原则初探[J]. 史海钩沉, 2018（6）.

[16] 刘建萍. 试析秦皇岛耀华玻璃厂的创办及经营（1921—1936）[D]. 保定：河北大学, 2015.

[17] 卢志民. 近代北京社会的"铺保"初探[J]. 中国社会历史评论, 2020（11）.

[18] 裴斐, 黄玉明. 英文历史档案翻译刍议——关于民国档案抢救保护与数字化的思考[J]. 档案学研究, 2017（6）.

[19] 彭博, 王莲英. 关于中比合办时期耀华公司企业性质问题的探讨[J]. 中华历史与传统文化研究论丛, 2018（10）.

[20] 彭博, 王莲英. 1921年—1936年耀华玻璃厂工人工资分析——兼论二十世纪二三十年代河北工人阶层工资水平[J]. 保定学院学报, 2018（31）.

[21] 郗宝山. 开滦那四万卷百年档案[J]. 档案天地, 2011（9）.

[22] 秦皇岛开滦外文档案耀华专卷（1934—1936）, 原卷号：M-18119, 新卷号：3789.

[23] 佟爽, 董劭伟. 从《耀华公司筹备情形报告书》分析民国耀华玻璃厂选址问题[J]. 社会科学动态, 2018（5）.

[24] 汪敬虞. 中国近代经济史（1895—1927）[M]. 北京：经济管理出版社, 2007.

[25] 王海沙. 民国时期证券经纪人合同文书浅析——以两份合同为例[J]. 证券市场导报, 2013（10）.

[26] 王莲英. 民国时期耀华玻璃公司董事会议事录摘编[J]. 中华历史与传统文化研究论丛, 2016（8）.

[27] 王莲英. 民国时期耀华玻璃公司董事会议事录摘编（二）[J]. 中华历史与传统文化研究论丛, 2017（12）.

[28] 王莲英, 董劭伟. 耀华玻璃公司产品商标变迁考述[J]. 中华历史与传统文化研究论丛, 2018（10）.

[29] 王庆普. 秦港近代档案漫谈[J]. 档案天地, 2009（11）.

[30] 王庆普. 秦皇岛港口志[M]. 大连：大连海事大学出版社, 1997.

[31] 威妥玛. 语言自迩集[M]. 张卫东, 译. 北京：北京大学出版社, 2002.

[32] 熊性美. 开滦煤矿矿权史料[M]. 天津：南开大学出版社, 2004.

[33] 耀华玻璃厂志编纂委员会. 耀华玻璃厂志[M]. 北京：中国建筑材料工业出版社, 1992.

[34] 曾泰元. 张家口的Kalgan往事[N]. 文汇报, 2022-02-19.

[35] 张德琦. 威妥玛与汉语拼音——谈中国地名人名英译问题[J]. 大学英语, 1986（1）.

[36] 张阳. 秦皇岛港藏"滦外档"之顾振等人事档案解读[J]. 中华历史与传统文化研究论丛, 2017（12）.

[37] 张阳. 秦皇岛港藏民国档案之外文书信等选译和题解[J]. 中华历史与传统文化研究论丛, 2016（8）.

[38] 照译开滦矿务总局十九年九月份营业报告, 耀档：室卷号 3-3-145.

[39] 照译开滦矿务总局总理来函, 1930年8月4日, 耀档：室卷号 3-3-146.

[40] 照译开滦矿务总局总理来函, 第零一六九号, 1930年12月12日, 耀档：室卷号 3-3-146.

[41] 照译开滦矿务总局总理二十三年一月份营业报告, 耀档：室卷号 4-2-216.

[42] 照译开滦矿务总局总理二十二年度营业报告书, 耀档：室卷号 4-2-219.

[43] 周锦章. 论民国时期的北京商业铺保[J]. 北京社会科学, 2011（3）.

[44] 祝庆祺. 刑案汇览三编（全四卷）[M]. 北京：北京古籍出版社, 2004.